I HOPE you ENJOY our book much LOVE TO you, Jujuolui Zitt

We Are Among You Already

True Stories of Star Beings on Earth

Compiled by Jujuolui Kuita
representative of
The Faquian Council

EARTH STAR PUBLICATIONS

We Are Among You Already

True Stories of Star Beings on Earth

Compiled by Jujuolui Kuita
representative of
The Faquian Council

Earth Star Publications
Pagosa Springs, Colorado

FIRST EDITION
January 2010

Library of Congress Control Number: 2010920644

ISBN 978-0-944851-31-9

Printed in the United States of America

Design and Artwork Credit

Book design (front and back covers) created by **Hartmut Jager**

Book covers, ET artwork provided by **Kesara**
(Front "from left to right": Gray, Pleiadian female, Reptilian. Back: Reptilian face)

Book cover (Earth) courtesy of **NASA** and **Visible Earth** (http://visibleearth.NASA.gov)

Bald eagle picture, Arroylos' story, **Carolina Raptor Center**

ET sculpture pictures provided by **Cynthia Crawford,** ET Sculptor

Dedication

We, The Faquian Council, dedicate this book to the following:

To the Star Beings who incarnated for "Mission Earth," who are assisting all life forms, including Gaia, Mother Earth herself. They knew it would be a hardship tour and that they would go through a type of amnesia until their planned awakening, and that they would be subjected to third-dimensional limitations and challenges, including the Human enculturation, which is much different from their own.

To the ET and Spiritual Guides of those Star Beings on Earth, who watch over them closely with much love and compassion, who had the courage to learn the ways of life on Earth in order to guide their loved one on their paths and in their missions.

To the Star Beings of Light who contact the people of Earth, who risk their own lives coming to Earth, out of their love for all lifeforms, with their intentions to help Gaia and Humanity in their evolutionary shift (despite the still-active USA "Shoot Them Down" policy, enacted by President Truman).

To all Star Beings who physically died during their missions to assist Gaia and her people. To those who died on a foreign planet, in their ship or in a military lab, without relief of pain until their passing. Especially to those who most unfortunately suffered at the hands of Humankind, receiving no rights, no respect and no courtesies as a result of being feared.

You are loved, and we give you our most heart-felt "Thank You!"

In Appreciation

We wish to show our deep appreciation to the following:

Hartmut Jaeger and Kesara, for your beautiful art work that your shared to help create our book. Your flexibility and kindness was a blessing to me.

Stacey Barlow, Cynthia Crawford, Quabar and Jackie Zandrews, for your friendship and support during the creation of our book. Without your help, the book would not be what it is.

To my mother and father, who surprised me with their loving support of this book, while it greatly differs from their beliefs.

Last, but not least, to Ann Ulrich Miller and Earth Star Publications, for all of your time and energy and desire to publish our book.

Sale proceeds of our book go to the following:
Southwest Light and Learning Center — "An extracurricular institute for higher awareness, based in Pagosa Springs, Colorado. With its year-round attractions to people from all walks of life, Pagosa Springs is the perfect place for gathering to learn more about ourselves and to share the gifts that will enable us to move into Earth's Ascension. We offer six-week classes seven times a year that meet once or twice a week, as well as seminars, weekend retreats and the semi-annual Love and Light Conference." Web site: http://www.southwestlight.org

Heifer International — "Bringing an End to World Hunger Through Unimaginable Blessings. Helping children and families around the world receive training and animal gifts that help them become self-reliant. Heifer has learned over the years that a holistic approach is necessary in order to build sustainable communities. So we've developed a set of global initiatives — areas of emphasis that must be addressed if we're to meet our mission of ending world hunger and poverty and caring for the earth." Web site: http://www.heifer.org

Introduction

"There is no proof. There are no authorities whatsoever. No president, no
academy, court of law, congress or senate on this earth has the power or
the knowledge to decide what will be the knowledge of tomorrow."
— *Wilhelm Reich*

In June of 2009, I was sitting in my lounge chair, enjoying the warm sun and
a special book. I am always reading some non-fiction book, and this one really
had my attention. I believe it was a *Kryon* book and my frequency was being
elevated from the information I was reading. All of a sudden, mid-paragraph in
the book, I received an "assignment" from my people, the Faquians. It was a
second-long, telepathic message, including both verbal and visual communication.
They said, "Organize a book containing the personal stories of Starseeds and ET
Hybrids incarnated on Earth. This will help other Starseeds awaken, unite
Earth's Star family and help expand the minds of Humanity."

I froze while receiving this message from my people. I carefully placed the
bookmark where I stopped reading and was excited to return to it once I
finished this communication. I put the book down and said,"What!? How am I
going to do that? I have never organized a book before." Before I could finish
my sentence, I received additional input, "Call Cynthias," they said, "we will
co-create the book with you." (Cynthias is a close friend of mine, who is also a
Hybrid.)

I instantly knew at that point that it would be done because I could see the
book already created in my third eye. So I said back to them, "Okay, but after I
read this book."

Wrong answer! *"Call Cynthias!"* they emphasized.

So I immediately got up, walked to the phone, called my very good friend,
and it all started from that moment. Six months later, we have compiled 18 stories from those Starbeings who were guided to be a part of this outreach project.

*   *   *

Main societies concern themselves with "First Contact" from an Extraterrestrial race. The funny thing is, depending on who you ask, first contact happened long ago and many times over! What experience would you qualify as "First Contact"?That may sound like a silly question, but what type of event would you consider "contact"? The definition is different for each person.

It would be wise for people to drop the expectation of ETs coming in their huge ships and landing near major cities of the world (as the TV series "*V*" portrays). This may actually happen one day, but we are here to inform the people of Earth—we are among you already!

There is a Universal Law that opposes the direct interference of a species by a more evolved and advanced race of beings. It is Universal law that a free-will species develops on its own, unless assistance is asked for by the majority of their group consciousness. Therefore, we could not just land on Earth in our huge ships and merge into society, the people of Earth are not ready. We have to incarnate among Earth Humans in order to help without violating the Universal Law of Non-interference.

This book is a compilation of very personal, individual, life stories from those who are Awakened Starseeds. A Starseed, or Starbeing, is a being who lives on Earth, but whose soul is of Extraterrestrial (ET) identity and origin. This self-awareness and knowledge of having ET origins is what we call being awakened. Awakening to one's true self is a very personal, spiritual and self-empowering journey. This path is most often lonely, challenging and not under-stood nor supported by mainstream society.

Included in this book is my own story, listed under my Star name Jujuolui Kuita. My people from Faqui, known as the Faquian Council, telepathically assisted me along the journey of compiling this book. The Council members are: Jer-mi, Jo-sah-fi, Kayac-tah and myself (Jujuolui). I am the Council's Earth representative. As I worked with each story, I could feel the energy of my people and something surprised me—I also felt the energies of some of the Starbeings' people helping me! I was delighted by their contributions. Some of the ETs or Spirit guides that were helping had very strong energy! I had to take many breaks.

Starseeds have incarnated in various ways on Earth and appear very

Human, to the average person. This was deliberately intended! Starbeings normally plan on integrating into society, becoming inculturated to fit in, while working on their missions. If Starbeings physically looked more like ETs, society might not allow them into Human culture, but instead, they could end up in a museum, a freak show, killed by fearful Humans, or worse—taken to a secret government lab. If you have seen movies like *District 9*, you will understand this better. Because of the Universal Law of Non-Intervention, Starbeings have their best chance to help in the ascension process by incarnating among the Humans.

There is a common theme among Starbeings, such as believing they are adopted, feeling that Earth is not "home," knowing they are different than others, having an invisible friend as a child, having metaphysical abilities that other people don't seem to have, speaking or writing in a different language, having vivid "dreams" of being an ET, being on another planet or within a ship and feeling love and empathy for all life forms. Starbeings are also not comfortable or able to understand violence, war, hate, prejudice, fear and the negative treatment of other life in general. Commonly, they have very open minds and more easily accept esoteric ideas. (See the "New ET Quiz" created by researcher and Starseed *Scott Mandelker*, under "Last Thoughts.")

Starseeds can also be genetic Hybrids, which is a mixture of Human and ET DNA. Only with psychic abilities, or training and a keen eye, can one tell the difference between a Human and a Starseed. Some ET DNA produce dominant traits and may be visible in a person's physical characteristics, whether a Starseed is a Hybrid or not. We are still learning what those specific traits are, since it is a limitless gene pool that started at the beginning of Human creation. ETs have come to Earth from every corner of this Galaxy, from other Galaxies and even other Dimensions. They consist of all different types and species. Some of them are known to Earth people, most of them are not. Some of them even live within Earth herself.

There is much confusion about Hybrids. Even in the field of Ufology it remains "taboo" among many researchers. Many have problems with this concept in Ufology, since it is not something they can prove, yet. There are many ways of creating a Hybrid body. The body is considered a "container for the soul" and may be genetically created by an ET species or by the secret military (sometimes in cooperation with another ET species). This may be accomplished as a result of an ET contact experience or by the more nefarious military abduction (MILAB). Simply put, geneticists combine the DNAs by a type of gene-splicing technology and "Petri dish." "Genetic engineering can enable the transport of genes between unrelated organisms (transgenesis) or related organisms (cisgenesis) that would otherwise be unable to occur naturally, due to differences in anatomy or the incorrespondence between the DNA structures." [1]

The body can even be manipulated by geneticists during gestation or after the being is born, usually at a young age. They can determine which genes to activate and which ones to keep inactive. The results are quite endless. Some species are more compatible to genetically mix than others. The Insectoid species, for example, like the Grays and Praying Mantis beings, faced many challenges while creating a healthy Human Hybrid because their genes are not compatible with the mammalian species. Many Insectoid Hybrids suffer with weaker immune systems and have small, frail bodies, but have many psychic abilities and are very intelligent.

The Reptoid species, on the other hand, is a much better DNA match for Humans because Humans already have Reptilian DNA (brain stem and tail to name a few), in their genetics. Reptilian Hybrids are known to be more athletic, healthy, strong and live longer lives, but seem to be more challenged with their ego and with "negative" emotions.

The best DNA mixture, of course, is with other Humanoid species, such as those from the Pleiades. These are by no means the only types of ETs that are incarnating on Earth or creating Hybrids. Genetic engineering programs are a very realistic and a serious professional field among many, many ET species.

Most of the Starbeings' stories were collected by interview method while asking questions from a created questionnaire by the Compiler. Each Starbeing was requested to only share what they knew to be true and to share as much as they felt was appropriate for the book. Some beings were told by their Star families not to discuss certain things at this time while others where encouraged to share their knowledge at this time.

Each story was recorded, transcribed and edited for brevity and clarity before going to the publisher. Each being was sent their edited story to make any desired changes and to finally approve their story. The intention of writing each story this way was to give an intimate feeling into each Starbeing's life and to keep the vibration of this book at its highest. Some of their stories include references to their own books, DVDs, music or services and businesses only because it was relevant to their stories. There was no intention, nor allowance, for self-promotions which would only diminish the vibration of the book.

Each story stands alone and is listed under the Starseed's name (or pseudonym). They are not placed in order of importance or ranking of any kind. The Starbeings in this book range in age, gender, sexual orientation, nationality and more. For the most part, each Starbeing chose a pseudonym to protect themselves from unwanted discrimination or harassment in their lives. They are each awakened, but not necessarily "Out of the Closet" to co-workers, parents, friends or the children in their lives.

You will read how each Starbeing is very different from the next and each has their own life perspective. They do not all agree or see things the same way and there is much diversity between each story. The key to remember when reading these stories is to be aware of how you feel about what you are reading. Feelings are your own keys to what is right for you. Try to remain open-minded and open-hearted!

Listed at the bottom of each story, the Starbeings have remarked on books, movies, websites or people that were significant to them. This was intended to help you in your own research if you connected with a being's story. Most importantly and respectfully, each Starbeing has left a way to be contacted, usually by email. This was intended to allow you the ability to connect with the Starbeing(s). Most of the emails were deliberately created just for the readers of this book and were created under pseudonyms for their protection. Feel welcomed to contact them! If you have any trouble using one of the email addresses or in getting a response, please email me: faquian@gawab.com.

The stories in this book are not trying to convince you, convert you or prove anything to you. Your own beliefs and understandings are respected. We do not wish to change you, only offer you information. Most Starbeings have moved beyond the need for proof as they evolve spiritually. Proof is a matter of perception and it is weighed differently for everyone. Proof or belief in some-

thing only comes from within yourself, so use discernment; it is your best tool
in life. Your intuition will guide you to your own truth, when you listen. Think
for yourself. Follow your heart and inner guidance. Question everything!

"Trust, but verify."
— *Ronald Reagan's signature phrase*

To our Starseed readers:

The intention for sharing our stories is to assist you in furthering your own
awakening and connect you to other Star family on Earth. Some of you may be
questioning your off-world origins or it may never have occurred to you that
you might be a Starseed. Spirit has guided you to this book and you can benefit
greatly in expanding your consciousness when reading these stories with an
open mind. You may also find answers to your unexplained experiences. Be
ready to explore your truth and set your intentions before you begin reading.
Once you allow the information into your consciousness, you are on a new path,
a path of awakening. Ask your guides to be with you and assist you on this
journey, they know you best. Each Starbeing included personal contact information at the end of their story so that we may be of even greater service to you.
We each welcome you to contact us for any respectful and sincere reason.
Please remember, Starseeds, self-discovery is very empowering and every life
form is equally valued by Source. The intention of awakening is not to separate
yourself from others, but to evolve.

I wish to share with you a powerful mantra, a protective shield to use daily
and before you read on:

"I am a sovereign being
exercising free will as I ascend the spiral of Spirit;
I intend that the Higher Purpose be served and
that the Light prevail..." [2]

To our Human soul readers:

We thank you for having the courage and desire to learn by picking up this book. It, too, was guided to you for a reason. This does not mean that you must believe everything you read, that is blind faith. We wish that you read everything with discretion. Take what you feel is true and disregard the rest.

Every soul is created from Source, but there are unfathomable amounts of "soul groups" that have taken their own paths of soul-evolution. The Human soul group of Earth, and Earth herself, both sent out an S.O.S. call to Starbeings everywhere, to assist in their ascension. Please remember, no soul is greater than nor less than another. We need everyone working together to complete Mission Earth. Our intention for sharing our stories with you is to present information to you that may help expand your mind to new realities and broaden your perceptions. We wish to be called brother and sister to you, not Alien.

"I believe (and hope), that I speak for each Starbeing in this book when I say that we place ourselves alongside Humankind, not above and not below. We especially discourage being idolized in any way. We are all equal in importance and we have a mission to accomplish together; to see Earth and all sentient life upon her, into the next phase of evolution!"
— Jujuolui, The Compiler

"You must **be** the change that you wish to see in the world"
— *Mahatma Ghandi*

Marcia Schafer once so eloquently stated: *We were born as part of a mass contingency, we decided to be here at a time to help in a strategic turn-around on this Planet. Let go of mediocracy, let go of being a sheeple, become self-empowered and remember who you are!*

"Few men are willing to brave the disapproval of their fellows, the censure of their colleagues, the wrath of their society. Moral courage is a rarer commodity than bravery in battle or great intelligence. Yet it is the one essential, vital quality for those who seek to change a world which yields most painfully to change."
— *Robert F. Kennedy, 1966 Speech*

"No problem can be solved from the same
level of consciousness that created it."
— *Albert Einstein*

The Compiler, Dec. 2009

1
— *Sustaining Life.* Oxford University Press, Inc. 2008. ISBN 978-0-19-517509-7

2
— From Speakers of the Sirian High Council, "No more Secrets, No more Lies," by Patricia Cori.

Contents

Star Being **Page**

1. Don Anderson 15

2. Raj 41

3. Sanni Ceto 53

4. Kesara 65

5. David Armstrong 75

6. INO 89

7. Bhodi 99

8. Jujuolui Kuita 109

9. OM 127

10. Serena Starlight 141

11. Arroylos 151

12. Cynthias 165

13. Laselena 183

14. Shenai 191

15. Niara Terela 197

16. Peanut 217

17. Norji 221

18. Jaeya 237

   Last Thoughts 243

Don Anderson

I had people ask me what my ET name is before and the first thing that popped into my head was 'Adamus.' I had no idea what that name was then, but I believe it is an old Greek God or something. I don't know if I really resonate with the name Adamus.

I was going through my awakening process at the time, which was very confusing for me. Names were never very important to me, but faces and personalities are. I have never asked what my star name is and maybe I don't want to know. I do know, most assuredly, that I am a Starseed.

I have done a pre-Earth regression. Before I was born here on Earth, I was being escorted by two Gray ETs. We were discussing the importance of "the mission" and how things should work out. I didn't get any specific details. The Grays looked at me and pointed down, towards Earth. That was the last thing I remembered.

I was born from a mother, but have absolutely no connection to her or her family. I can stare at her picture and wonder who this lady is that raised me. There is no emotional connection to her or her family. I always felt like I was born in a house full of strangers. Sounds familiar to other Starseeds, I know.

I have also been called a Hybrid by some. I have had a definite type of "walk-in" experience once. I call it more of a transition where one Don traded places with the other, like a change in energy patterns. The ETs I used to communicate with in meditations prior to that experience no longer recognized me and would consistently refer me to other places different in nature.

All in all, it has been up to this point, very confusing. I do feel like a genetically mixed hybrid. Shamans tell me that I am, and recently I came to that feeling for myself. It has to do with some experiences I have been through and how I've been treated by other ET beings. There are times I will look in the mirror and see something that is not familiar to me. One time looking in the mirror, I saw a Gray-looking being with a triangular-shaped head and tan-colored skin. A different time I saw my Nordic self: blond hair, blue eyes, and about 6 feet tall. I have also seen another being while looking in the mirror at myself.

The more I understood about my contact experiences, the more unusual I realized I was. After I had had more than my share of experiences and knowledge from these contact experiences, I realized I was not exactly cut from the same mold as humans. There are many times when I was with friends who have had the same type of experiences that they would start asking me, "Who is we?" when I talked, and I realized I was unconsciously talking in the plural.

Shamans would look at me and call me their "alien friend." It was after I had experienced some of these things that I came to understand and accept who I was. It was just a natural understanding that I am not from here. This is my home and I live here currently, but when my body goes, I am not going to any type of heaven realm. I am going back to my cosmic origins.

If you were to see me on the streets, I would look just like anyone else, although I have been told many times there is something different about me. I try to fit into society just like anyone else and I can communicate on a level with most anyone. My IQ is in the mid 140s. I have taken a MENSA pre-test and I passed. I suppose I could take the real test if I had the desire and I would pass it. I can talk sports, politics, religion, economy, and pretend to fit in. That's as far as it goes.

I know I am from another star system because as well as I can pretend, I just can't process or internalize the things of importance to people here. Sometimes I play the game really well. When I completely shut out the ET side of me, I can immerse myself in society and do okay, but sooner or later, I cannot keep it from coming out. My connection to the stars is just too great to ignore. I feel the deep, intense love, the feeling of something always missing and the understanding on some level that the pursuit of things just isn't worth it.

My Earth life is like reading from a book, understanding the concepts, but failing to get any deep meaning from it. Life can be all nice and fluffy if I'd fol-low the rules and ignore the cosmic side, but it leaves me feeling shallow. Similar to kissing your sister, it's a nice gesture and well meaning, but it is lost when real love comes along.

I don't know for sure what planet I came from, although I know my species are of a Nordic race. Two planets resonate strongly for me: Alpha Centauri and Sirius A, in the Sirius Star System. An experience I find myself in is waiting out on my driveway late at night for a ship. Once a ship comes, I am taken to Alpha Centauri, but other times I get a very strong connection with Sirius A. I do a lot of "reverse speech," where you replay what someone says in reverse. In this manner, I would ask various questions and Sirius A keeps popping up as a big connection for me.

Alpha Centauri is a planet I have been to many times. I don't always get there by ship, although I have gotten there by a typical "saucer-shaped" craft that I watched come in towards me and I blanked out. On other occasions, I can see my aura body where all of my chakras light up the colors that they are and they shoot me out of my body. It looks like a rainbow arch and I instantaneously flash over to Alpha Centauri. It doesn't really feel like a place I would call home, but more like a meeting place where I remember communicating with a group of beings.

I can remember looking out over the planet. It didn't seem to be very big, since I could see the curvature of the planet. Alpha Centauri is a darker planet because they do not have much of a sun. The only colors on the planet are hues of violet-purple. In some ways it resembles Earth in that human-like beings occupy it, though small in numbers. There are buildings there as they are needed and technology is light-years in advance of Earth. The countryside was pretty rocky and barren, more desert like. There were about half a dozen houses in this little community that I associate with, especially one house in particular.

It was a little adobe cottage, made out of white and purple materials; the inside was white and the outside was purple. I saw a walk path and something that looked similar to lawn and shrubs. This setup was nothing like on Earth; no lights, no refrigerators, no electricity and no running lines. The houses all looked the same, although It looked very professional and very well made. It was just different than what we have here.

There are no doorways on anything, you just walk right in. I remember walking down this hall as the lights just kick on for you as you walk, and I don't know where the lights are coming from. I walked into this back room and saw a couple of beings sitting there waiting for me. I asked them what this particular room was, and they told me that I would probably describe the room as the kitchen, where we go to eat.

They told me, "We don't eat food, but your physical bodies require it and so we have a place provided for you." I believe they created this to make me feel at home on Earth. The two beings in the room were "Nordics," both a man and a woman.

After this greeting, the three of us went over to a main building that had a dome-shaped top that was a gold color. This was our meeting place, not extremely large. Inside of this building was elevated seating going up towards the ceiling. All of the seats were arranged in a five-pointed star pattern, which was weird. I was the speaker and I would sit in the center of this star on a platform that would raise up. Then this holograph projected me so that I was facing everyone in the room.

The last time I went to Alpha Centauri, everyone was standing up and cheering. I have never been filled in on what is going on in these meetings. I always ask them what is happening, what the big deal is, what the meeting is all about, but I just get stonewalled. They will talk to me about anything under the sun, but when I ask about those experiences, nothing.

Once, while I was meditating, I was taken to the planet Sirius A. I remember meeting up with my Earth friend, Dawn, while meditating. She would take me to places like Machu Pichu and Area 51. I call it "Consciousness Sharing," which is different from remote-viewing. I would see signs and landmarks in the area during these experiences and I would later see these same signs while driving in the area. At Machu Pichu, I saw this guy sitting behind a desk with a bunch of books. He looked very much Caucasian, but he dressed in South American clothing. This guy would wave us toward the back of the building where there is a great big cave. Dawn would take me to a big pedestal in this cave where a type of portal was. We would jump into this portal and we would be at my home planet on Sirius A. It was like flying through the skies, down through a couple of mountains, and we saw a house down below.

I asked Dawn what it was, and she told me, "This is where we lived together, just the two of us." The house was similar to the European houses, an Alpine, Dwarvish style house. It was sitting out in a big, open green field. I could see an energy field around each blade of grass.

Then I saw mountains in the background and, off to the side, there were cliffs and a big ocean. As you look at the waves of the ocean, you can see the energy of the wave itself, like seeing its aura. It was the same with the Earth-looking plants as well. It was a very peaceful and calm energy there, even the air was lighter. The color of the sky was a bright blue with no clouds. I couldn't see any suns or moons, nor any ships or vehicles. There were no other buildings nearby, but I do remember seeing a village during a another visit to Sirius A. That village was a very clean, Alpine-styled area. I saw people living there who were about 6-to-7 feet tall and some had brown hair instead of blond. Lately I have run into an Indian guy who has told me about also seeing the energy aura on this planet.

A contact story I wrote:

"MOMMY!" A blood curdling cry rang out through the darkness of the night. "MOMMY!" The voice rang out again with the urgency of a terrified child.

Opening her eyes from a deep sleep in the hot summer night, her heart pounding with adrenalin—the adrenalin of a mother whose child was in danger—she momentarily froze. *Donald!* she thought to herself as she sprung from her bed. The urgency in his small child's voice echoed down the hall. *Donald!*

She flung open the bedroom door and sprinted down the hall toward the boy's bedroom. Flinging the door open, she nervously flipped on the light. It took a moment for her eyes to adjust to the suddenness of the lit room, but once they did, she glanced around the room, expecting to find an intruder—perhaps a robber? Who knows?

Instead, she saw me curled up in a ball, my arms clutched tightly to my legs, which were pressed firmly against my chest. It was a bunk bed, and my bed was on the bottom bunk. You could barely make me out in the shadows of the upper bunk, my tiny body rolled up in the corner in the shadows. Tears were rolling down my cheeks as I slowly rocked back and forth on the mattress, my covers piled in a lump on the other side of the bed.

"Donald! What's wrong?" she asked rather tepidly. She sat on the edge of the bed and gently pulled me towards her. The pajamas I was wearing were drenched in sweat. Grabbing her tightly, I clung to her neck. "Did you have a bad dream?" she said, relieved I was okay.

My little brother, awakened by all the commotion, stuck his head over the bed rail, staring at me curiously, his little blue eyes gazing at me. "Did you have a bad dream?" he said, echoing our mother.

"It wasn't a dream," I replied as I laid my head on my mother's chest. "There was a man outside my window. A really big man! And he had a flashlight. He shined it in through the window to my bed. He was a big man, Mommy! A really big man!"

She froze in terror, staring out the window, half expecting something or someone to come busting through the glass window and rolling across the floor. Perhaps brandishing a knife and demanding money, or worse! Her imagination ran wild before she finally got hold of herself and came to grips with reality.

Grasping me in her arms, she slowly got up and turned out the light. Cautiously walking to the window, she gazed out through the darkness of the night, slowly scanning the backyard for any type of shadow or figure that may be hiding in the darkness. A lone streetlight lit up the corner of the property. She could see nothing—even in the light of a full moon and with the help of the streetlight. Now she was just plain scared.

Within minutes the police had arrived. It was a rather small town in a rural community. Not much happened here and chances were the police were in bed when she called. They knew almost everyone in town, and they knew she was a single lady. So in the wee hours of the morning, they had come to investigate a possible intruder in the area.

After an hour of checking the area with flashlights, looking for footprints in the freshly irrigated yard and combing the neighborhood, there was no sign of an intruder.

Soon there was a knock on the front door. Passing the clock in the hall as she went to answer the door, she saw it was 4:30 in the morning. *Too early in the morning for all this*, she thought to herself as she opened the door to the sight of the policeman on the porch.

"I am sorry, ma'am," he said rather apologetically, "but we have done a really thorough search of the backyard and the surrounding neighborhood and have not come up with anything. Your lawn and backyard have just been irrigated, so if there was anything out there, it would have made some clear footprints."

"Thank you officer," she replied. "I am not sure what happened, but it is not like him to wake up so terrified. He has always been such a good sleeper.

When he woke up screaming, I was really concerned."

"Well, that's understandable considering the circumstances," he replied, "If I were in your situation—meaning a single lady and all—perhaps I would do the same thing. Keep your eyes open and if you notice anything suspicious in the morning, any locks jimmied or something out of the ordinary, give us a call."

The next three nights produced more of the same, each night the screams in the middle of the night, each night the followup with the police department, until finally on the fourth night the police had told her she just couldn't keep calling them about the same incidents.

"Ma'am," he said after the fourth visit, "there just is nothing there. I hate to say this, and I don't want to sound disrespectful, but your boy is just having nightmares. Now I know he is scared and all, so there is something that is really bothering him, but we can't keep coming out on these calls. There just ain't nothing there."

She sobbed as tears flowed down her cheek. "This isn't my son. Something has him terrified. Something has been spooking him in the middle of the night. Always the same time, always between 2 and 3 A.M."

"How about you give Doc a call in the morning and see what he can do? Maybe it's medical, couldn't hurt," he said.

She nodded her head in agreement, even though she did not agree. What else could she do?

The next night I crawled into my bed, pulling the covers up tight against my chin and cowering next to the wall. "Good night, boys," said Mom as she turned to walk out of the room.

"Mommy," I said as she turned out the light, "can you leave the lights on?"

"No, Donald…But I will leave the door open, okay? I'll be right down the hall with my door open. You'll be okay," she said, almost believing herself.

I was not sure what had awakened me in the middle of the night, but quite suddenly my eyes popped wide open and I found myself staring at the large bedroom window across the room. Perhaps I was waiting for the large man with the flashlight to shine it through the window and illuminate the room as he had been doing the previous nights. I just held the blanket tightly under my chin and drew closer to the wall, as far away from the side of the bed as I could.

But no man with a flashlight showed up. This time it was different. I watched—terrified—as some sort of little creature suddenly materialized through the wall. No lights, just a 3-foot-tall, troll-like creature. I huddled up in a ball, my eyes growing as the creature slowly waddled towards me, like a duck would walk. It didn't look like it had actual legs—rather just two attachments hooked to his short, stubby torso that was almost as wide as it was tall. It had black, rough-looking skin, sort of like a crocodile. Its arms were skinnier than they should have been for something of its size, and they sort of dangled next to him and swayed as it walked. Its head, really quite large for its body size, just sort of stuck on its torso with little or no neck, making it very difficult for the thing to view anything that was not straight ahead of it.

And its eyes…its eyes were like big red saucers, larger than normal, but in proportion to its head. (Years later I came to recognize this being as the same being in Whitley Strieber's movie *Communion*. It was the little being Christopher Walken danced for in one of the scenes.) It stopped at the side of my bed and just stared at me with those huge, red eyes. A weird type of grin revealed through its large fat lips. It reached its arms up and slowly pulled the covers away from me.

Then, quite surprisingly, it reached up under my arm pits and gently tickled me with his stubby fingers. I was terrified. I couldn't laugh. I couldn't cry and I couldn't scream for my mother either. This strange little creature stepped though the wall and was suddenly tickling me under the arms. I couldn't understand what was happening to me. And worse than that, I couldn't move. The little being managed to scoop me up in his arms and lift me from my bed. Almost immediately afterwards, a brilliant blue light was shining through my bedroom window, illuminating the room in an eerie iridescent blue.

I managed to see my little brother sleeping peacefully on the upper bunk. The little being shuffled me across the room next to the window and into the light. I realized now that this was the man with a flashlight. Away we went into light, through the window and out into the night air.

This story, though it may seem like more of a night terror and scary abduction experience, was not so much an abduction experience as it was a teaching moment. This is the time when they—my teachers—would come to get me and help me to awaken my DNA. Years later, I consulted with a certified hypnotherapist and underwent several sessions. I realized that all the experiences

I had over the period of that month and a half were in the pursuit of training me.

Games were devised with various beings where I was taught how to levitate objects and operate different types of machinery. I was always gifted with fantastic eye/hand coordination. All "abduction" experiences are not bad…they are just misunderstood simply because the human mind has been taught fear of things it does not understand.

One night my mother's new husband offered to take everyone out for a ride. This time Mom refused and wanted to stay home to finish cleaning the house, so we left without her. We came home a couple of hours later to find her terrified and locked inside the car in the driveway. Every light in the house was on and the radio and TV were on full blast.

"I will not go back into that house by myself!" she exclaimed emphatically. "Something is not right!"

Those kind of things happened on a regular basis for us. We would go on a car ride and come home to every light in the house on and all the electronic equipment turned on full blast. The doors would always be locked from the inside and all the windows shut tight. Sometimes the neighbors would even ask what the lights over our house were. It was always a mystery and kept up until we finally moved again.

When I was about 8 years old, I remember being at a friend's house, viewing the night sky which had all of these really colorful balls or Orbs zipping across the sky. Suddenly we saw the front end of a ship appear and we freaked out. We ran into his Mom and Dad's room and these Orbs began popping up inside the room. I was shaking his Dad, trying hard to wake him. The last thing I remember was hiding behind a chair, looking out the screen door and watching some Grays floating towards the house.

I had a "screen memory" experience when I was 14 years old. I got stuck up a canyon while I was at a party. The funny thing was, I didn't remember how I got up there. I do remember hitch-hiking, but then—all of the sudden—I was walking up the road to the party. Everybody was drinking and surprised to see me there. I had one drink, got sick to my stomach, and that was it for me.

The next day I was left at the canyon all by myself. There was no moon that night, and under the cover of the pines it was quite dark as I made my way down the campsite road. But that night did not feel right and I knew something was off.

Suddenly, in the distance, I could hear the sound of footsteps on pine needles, crushing under the feet of whoever was following me. First I heard footsteps on the one side of the road, and eventually on the other side of the road, not far behind me.

As a 14-year-old boy, alone by myself in the mountains at night, I panicked. Images of coyotes suddenly emerged in my head as I broke into a run down the road, the footsteps gradually fading off into the distance before I slowed down and stopped. I realized I had no place to go and that whatever was following me would eventually catch up to me before I could reach the mouth of the canyon and arrive at the safety of the park superintendent's house.

I contemplated my situation. The only option was either to climb a tree or lock myself in the outhouse just down the road from where I was standing. At this point I had also come to the conclusion I was being chased by a herd of skunks. I again had images in my head of skunks confronting me down the road. So I decided to hide in the outhouse and it was in there I was taken by a UFO.

I later underwent hypnosis to get more information out of this experience. I found out that I was taken that night by a disk-shaped craft. The inside of this craft matched exactly what prior-Area 51 employee, Bob Lazar, described inside a disk ship. I saw a big silver screen that stretched all around the inside of the ship. All of a sudden, this screen gave way and I could clearly see outside.

As I looked outside, I could see all of these beings walking around and between the trees. These beings were actually the "Grays." Next, they took me to the middle of the Milky Way Galaxy and parked in the middle of a huge donut-shaped ship that was there. I was escorted into the donut-shaped ship by a Nordic being whom I believe was my Dad, Raphael. There is such a strong connection between us. These Nordics are all tall, have blond hair and blue eyes.

Inside this huge ship there are long walkways that run from the center and into different places within the ship. In this one particular room, Raphael and I walked inside and I saw a classroom that had something similar to a chalkboard. There was an old guy, the instructor, sitting at the chalkboard and 15 to 20 children sitting nearby. The children would look at this chalkboard and I saw these characters of a different language pop up and the children would respond to it. They would tell the instructor what they were seeing.

The instructor looked ancient, he had a shriveled face and seemed to be a Human-Gray hybrid. His skin was a tannish color and his eyes were human looking, but really deep. They reminded me of looking into a Gray's eyes; you can see the universe and it is overwhelming. I have never seen this language before, but it looked similar to Sanskrit. I have also seen a similar language in a book written by B. Andreason.

One time while I was lying in bed, there was this symbol that suddenly appeared in front of me. Inside of this symbol I could see the universe. Then I noticed the Pleiades and then Sirius shining through. The symbol moved towards me and right into my forehead and disappeared. This made my forehead tingly. I later talked to someone else who saw something very similar.

Once there was a lady I had an instant connection to. I was told before we met each other to "look for the blond-haired lady." She walked up the driveway at a MUFON meeting one day and everyone thought we were together because of how we instantly connected.

Unfortunately, she recently got out of this field of study, because she had had enough. Although we had a lot of experiences together, she just decided to turn it off.

I am a part of the Nordics, but the Grays are my teachers and friends. Of course there are different species of Gray; some of them are biological units as far as I understand. Some of these will work for benevolent beings and others work for malevolent beings, and these units will tend to pick up the traits of whomever they work for. There is only one being that I have a clue about; his name is Jaron. Jaron is a Praying Mantis ET, and he is with me quite a bit.

I have run across the "Cat people" before, too. They are very humble, loving, and seem timid. The Cat people were very sure of themselves, but reserved. They don't like to get out and be recognized much, so they stay clear. They also don't really like to associate themselves with a planet.

I recall one experience with this species while I was sitting in meditation. I said, "Okay, take me to the nearest ship." *Boom!* I was sitting on this ship and the feline people were there. They were having a problem with their propulsion system or something. It seemed as if they were having a hard time figuring out how this machine worked technologically. I walked over and spat out some really bizarre technical term or jargon at them.

They just looked at me, took off to another room and said, "Thank you very much." They spoke telepathically, as most ET beings do.

Certain races of beings work off of the fear emotion. A true cosmic being is devoid of fear and does not respond to it. In a word, you are responsible for your actions. There is no single entity that is responsible for the decisions you make and the life you live.

Some not-so-nice entities can—and do—try to influence your actions and can become quite successful, such as with drug addicts, alcoholics, substance abusers, most addictions, etc. There are beings that are on "the other side" that can and do whisper in auras and attach themselves to people. They can become quite powerful, especially the ones that have existed through the ages. There are many realms of existence out there quite close to ours that can influence us, just as we can influence theirs.

I have had many shamanic experiences where I would sit up in the mountains for four to six hours and just observe things. I would see a dead tree and feel tears stream down my face.

I have had Indian people come up to me, asking for help when their own brothers are shamans. I feel a strong connection to an Indian side of me. While advancing this side of me, the "Consciousness Sharing" experiences became important. One year at the "Area 51 Conference," I did some soul-retrievals and similar shamanic duties. Directly afterwards, these abilities came to a halt.

I believe this happened possibly from outside interference because a year before the conference, I was told by the Reptilians not to speak. As a result, I died a shaman's death (a traumatic experience where you die or are overtaken in another world and, when you come back alive, you come back stronger and better prepared). There was a really strong entity that attached to my soul. When I finally got rid of it, my head felt empty and I almost went insane.

While going through an awakening, most people are very naive in thinking that nothing can hurt them and that they are protected. In the shamanic world, one must know about these entities and must understand them. There are many different levels of reality and many different types of beings. They are not all nice. Some people are meant to walk the peaceful path and some are meant to walk the warrior's path.

I did energy work on my son before, when he had two powerful beings attached to him. These beings feed off of the energy of others. Since my son was addicted, these entities were feeding off of his addictions. His life wasn't his own at that time. The beings are attracted to the vibrational patterns of a person when they are high or drunk. Many others share this problem.

Because of my ET side and my shamanic side, I am able to connect to beings in other realms. There is a group of Inner-Dimensional beings I work with called "We." It is a collective consciousness of beings and I believe they are my family.

Sometimes I will start breaking out talking in the plural, saying "we." They are source material for me and have told me that they look after me. They showed me what they are capable of; my bills were paid up to where I didn't have to worry about them for months, everything was working out for me really well. There is one I call the "psychic being" and he helps me with the energy in my meditation work.

I also work with the Angelic Realm when someone needs their assistance or guidance. Another type of being I call the Kabbalah being. These are the beings that work with the Jewish people. The energy they have is very powerful, very raw and direct. Everything is a matter of fact with the Kabbalah beings, no fun or games.

I recall one instance working with them involving weather. I was walking near my street when this voice told me that I had the ability to manipulate the weather. Using my third eye, I saw this very tall Indian sitting on a big horse with a rod in his left hand and the reins in his right hand. I humored this being and told him to give me a thunder and lightning storm, but not to hurt anyone. Instantly, I watched this Indian gallop up to the top of the mountain, swirling the rod in the air above him. I saw clouds start forming over his head.

I thought to myself, *I have seen this type of show before, you guys are masters of illusion.*

I walked home, thinking nothing more of it until the next day. I saw on the news that a massive storm occurred, involving much damage to property, but not one person was hurt. Since then, I have learned that tapping into these energies is natural for me. Later, I saw one Kabbalah being ride his horse into the infamous Hurricane Katrina. Although the Kabbalah are sentient beings, those who learned to use them can manipulate them to be used for whatever intentions.

One July night there were four of us at a campsite trying to have a contact experience. One member in our group, a shaman, had a strong ability to communicate with the ETs, and we all decided to call in the Praying Mantis. Our shaman began by calling in the four winds and spoke an old Indian language.

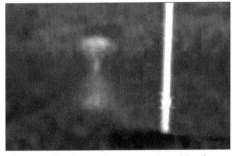

We were sitting at our campsite when—suddenly—the cloudy sky gave way directly above us. A perfect circle of clear sky became visible where we could see the stars and a triangular ship. I could tell it was triangular because as it moved it blocked out the stars.

One of the girls in our group walked towards the outhouse and suddenly we heard her screaming. She was calling out to the other female to come take a look. Then the two girls called out for us two guys to come as well.

I saw all of them stretching out their hands in a section of air above a path. I felt the air pocket with my own hand and it felt about 15 degrees colder than that night's air.

It was at that time I heard the clicking sounds. I could make out shadow shapes running around, I saw bodies which resembled huge Praying Mantis, red-colored eyes the size of saucers, and they walked on four legs. They kept making these clicking sounds and, once in a while, I would also hear a *whirr*, like feathers.

I later learned that the Praying Mantis have a breathing apparatus on their stomach which sounds like a feathering when they breathe. These beings stood about 8 feet tall and had two "arm" appendages. It seemed that they never fully came out of their higher dimensional state, although I could make that much out. The Mantis beings have a very cool, electrical energy about them. They also have a dry and witty humor, as if they don't understand they are being funny. It comes out really bizarre. They ran in packs of three and there were about nine of them running around.

"Watch," exclaimed the shaman as he calmly walked out into the middle of the yard. "I am going to have one of them hide me and as they do, I will disappear." True to his word, the shaman disappeared, only to reappear a moment later. "I am going to have them do it again," he said as his torso disappeared, leaving only his legs showing from the knee down. Again he reappeared a few seconds later.

We all stared in amazement, nudging each other as he disappeared and reappeared. "You see?" the shaman said, "They are real." I believed him, yet I wanted them to show themselves to me personally.

"I want to see you," I exclaimed aloud. "I want you to appear to me in full form, not shadows as we now see you, but in full form."

Instantly I felt the presence of one of the large beings standing next to me (I felt it was a male energy); his voice telepathically echoing in my head: "Are you sure you want to see us?"

"Yes!" I responded emphatically.

"Are you sure?" he responded.

"Yes! I want to see you!" I replied back.

"Nope!" he added in an amusing manner as he scurried off down the road. I felt he was being comical towards me.

I then walked back to the group, feeling disappointed. When I met up with the others, I saw one of the ladies raise about 3 feet off the ground, lifted by some unseen force. I could not see anything underneath her, just air. Her head was tilted back, as if the Mantis beings were talking to her. Then she slowly drifted back down to the ground.

I then became determined to see the Mantis beings. This is how I meet Jaron, my guide. He popped in next to me again, like before. He asked me again, "Are you sure you want to see me?" I repeated how much I wished to see them.

This time I felt an arm drape across my shoulder. A cool electrical type of energy flowed over my shoulders and slowly crept down my back. The most unbelievable feeling of love came over me as he responded, "No, little one, it is not yet time." The most sincere and caring response I had ever felt while hearing 'no,' and it filled me with compassion and understanding. I felt the arm removed from my shoulder as the sounds of steps faded off into the distance. I had no qualms about his answer. I felt complete and total ease and knew that the time would come.

Complete joy filled my soul as I listened to the sounds of their activity. "They are leaving," said the shaman sadly. Tears filled his eyes and you could tell he was choked up over their departure.

"What's the matter?" I asked him.

"You don't understand," he responded, "These are the supreme beings of the universe. It is a big deal for them to show up."

I noticed by now that the clouds have filled in the circular clearing and I no longer heard the Mantis being's clicking sounds or running around.

We noticed footprints all over the yard that were similar to deer tracks, except reversed. We all sat there for a while, taking in our grand contact experience, and then suddenly we all jumped up to go to bed. I think we fell asleep within 10 minutes. I slept soundly until around 3 A.M. in the morning.

All of a sudden, I woke, drenched in sweat. I was burning up. My sleeping bag was drenched, my pillow was drenched, and I couldn't get back to sleep.

In the morning the shaman asked us, "You guys remember anything after you went to bed?"

I shook my head no. "Only the fact that my body felt like it was on fire," I said.

He smiled at me and said, "You guys sure were busy."

"What do you mean?" I asked.

"All of you woke me up as you walked by me and across the deck. The ladies were gone about a half hour each. When one of them came back, the other one left." Looking at me, the shaman said, "You were the last. You came back about 3 in the morning, I guess. You all took off and walked up the road."

I looked at him and smiled back. "That must be why I had cedar gum all over the bottom of my socks this morning." Usually I don't sleep with my socks on. I still don't know why I did. "What do you think they were doing?" I asked him.

"Ahhh, just a little tuneup," he stated nonchalantly. The reason we were burning up, I believe, is because the Praying Mantis had this intense energy. Our physical bodies tried to adjust to their energy while on the ship. Some people even return from their ships with blisters. For a little while after that experience with the Mantis beings, our group of four could receive and transmit telepathic thoughts between us.

Later on, I regressed this event and found out that after falling asleep and walking into the triangular ship. A Praying Mantis being was there leading me along a catwalk. I came to understand his name was Jaron.

Jaron was standing next to me as he led me on somewhat of a guided tour. At least as much of a guided tour as he was allowed. The catwalk led to a podium centrally located with two other catwalks which led to their respective corners. The room was triangular and met in a dome shape over the podium. Underneath the catwalk was a large orange-colored ball, which was brightly lit and surrounded by a white light. I got the impression it was some sort of power generator and it was directly beneath the podium we were now standing in front of. I also believe this to be the center "red light" witnesses describe seeing in the triangular ships. On top of this podium was a little black ball with an impressed handprint of two fingers and a thumb.

Jaron motioned me to place my hand in this imprint. When I did, a huge, flat screen popped out right in front of me. This screen showed me scenes of my life and I could see myself on the screen. I looked at Jaron and asked him what this was. He told me, "*Deja vu*." All of the sudden, I could see that we were in space, and a ways out.

Jaron then took me to the top of the ship, in the bubble or dome. He asked me if I would like to see it. I said, "Yes."

The bubble then gave way and it was like I was sitting out in the universe by myself with thousands upon thousands of stars all around me. At that moment, I felt no ship, no rooms, no floor, just Jaron and me in the open cosmos. I stood perfectly still, allowing the universe to flow through me, and the stillness of it was overwhelming. In this stillness was something that developed that seemed like a song. I could feel something like a breeze travel right through my body, touching every cell.

Then I heard the glorious *Tone of the Universe*. It was one of the most amazing things I have ever felt. I closed my eyes to fully enjoy the experience. When I opened my eyes again, the scene was gone and we were back in the ship. That experience changed my life in such a way that all I wanted to do was get back to that state of being.

Jaron then led me into a little room where a little camera "eye" sitting in the corner of the walls shot a violet-colored laser up and down me as if I was being scanned. Jaron cocked his head as if thinking of how to explain this and he said, "Soap, soap."

I got the impression it was a type of ray that sanitized the body of any impurities. Then he led me to another room where 26 people were sitting at a kidney-shaped table near a smooth, silver wall. They were all human looking and I did not recognize anyone. I had the impression they all had something to do with Planet Earth. There were two sides of the room that were like windows and I could see forever out into space.

In the center of this table there was a great crystal ball sitting on a black pedestal. The ball itself was perhaps a foot in diameter and everyone seemed to be focusing on it. I also found myself focusing on it, and the more we all focused on it, the more light it started to emit.

Quite suddenly, I felt myself tingling at the top of my head. With the exception of Jaron, each of these 27 people (including me) had a rainbow of colors from their chakras come out from the tops of their heads and merged as a beam of multi-colored lights into the crystal ball. This light swirled around in a kaleidoscope of patterns and designs. Once the colors mixed, the crystal ball shot the colors out and entered back through the top of their heads.

Then I was led back to the trailer, where we were all staying for the night. I feel that these 27 people are a special group and are meant to do something together. I also have an intuitive feeling that it is a "Sign of Perfection." It is interesting that our group of 27 is divisible by three, which is a recurring number among the Mantis beings. I am not sure how it all ties in yet. The Mantis beings think at such a different level; it is hard to understand what concepts they have, why they are doing something, even why they try to make it easy for us.

This was the most singular, spiritual experience of my life. I can find no words, no experiences, no concepts or ideas that can describe the feelings associated with this experience. Of all the experiences I have ever had, this encounter with the Praying Mantis Beings has been the highlight of my life. It is one of those experiences I am forever trying to get back to and forever trying to capture again. Everything else pales in comparison.

My awakening happened gradually over a five-year period. During that time I was very religious, 100 percent Mormon. In 1984 I had my first experience with my people, the Nordics, at the age of 24. They just came down and pretty much knocked on my front door to take me. I was told by them that I was different and that I was an unusual one.

It was similar to a near-death experience in that everything up to that moment was instantaneously recalled. Suddenly I had memories that I hadn't remembered before and things that I only partially remembered were then fully remembered. I then found myself upon the ship, escorted by a female Nordic being named 'Andromeda,' whom I believe is my mother.

Two events in my awakening were very significant to me. The first one happened when I was coaching a competitive soccer team. Soccer was a passion of mine, deeper than anything I had ever known, and I was doing it nine months out of the year. I loved the competitive side that came out in me as I taught these teenagers how to play the game.

I was sitting on the back porch, watching the sun go down, and I heard this voice pop into my head that said, "Don, it's time."

I said, "Okay. How is this going to affect the relationship with my son?"

They said not to worry, that it will only increase in my love and under-standing of him. There was no explanation needed, no argument, no attempt at trying to understand what I may be ready for and no logic behind the actions or words I heard.

I walked inside the house, called the soccer league office and quit my position with a league I had helped to form and was instrumental in getting off the ground. I never even looked back. This was the start of my awakening, and it took years to get through. This experience was as if someone cut my head open, took a spoon and mixed my brain up and put my head back on. My life turned around 180 degrees in that moment. For years after that, I read everything I could about the UFO/ET topic, sometimes five books a day. The information I received during this period was an awakening itself.

The second one was during a time when a lot of supernatural things were occurring to me. This experience had great importance in my life because it led me to conscious awareness that we are not alone in the universe. It left me questioning everything I knew about my place in the universe. They knocked on the door and introduced themselves!

I was lying in bed at night, watching a show called *Ancient Mysteries*, and I fell asleep. My son was sleeping in the room with me. Quite suddenly, I sprang to an upright position in my bed. I went from a deep sleep to instantaneously being wide awake. I was not groggy in the least little bit. I was a little confused at why I would sharply wake up. Perhaps I was late for school.

I glanced at the clock next to the bed and noticed it was 1 A.M. Then I was aware that I was not alone in the room. Directly in front of me, suspended in the air just below the ceiling, was a slender Gray being, perhaps 3 feet tall. His long skinny legs dangled in the air, one arm next to his side and the other extended out and pointing at my son, who was now playing with a toy truck at the head of his bed. I got the impression he was trying hard to ignore this intruder who was hovering in the air.

I returned my gaze back to this small slender being as our eyes met. His large black eyes, too large for his head (in spite of his extremely large head), was staring through me. I felt the endlessness of the universe flowing over me as their gaze penetrated my soul. I instantly understood what the Gray was doing.

"Let me go with you. If I go with you, he will not be frightened. He just needs to know I am close by," I said matter-of-factly. I knew this being. I had the feeling I had met him many times. He was like an old friend who had just come back to visit.

Now he was taking my son—following the genetic code, so to speak. But he was also my teacher and acted like a guardian to me the many times I had been taken in my life. (This I did not realize until much later in life, after some intense hypnotherapy sessions). My son and I both stood up and, holding hands, we followed this Gray being into a bright blue beam of light that shone through the cement basement wall. I watched this being as it drifted through the basement's cement wall and ceiling with ease. My son and I trailed close behind him. I was amazed at how easily we passed through as well.

Once outside, I was taken aback by how deathly quiet it was. No crickets were chirping, no wind was blowing and most surprisingly, no dogs were barking. I could only hear the *whirr* sound of the ship itself; it was like being in a vacuum. I could see the bottom of a huge saucer-shaped ship which was silently hovering in an empty field directly across the street in front of our house. I believe it was 40-to-50 feet wide and about 100 feet above the ground. It struck me as very odd that no one was noticing the ship or the bright lights emitting from it. How could no one see this?

Then I felt a tingle as we floated through the electrical lines and I thought how weird it was I did not get electrocuted. I stared at the house next door and noticed the ship's lights strobing off their roof. First a red light flashed, then blue, similar to the way a police car's lights flash. Wasn't this waking anyone up? How could anyone sleep the way these lights were flashing through their windows?

Once on the ship, I found myself walking along a circular path, what is perhaps the outer edge of the ship. I was walking on a rubbery mat that cushioned my step and felt slightly sticky. The ceiling and walls were a shiny metallic metal of some sort, like polished silver. I then noticed next to me was my Nordic Mom, Andromeda. She was rather tall—perhaps 6 feet—with long blond, shoulder-length hair and bright blue eyes. She was wearing what looked like a jumpsuit that appeared almost camouflaged with brown and orange coloring. She didn't talk, but we communicated telepathically.

We came to a stop and on my left an arched doorway appeared. Inside the room was a shiny silver gleam of metal, empty with the exception of a single column—perhaps a foot in diameter—running vertically through the center of the room. Instead of the strange, rubber-like matting material on the floor, there was some type of metal grating surrounding this column. A device much like a shower massage was hanging from this column. It, too, looked like it was made of a polished metal of some sort with a coiled cord attaching it to the column.

I watched momentarily as my son showed up with another young boy roughly the same age and height, both struggling for possession of the shower massage unit. When one of them grabbed it, they would place it over their heads as if taking a shower. Then a blue pulse of what looked like electricity would surge over their body, sending streams of this energy over them and down into the grating on the floor underneath them. Then the other one would hurriedly grab it and perform the same trick while the other would watch and break out in laughter.

I watched for a few moments before I was motioned on by Andromeda. I did not have a clue what they were doing. And for whatever reason I did not ask. As we continued our walk, I remember asking her about a health concern I had been experiencing. "Can you cure my stomach problems?" I asked her in the most sincere manner I could.

To my surprise, I heard laughter echoing throughout my head and I felt hurt. I was really thinking she could help me with this problem that had been bothering me so badly as of late. She must have realized I was not reacting well because she stopped, lifted my chin up and looked me in the eyes, saying, "You will be okay."

Next I was shown a lady with long brown hair, slight features, about my height, but her face was blotted out. "This woman will change your life," Andromeda's voice echoed in my head. What this meant I still do not know. But it had a tremendous impact on my life and took me several years to deal with.

Finally, I found myself outside the craft in what appeared to be a garage of some sort. There were boxes stacked along a wall and in front of me. The garage door was at the far side of the room. Although it was dark outside and darker inside, I could make out all the features of a two-car garage. I am guessing it was from a house down the street, but in reality it could have been anywhere in the world. Standing next to me was the same Gray being that had originally appeared to my son and me when we were awakened in the basement. We both stood there quietly as I wondered what was going on and what would happen next.

Then it appeared, a shadow figure moving through the garage. Something that looked a lot like a man, but without the features you would normally see in a person. I watched as it slowly moved to the end of the garage next to the garage doors and then slowly turned, moving its way to the opposite wall. When it hit the wall, it made a 180-degree turn and headed to the opposite wall.

The Gray being raised his arm, pointing towards the shadow figure with an outstretched finger and said telepathically, "It is forbidden to walk through those!" I felt the Gray was showing me that I don't want to share space with these type of beings, it would be like a possession.

Quite suddenly, I found myself, my son, his companion, and perhaps 10 other people standing in the living room upstairs in the house. I could hear a low hum from the ship through the screen door and I could see it hovering outside the house. Its blue and red lights were strobing off of the faces of the strangers standing in the living room. I saw an older man and woman standing on the other side of the room. They looked catatonic, completely tranced out, unaware of their surroundings, and were standing naked in the living room.

I could hear some laughter from my left and as I turned around I saw my son and his friend tussling on the loveseat, jabbing at each other playfully as we waited for whatever was going to finally happen.

Next, I woke up in bed and I had an explosion of memories of all my events. It blew me away. I suddenly recalled all the times that I had been taken. I didn't know what to do with this information at the time. I was highly religious and all I could think about was why did God "let this happen to me."

I turned on the light and checked where my son was sleeping. There on the floor next to his head was the toy truck I had seen him playing with, the fingerprints clearly visible in the top of the truck through the thick layer of dust that had been collecting on it over the last year. It was all real and I was stunned. I just laid in bed for the rest of the night, going over all the suddenly remembered incidents I had had over my life. To say I was bewildered and taken back would be too kind. I was totally blown away. I had viewed myself as a very religious man, having been raised, drifted away, and then reborn again, so to speak, in the Mormon religion. *This was just not possible,* I kept thinking to myself over and over again, *how could God, or my version of God at the time, allow this to happen to me?*

There was really no one I could talk to. I couldn't get my mind off what had happened and I knew I had to find some answers. So instead of driving to school the next morning, I drove straight to the local library. I had to see—had to understand—what had happened to me. I had to see if there were any other type of people who had had an experience like this.

I was a little surprised to see there were three books about UFO abductions. The one that stood out most was the Betty and Barney Hill case. I did not leave the library until it closed at 5 P.M. and I had read all three UFO books.

When I arrived home and walked up the stairs to the back door, my son emerged. I smiled at him as he stopped on the steps to say hello. "Daddy!" He said excitedly as he escorted me into the house. "I had a nightmare last night. Do you want to hear it?"

I froze as he motioned me to sit on the stairs next to him. "Sit down, Daddy. Sit down," he said impatiently.

Sitting down next to him, I listened with a mix of curiosity, nervousness and fear. I listened how in his dreams he had battled the bears that had come to take him away. He grabbed his BB gun in order to shoot them, but they were too powerful. In the end they just grabbed him and he couldn't get away. I had just read in the library books that many times "aliens" would hide their appearance in the form of animals of some sort. I also read that many times they would leave 'scoop' marks. These were small, round indentations in the skin, like a melon spoon had scooped it out, or half crescent shapes. They would heal very rapidly over a period of 24 hours.

"And something else,Daddy," he said curiously. "I need a Band-Aid. I think I cut the back of my leg. Must have been crawling under a fence, I think. I don't know."

I took him in the house and gently brushed the back of his leg off with an antiseptic wipe. On the back of his leg, in the middle of his calf, there was a perfectly formed half-moon, crescent scoop mark. My hand shook as I applied the Band-Aid and sent him off to play. I had my answer and I knew it had happened, but my religious faith was firm.

For the next 13 years I just placed this experience aside in the far corner of my mind. I could never quite figure out what to do with this experience I had gone through. It never scared me or intimidated me, I just couldn't figure out where it fit into my life. I would sit in Sunday school class all those years and wonder how Christ could fit into all this and how would any beings of such a high intelligence ever buy into such a backwards notion of religion.

One day I looked around me and just decided I had had enough. Religion could never provide me with the answers I needed. I glanced around the congregation and just sighed. I did make an attempt to reconsider leaving my religion. I found the local clergy leader and wrote him a letter. As close as I can remember it went something like this:

"Dear Bishop, I am writing you in regard to an encounter with alien life forms I experienced a number of years ago. Most would call it an abduction. But I prefer to refer to it as a contact experience with alien life forms. I am truly puzzled by the nature of these beings and would like some understanding and clarification of how your view of Christ relates to a cosmic perspective. If you cannot help me, I would like my name removed from the church roles. Sincerely, Don Anderson"

One week later I was quite surprised by the response in a return letter:
"Mr. Anderson, I have submitted your petition for your name to be

removed from the Church of Jesus Christ of Latter Day Saints records. You have
one month to reconsider your actions. After one month you will receive a letter
from church headquarters in Salt Lake City, informing you your name has been
removed.

Sincerely, Bishop _____
Provo, Utah branch"

Just three days later, I received another letter:

"Mr. Anderson, per your request, your name has officially been taken off
the roles of the Church of Jesus Christ of Latter Day Saints. All the priesthood
rights and privileges have been removed and stripped from you and your temple
ordinances are no longer in force.

Sincerely, _____
Office of the presidency of the Church of Jesus Christ of Latter Day
Saints."

I have been told by forces out there (the shadow government/ Reptilians), not to talk about things. They do not want people knowing about things that transpire with contactees vs. abductees (those taken against their will). They have made it abundantly clear—verbally and by demonstration as well—that I should be quiet and play in their world.

But they do not understand me too well, or perhaps they do? More than I would like to admit. A Praying Mantis being told me at one time that he was hiding me. I didn't understand why. I know the secret military and the Reptilians would rather me keep my mouth shut about stuff. I have been taken by this military/Reptilian group once upon a time and they have done something to me.

My mission is still something that eludes me. I talk to Jaron about it, my Praying Mantis guide, but I don't have all the answers. I live more in the ET world than in the Human world.

I always have had a particularly hard time writing about myself and my awakening process; I never used to. My ego used to be the size of a blue whale. I used to love to talk about myself and my experiences. I used to think I was "the bomb." I had all the answers and I knew the shizbang of all shizbangs. The importance of who I was, the experiences I have had, along with the importance of my mission, and the driving force of something I needed to do, all drove me crazy.

I never wanted to come here, I do know that. I agreed to come here to accomplish something. I'd like to say I came here voluntarily kicking and screaming. I was quite happy where I was at, and the memories of past lives have not been so enjoyable. With the exception of one or two, most lives I have lived have been quite dreary and without a lot of fanfare. So I was not excited about it. I call it a journeyman's existence.

Let's go get the job done. Perhaps that is why I am still ignorant of what type of job I really have here.

Books that were significant to me:

Delores Cannon's *The Convoluted Universe* series and especially her *Conversations with Nostradamus*; I have found myself connecting really well with this book.

Courtney Brown's books *Cosmic Voyage* and *Cosmic Explorers*. When I read *Cosmic Explorers*, I was so stunned, not because of what I had read and what he touched upon, but more that I already knew what he was writing about. These are free downloads, by the way, on his Web site. I would highly recommend them if you have not read them already.

Web site that is significant to me:

Coast to Coast: www.coasttocoastam.com

Contact me at:

Donaa44@msn.com

(Phone number will be provided upon email communications)

RAJ

I am from Sirius B and I came here from the end times of Atlantis with a woman companion. I was a scientist and worked in Atlantis with the Priest and Priestess that would put energy into crystals. It was my job to convert their energy into mechanics or machinery, or into whatever we needed it for. That is my first recollection on this planet, Earth.

If you are an old spirit from the beginning of Creation, why would you prevent yourself from knowledge or knowing? I asked my Spirit Guides how to see my past lives. I was told to relax as I was laying on my bed one night, then my eyes rolled back into the center of my retina and into my brain. This is how I learned to travel to the "Akashic Records."

I was able to see my past lives all the way back to my home planet, Sirius B. The Sirius System is made up of Sirius A, B and C. I remember how we came to planet Earth. We arrived in a spaceship, but we had to curve time and space. Our course took about six months from Sirius to Earth at that time, during the period of Atlantis. There were about 50-100 people that came with us on the ship. Our people have a light tan skin color, blue eyes and we are more physically endowed than humans are (more of a muscular build). I remember a lot of these details and some people would call that being enlightened, or similar. However, I look at my life as being served on a silver platter and that is because of my spiritual side. If you talk to people I know, they would say I have a spiritual nature.

In this life I incarnated as a spirit, but my birth was a ten-month gestation. I had a lot of medical problems when I was borne and I wasn't suppose to live. The doctors called me a 'miracle baby'. During this time I remember seeing all of these angels and beings watching over me. People and Doctors were praying for me too. A major medical problem I had was that my stomach was not connected and I couldn't hold down food. It could have been a result of my ET side, because my body was also rejecting my own blood!

*   *   *

I had an interesting childhood. I had an invisible playmate named Jaiya. I basically grew up with him. I could speak and understand his language. Sometimes that language will come back to my conscious recall. Jaiya told me that his family was in an accident and something happened to their spaceship. They were traveling through another dimensional plane on their way to Earth and somehow their ship crashed.

At the time of their crash, I was a little kid going to Cuba with my parents. Jaiya's family either died or was able to escape, I never knew. I don't believe he was dead because he was so alive to me. Jaiya was separated from his family when they crashed and he saw my "light." He told me he was attracted to my "continuity of connection," or as I understood it later, my highly evolved spiritual being. Jaiya also told me he was attracted to my energy as a baby and he stayed near my essence, even though he was trying to ascend his own.

Most of the time he was in spirit form, but sometimes I would see him as a child of about 8 years old. Jaiya was Human-looking, he had blue eyes and blond hair. He didn't grow up as I grew, he stayed adolescent for a long time. I used to know where he was from, but that was so long ago.

I always had the feeling that I could fly when I was with him. In first and second grade I always had someone to play with because Jaiya was always there. We always talked and played together. I would tell him what a word was in English and he would tell me what it meant in his language. I believe that we were sometimes in his dimension because my Mom would not be able to find me when I knew I was in my room the whole time.

Jaiya told me when he reached a certain age that he would be able to ascend. When I was in high altitude, I could see the gravitational field of his planet and eventually he was able to ascend back there. I remember the day when he ascended and left me, I was in the high Sierra Nevada Mountains and we were both running. Suddenly, I realized that I could not see Jaiya any more. I remember at that point that he did tell me that he was leaving. He had to wait for a specific gravitational field to occur near Earth before his essence could leave again.

Even after I had all of my encounters with the Grays, Jaiya was still there.

I also know that I have always been spiritually protected. I used to have spirits that would come to me and talk to me all night long. Their voices were not in my head, these beings were actually physical and next to my bed. I could have written a book just on what they told me. I get the impression they were "Archangels." This is why I probably have a different concept of humanity than most people. These beings taught me so much throughout the night.

I have had three different types of teachers including Jaiya, up until the age of about 13, then the Archangels and then the Grays at age 17. The type of Grays I dealt with were about 5 feet tall, had a darker gray skin color, their eyes were black and more oval-shaped, and they had two small nostrils with a very small mouth. These Grays were and are very gentle and protective over me. They taught me a lot about scientific technology, but they do not have the same spiritual quantities that we do. It is as if they try to quantify God instead of understanding the spiritual aspect. That is the impression I got and what I felt from them anyway. They do wear clothing, but I cannot recall what it looked like. Their clothing is not like ours. They don't show genitalia because I don't ever remember thinking how big or small they were compared to myself. I know other beings wear silvery uniforms that fit tight to their bodies, but I don't recall what these Grays wore.

I have seen lighter-skinned Grays that are smaller in size, about 3'6" tall. Those are more like robots, but I always called them "little irritants." I know that people say they don't really have a mind of their own, and say they have a "Hive" mentality. However, I would say that the Grays don't necessarily act independently upon their own thoughts and that they have an intuitive under-standing of survival. I believe this occurred because of their past and what happened to them on their home world. The Grays learned that if they continued to act independently, as Humans do, their society would have come to an end. They learned how to co-exist without a connection to a higher benevolent being. Even though they may look different—different species of Gray—they are still all related to each other. The positive and more negative types are still connected to one another.

There were a lot of things I used to do when I was young, that I didn't know I "wasn't supposed to do." I was able to astral-project, I was a great empath and clairvoyant, although I didn't understand it fully. I also had the ability to look at a person's actions and read from their heart so I could understand why they did what they did, without judgment. I used to astral-project to the Grays a lot when I was young. They always put me in these scenarios that would test me, to see if I would kill.

One time they put me in a room with another person and told us that only one of us could leave the room and that one of us had to die, or we would both die. I would always flunk the test because I would never kill. I told them in the test that they could not hold me spiritually responsible for their actions. The greatest thing I like about my youth is that when I would go to sleep at night, my Archangels would come to me. My whole day I would go through their teachings as things would be explained to me, such as people's actions, why they treated each other the way they did, and if I didn't understand something. Any questions I had, they would answer them.

I had a very old Gray mentor since the beginning of my experiences with the Grays. I don't know if he was assigned to me or what, but when I would see him, there was an instant recognition of who he was. At 18 years old, I was in my bed and I was taken onto the Grays' ship. I remember seeing the room I was in and talking to my mentor. He asked me if I would conceive a Hybrid child. The reason the Grays chose me is because they wanted the spiritual energy within their matrix.

So I gave my mentor permission and then I remembered laying on a table that looked like chrome, but felt like an air mattress. It conformed to my body shape and it did not feel like metal. I saw a door open in the room and this figure entered. I can't say that she was a Gray because she had a longer neck. She looked attractive, but I don't know if it was a screen memory or my 18-year-old hormones. As she walked up to me, her appearance would change according to what I was thinking looked attractive. She was very tall, taller than the Grays. Her skin was the color of white ash and I don't remember seeing any breasts on her.

She then mounted me and was looking intently at me. I remember emotions arose out of me during that time. For a moment, I felt a repulsiveness because of her being alien. As soon as I felt that, she turned back into the most beautiful human-looking female. A lot of things entered my thoughts and my spirituality reminded me that this encounter was really okay. That she is just different in appearance, but still a Gray. When my emotions calmed down, she would change back to what she normally looks like. During this rather short event, she had changed appearance four times.

When we finished, she began to leave the room. My mentor said something to me mentally at this point, although I don't remember what. I saw that she had her back facing me as she was leaving. However, just before she walked out of the room, she turned back around and looked at me. That has always stuck with me.

About a month later, I was called to the ship, physically. My mentor was there and we were talking. We walked into this one room and he asked me if I would like to pilot the ship. I said "Yeah!" There was one Gray sitting at the console and another Gray standing with a type of headband on. The room looked dark to me and I realized the Grays don't have bright rooms. The Gray wearing the headband took it off and gave it to me. When I put it on my head, it automatically adjusted to my head shape and size. It had a metallic feel to it, but it also felt like there was liquid crystal in it. As soon as I put it on, the entire room changed to the view outside the ship. I could see 360 degrees around me, up and down, all through the walls of the ship. If I looked at a planet, the planet would come toward me and into the view of the ship.

I didn't have to move physically, I just used my thought. I remember going to Jupiter, Saturn and I believe we went all the way out to Pluto and back to Earth. I was never in any danger because I can recall other Grays watching my performance. They were making sure we didn't crash into an asteroid or do anything dangerous. It was emotionally overwhelming on the Human side. My brain did not know how to process that information. Time is so weird in space. I felt this was a "reward" for my participation in making a Hybrid child.

Another time, when I was about 18 years old, I went to what I call "The Holy Alter," where I saw my spiritual self. I went down to the temple of God, where Christ and all these very high spiritual beings were. I told them that my life was too perfect, that I didn't understand the Human condition nor the way people treated each other and if I needed to make the decision on whether they live or die, I needed to walk in their shoes. I handed the silver platter in my hands back to Christ, saying I needed to walk in the footsteps of the Human race. I believe I came here for a purpose, but I couldn't fulfill it because of my spiritual protection and everything else that I knew of at the time. I couldn't make the connection with the physical being. Spiritual being I could understand, but I could not understand the physical Human entity. There is a reason for the Human side. After handing back the silver platter, my life changed drastically. I became less enlightened with the spiritual knowledge. I chose that path so I could learn what it meant to be Human.

I feel sorry for the Human race because, for all their greatness, they don't want to take that evolutionary step to be all they can be. When I deal with other ET races, they don't have a complex like Humans do. It was only when I started walking in the footsteps of man that I let fear, ambition and greed influence me. They call it "the seven temptations of man." I would rather be an enlightened being than a king on Earth. The material values in this world don't really mean anything when you understand the higher power. I know that when you are connected to temple, mind, spirit and higher self, the human being is capable of so much. The religious organizations, the government and even our own peers might be afraid of each other. When one entity has power over another entity, their mindset is in a different place. Human beings give up their power to each other. The ETs I visit know how to be equal to each other and in their expression of power.

Even being a Hybrid, we can't deny the physicality of being Human. I now understand the difference between the body and the temple. I see the physical body as a temple because I can put more energy into a temple than I can a physical being. I know this is my last time on this planet, I finally came to my evolutionary step of going beyond physical limitation of vibrational energy.

It has taken me almost twenty years to get back that silver plate, and it is still coming back. It is easier to give up your gifts than it is to get them back. I am grateful to achieve the gifts now, I respect them because they are truly a part of my psyche. I want to use them for the betterment of the Human race and that is the difference. I am very proud of myself now because I go out and teach other ET races. I have learned to become accepted among our ET peers.

Later on, I found out that I have a Gray/Human Hybrid daughter. The Grays did not want me to visit my daughter and I knew that decision was not correct, so I took the Grays to Council, something similar to "arbitration." Their Council is like a "Universal Grievance Council" and I remember walking in there not in the physical, but I could see the outline of my energy. I saw many different types of beings there as well. In order to bring a being to this Council, you have to know that being's name and rank. They all have identification, individual names and rank. The Council listens to both party's side, dealing with everything in absolutes and deciding what resolve would make the perfect balance.

That is why God is not gray. Species make themselves gray to represent the shortcomings to match their free will, but God does not play that game. It either is or it isn't. The Grays didn't want me to visit my daughter because they create Hybrids for a particular means and they did not want me to interfere with her. I understand that I was the perfect candidate because I never wanted children, but the circumstances changed because I was going through a hard time in my life. My Hybrid daughter came and actually saved my life one night, healing me of cancer. They put a lot of blocks on my memory, but I still can remember being in my bedroom when she showed up with two other Grays.

After that event I had a connection with her that I haven't had before. This was more of a spiritual connection—we bonded. The Council came up with this resolve; the Grays could not interfere with our decision of wanting to communicate with each other. The reason being is because we are individual spirits and because we are connected through the Universe. No entity has a right to stop connection between beings.

In the end, we are all energy of the Creator, these are just different physical bodies we chose at the time. As one of the universal laws go, a physical being cannot stop another physical being from developing to a higher spiritual being. The Council told me and my daughter that as long as we both wished to communicate with each other, no one could stop us. However, if at any time one of us did not wish to communicate with the other, they would have to obey that wish not to communicate. Their decision made perfect sense to me, that the Grays did not have a right to stop our spiritual development to the Creator.

I found out a lot about my Hybrid daughter. She is like a Gray Ambassador, she goes out as the Gray representative for exchange with other beings. The Grays deal mostly in technology and commodities.

My many encounters with the Grays helped me learn about astrophysics. I knew that planets were actually hotter than what scientists were saying. I knew about a lot of things before they were discovered. As I became older, my contacts with the Grays became more mental or lucid dreaming. The quality of my experiences with them shifted. I don't remember names nor do I event think to ask them. I was always focused on what I am experiencing at the moment. Names do not seem important to the ETs either. The Grays are not into socializing much, they speak matter-of-factly.

My daughter showed up another night with three other Grays in my bedroom. She showed up because I wanted to go to the Grays' home world after witnessing a Gray die. I was up on the ship in the hallway and I saw him just die. Another Gray happened to come along at the time of this Gray's death. He explained to me that they do die as a race, but they also live for a long time. So my daughter was there in my bedroom and suddenly everything went blank.

Next thing I knew, I was on another world. It was dark like twilight, even though it had two suns. My Gray mentor met me as I arrived. There was a lot of geometrical shapes on their home world. Their buildings are designed to absorb the little sunlight they get and are pyramid shaped. I remember going to a hospital on this world where there was another Gray dying. When this Gray was about to pass, another Gray took his hand. It seemed that he was sharing the death experience with the Gray that was dying. To me, that showed so much compassion. I realized then that beings cannot have a hive mentality and show such compassion; therefore, I do not believe they have hive mind. That is when I learned that the Grays live in cooperation of co-existence for the betterment of their species.

After the Grays took me to their home planet, they dropped me back into my physical body and my psyche got messed up for a while. It was messed up as a result of the space/time variable. There was a separation of my subconscious mind from my physical body. They both must vibrate at the same rate to function normally. When my subconscious was placed back into my body after that event, they were vibrating differently, causing me to be "out of phase." My mind wasn't working properly, the neurons and synapses were "out of sync."

I realized what had happened, but I did not know how to fix it. That was when the Grays introduced me to the Mantis Being. He was an off-color green or olive and stood about 6'2". They were attempting to realign my psyche so I would be vibrationally in balance again (I would resonate in the harmony of my frequency for this body). I remember they laid me on my back and I was being held down for my own good. Then the Mantis being's tentacles came out of his head and attached to my forehead. He basically re-calibrated the vibrational frequency for the Human body, including my aura and my electromagnetic field.

Since that healing the Mantis beings did for me, they would come into my life quite a bit. The Mantis beings are very benevolent and have a very deep spirituality about them. They introduced me to the beings that they felt I would like to know about.

One day I was teaching and I had a really bright bluish spark go off through my brain. Then I heard this voice telling me that I didn't have the "Demimyre" to teach. I looked up this word later on and the definition was "an inner active experience that is part administration and part seminar, where participants focus on new technology." At the time, I was teaching kids in a seminar, because I remembered the event. The kids looked like Gray Hybrids and had no social identity. They were about 3 feet high, they had a grayish-white skin and oval-shaped eyes. They had no hair and they all wore the same uniform. I was teaching these Hybrids theoretical propulsion systems for use in their ships.

The Grays are really good when it comes to science and they have taught me so much. They were my third teachers after Jaiya and my Archangels. However, they don't come around as much after taking them to the Council regarding my Hybrid daughter. The Grays and I are now at a mutual impasse with each other after that event.

I had most of my encounters in the '70s. Then they started up again in the late '80s until 1999. They went away for a while after that. The Grays are not consistent, sometimes I had to go after them. If you don't think about them once you get to a certain age, it is "Out of sight, out of mind" with them. On one of my attempts to go to them, I found out that the Grays know how to make a hologram of an individual. This hologram includes your frequency, energy and other things that you emit. They can pick up the energy a person emits with machinery in their ship.

I believe it is on their mothership where they keep these holograms. I astral-projected and found the Grays' mothership. I went aboard their ship looking for this hologram they may have taken of me. I realized that they did have a container of my "Poly-resonant vibrational frequency." It is basically our aura and other frequencies, plus our thoughts which are transmittable. They take these different energies we project and filter them into a biometric spherical stone. It looks like a round glass tube. Energy comes in to one end of this device with your bio-luminate form and then it goes out the other end. With this, they can monitor you anywhere you are because of this hologram they have of you.

They can also influence you remotely. If you can transmit energy, you can also receive energy and receive input of thought. I felt this was a way of controlling people. And I realized that as I got older, they didn't need to come to me because they had my hologram. I wouldn't even be aware that they were doing anything and I didn't like that.

What I did then, in my astral form aboard their mothership, was I damaged my container, or hologram. I had found the room in which my hologram was stored, along with many, many, many others. I tried to smash my container, but I couldn't. I found a pipe of some sort and tried breaking the container with it, but that didn't work either. So I went to the connection point where the lines came into my container and I smashed them with this pipe.

After that, my container just fell to the floor, crashing in thousands of pieces. The Grays entered the room at that point and they were not pleased at all. They did not have contact with me for a long time afterwards. This was a good lesson for me because I found a truth in all beings in general: If you do not give permission to an ET and they play with your psyche or stop your spiritual development, then they violate the Universal Laws of the spiritual connection to the Creator. I found out that breaking this law is not permissible.

I was out astral-projecting on another night and I remember running into this Reptilian somewhere. Reptilians have a "I am holier than thou" attitude sometimes and what they were going to do was kill me. This Reptilian stood about 9 feet tall, it had the darker scales, its chest was a grayish tone and the eyes were yellow with a black vertical slit. I don't remember if he had a tail because he was standing facing me. I looked straight at him and said, "You can kill me, but here is the problem, if you mess with the higher power of myself (Creative Energy), then what I will do is come back into your species and take retribution upon you."

The Reptilian being had to think about that for a moment. He realized that I was aware of my spiritual being and that I would do as I said. He decided to let me go. Depending on what planet or universal place you are a part of, there are different concepts and laws. We set down rules and regulations as Human beings, not spiritual beings, so we play by different concepts. So as a Human, if I play with your psyche, that's all right because I can say that it was part of your lesson, something you chose to do. That is all bull crap! But we find justification on what we do to each other. It is probably why we have to incarnate so many times.

I don't recall having any "MIB" or secret government contact. I have always felt very well protected by my beings. There is a spiritual forum that proceeds any physical beings' abilities on any planet. If you have a spiritual connection to the Creator, you almost have an immunity against true evil intent. It may have been there, but I didn't need to experience it, I wouldn't want to. I have gotten past my fear and now I can do so much more. I have intuitive knowledge about a lot of things and when I share them with people, they look at me funny. Later on, the scientific field will prove what I had already told people, and say they find it to be true.

I am working on my mission now. I am hoping to elevate the spiritual awareness that we all have back to its simplicity. Religion, for all of its good intentions, has actually divided the Human race from their true connections to each other. I wish to teach people that there are other life forms out there. There are rules of this world, certain laws that say what ETs can and cannot do. When we start breaking those laws against each other, those rules change. I would like to see the Human race go into space and live with each other instead of with fear and hostility. We may not make it because Humans feel they need to fight every species they encounter. Humans are becoming an extinct race and I hope "The Shift" will change this.

Eric Von Daniken's book *Chariots of Fire*, had an impact on me.

You may contact me at: *Prhdevice@gmail.com*

Sanni Ceto

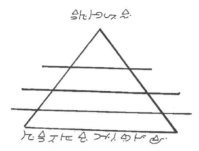

I am a Gray/Human Hybrid who incarnated on Earth in 1958. I very clearly recall my past life as the Zeta Reticulan Commander of the three spacecrafts that crashed in Roswell, New Mexico in 1947. I can still speak and write in my ET language. My story is told more in-depth in my two autobiographies, *Stranded On Earth*, and *Zeti Child*. I am a relayer of communications from the Zeta Reticulan Council and I am most often in contact with my Zeta father and guide, whom I call Khinyeo.

A Hybrid is technically a cross between two different species of plants, animals or beings. ET Hybrids comprise a blending of characteristics from both species. In the case of an Essasanni—a cross between a Human and a Zeta—such traits may include a larger skull, pointy chin, larger eyes, small ears, trouble with ear canals, altered skin texture, albinism, frail immune system and altered vertebrae, to name a few.

Gray Hybrids are not as robust as their full-blooded parents, due to inter-species incompatibility between Insectoid and Human DNA mixing. Hybrids are created to prolong the Zeta's existence as a way to carry on their dominant DNA into the future. This may ultimately enable the Human DNA to survive as well, in the event planet Earth is destroyed. My people, known as the Zetas, are a benevolent and peaceful species. We are curious scientists and space travelers,

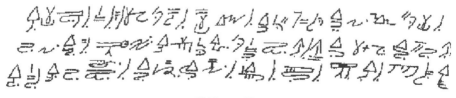

Kebben writing

and we wish to assist Gaia and Humans in their upcoming ascension.

My home planet, Serpo Jadui, is in the Zeta Reticuli Star System. It is a binary system of over 500 planets which orbit *Tiu 1* and *Tiu 2* (our suns). The soil of Serpo is a reddish brown and looks like Mars when seen from space. Its

Zeta Home World

size is three times the size of Earth. Serpo's climate is mostly arid to semi-arid and has two seasons. Each season lasts about six months in length, with the first month of each season being less intense than the rest. The windy season is called *Nui*, and is like a dust storm. The wet season is called *Zui* and occurs over the mountains. Most structures on Serpo are under "biodomes." Our bio-domes are hexagonal and pyramidal in shape. They come in different sizes and resemble clear glass; however, some blend into the desert environment, which is deep red and tan.

There are three moons that orbit Serpo. *Tias 1* and *Tias 2* are large rocky moons with *Tias 1* being about three times larger than Earth's moon. The second moon is about the size of Mercury and is a barren world, used to store large crafts inside underground hangars. *Tias 3*, the third moon, is a large mining colony, used to collect ores of Elements 114 and 115. This is our largest moon and has an atmosphere which supports minute plant life and micro-organisms. *Tia 3* has several cities that are operated as a mining base and they also control the flow of ores and minerals to the different trade routes that link the other planets in a vast economy network. The people who live on this moon base are mostly an Insectoid species.

Each city, or unit, is controlled by the hive or *Kiguish* (Praying Mantis beings), which is the ruler-ship on our world. Our economies are based upon a barter-and-trade system. The transit system on Serpo Jadui is like Earth's monorails and trains that run on electromagnetism, combined with a crystal generator that creates energy from deep inside the planet. Most people use the large subterranean transportation because we don't go above ground except while inside the bio-domes. There are three different types of trains; one is for transporting people, the second is for use in the mines and these are similar to "box cars" and "hopper cars" used on Earth. The third is for ship and dock-loading of the vehicles, which are similar to "hover boats" on Earth's waters. The rails are buried, separated by magnets and crystals that pull and stop the trains at different locations. These locations are programmed into the main operating system. This type of transit is used on the mining bases on the moon as well as the neighboring worlds. Another type of transport on Serpo is like an "aero car" that rides on a cushion of highly charged particles and lacks wheels that Earth cars have. The door is a bubble that folds back from the top and you are levitated into your seats. These vehicles do not burn any fossil fuels and are made to harmonize with the environment. The roads on Serpo are like criss-crossing tubes that the vehicles go through and they link different cities or units together. Each city has its own structured system of controlling the usage and amount of aero cars and trains. Each grid work is set up to allow a certain amount of traffic to pass through. It is better and more efficient than using traffic lights.

Here I shall describe a few species of my people, the Grays:

1. **Kebbens** are a cross between the Ebben species and the Keb species of Grays. Kebbens are a slender people with long, narrow heads, pointed jaws and large wrap-around eyes. Their basic skin tone ranges from a soft gray to a steel gray. Some have a tan color mixed with the gray color. Most of our people reproduce via cloning and genetic-splicing technologies. Khinyeo is mostly a Kebben Hybrid with some Ebben and a little Kiguish (Praying Mantis). Their Hybrid children, with a Human parent, is called an Essasanni. Kebs or Kebbens stand around 4 to 6 feet (male) and about 4 to 5 feet (female). Their lifespans are around 980 years (males) and about 960 years (female). There are around 48 different species of "Gray," along with subspecies. They are mostly Insectoid, but a few have created species that are Mammalian as well. Most Grays are native to the Eridani and Zeti Reticuli Star Systems and most of their worlds orbit binary stars (two suns). These worlds are Earth-like in composition as well as their climate, which is mostly arid to semi-arid.

Currently, our missions have been to monitor the underground bases in the Western USA, as they are creating new aircraft. Plus, they are working on an artificial black hole, or worm hole, to be used in creating events for the year 2012. Most of our work involves flying our crafts and doing reconnaissance

work. Recently we have been back to our lunar base on Earth's "moon" since
Humans are trying to re-establish a military presence there. Most of my events
are physical, although I transform into my true form; I do not go astrally when I
am with Khinyeo.

2. **Ebbens** originally evolved from primitive Insectoids who were helped in
their evolution by outsiders such as the Meropians, who are from the Pleiadian
Star System. Ebbens are about 4 feet tall, have thin to slightly muscular body

Ebben

structures, a large, rounded head like the Cheridani Grays,
a tiny chin, prominent round eyes, long arms, large hands,
feet with four digits each, and the genitalia is mostly
internal. Ebbens are more robust in structure, since they
are an explorer race that colonizes and takes control of
other worlds where there is no other competing species.
There are two main groups of Ebben species; one is tan in
color and has more Humanoid eyes with a brown lens
covering and a wide forehead. This group was later used to
create Hybrids on Earth and other colony planets. This
group is more aggressive than their Kebben cousins, and
most carry a laser-type weapon on their uniforms. Their
lifespans are about 690 years and their reproduction is similar to higher evolved
mammals.

3. **Betelgeusian Grays** are a subgroup of the Kebbens who fled the
Reticulum Sector earlier in their history as a species. They were forced to flee
after their home planets were destroyed via nuclear strike from the invading
Orion and Draconian fleets. The Betelgeusians colonized the "B Sector" in
Betelgeuse and hybridized with the native species of small, mammal-like
Insectoids called Dra-Hids. Betelgeusian Grays have about five main sub-
species. Kebbens are an off-shoot of a subspecies known as the "big-nosed"
Grays. The Dra-Hids later died out as a species, due to genetic incompatibilities
between the dominant Betelgeusians, who were more adapted to the evolving
planets in B Sector. B Sector is located in Quadrant 7, which includes Zeti
Reticuli and Serpo Jadui. After the inter-planetary wars, different groups were
dispatched to help assist the Zetas, the Cheridanians and the Kebs, who were on
Zeti Reticuli in tiny groups. Many Human species (mostly Pleiadians,
Alcyionians and Meropians) came to help the Insectoid people rebuild. Along

with their efforts, the Human species established a scientific and economic structure which was incorporated into the ruler-ship of the Kiguish. The results were the creation of Esassanian people, a Hybrid race of Human and Insectoid.

Our ships come in several sizes and their usage is based upon their functions. Here are a couple:

1. The small, disc-shaped ships are used for surveillance and range in size from 35 feet to 100 feet in diameter. The composition of the hull is titanium-magnesium with aluminium. The propulsion is an anti-matter and anti-gravity generator and is located in the center of the hull. This ship's capacity is from four to 25 crew members. The reactors are like a ball of putty and are Elements 114 and 115. The reactor core has a lifespan of about 200 years, depending on its size. Most disc ships have a circular, inner toroidal ring, where the super-charged particles are amplified, then sent across the outer hull and inner hulls. This creates a "force field," shielding the craft from many things and from re-entry into a planet's gravitational field. Most disc ships have a tripod landing gear arrangement and some use a tube-like elevator to land with.

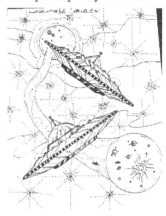

Zeta ships

2. Delta-Wing ships and Wedge-shaped ships are a type of modified triangle craft, with swept-back wings and which utilize anti-gravity propulsion. These vehicles require a "Mothership" to ferry them into a solar system, and most range in size from Earth's Space Shuttle to much larger, having a capacity of 12 to 50 crew members. These crafts are mostly manned, though a few are drones controlled by a larger craft nearby. Landing gear arrangement is one leg in front of the craft and two at the rear. These craft are used for surveillance and collecting samples from a planet's surface. All crafts are built by Zetas and Pleiadians.

*   *   *

I had many abilities when I incarnated. I used to have telekinesis and be able to bi-locate. These abilities were damaged by psychotropic drugs I was forced to take when I was young—an effort to erase my memories. I have the gift of premonition, or of seeing things before they occur. I see things as if watching a movie. I am able to "scan" people, read inside the body and see auras. I communicate with nature, the animal kingdom and plant kingdom. I am also an intuitive and an empath.

My awakening first occurred when lightning struck our front porch when I was around four years of age. When that lightning hit, I was seeing movies inside of my head that were actually flashbacks of my past life. I was a ship pilot, a "lieutenant in-charge" over three ships. In the flashbacks, I saw myself, along with my crew, seated at a semi-circular console that was the cockpit area of our aircraft. We were all dressed in silver uniforms with matching boots and we were bald. These flashbacks were too vivid to be so-called dreams, as I would have hundreds of these during my awakened state. Growing up, I had many events that caused me to question the Earth reality around me as these events involved UFOs and my dad's people, the Grays. I questioned many times if what I was being shown was real or hallucinatory in nature. My dad would tell me, "Child wake up! This is reality and we do exist. It is the humans who are a hallucination."

As I got older I went through hypnotherapy to help uncover what the ugly veil had blocked from my memories about my crash in 1947, and to help remove the guilt that still lingered from my actions that night. When I got older, I went through a very skeptical period about my experiences. My dad's people gave me a choice, to either believe that they were real or to have no other contact with them or UFOs. I decided to be skeptical and not believe. By not accepting the truth about myself and my people's existence, I became very ill and hospitalized. I then begged for them to return and it was then that I opened my eyes to see beyond the conditioning of an Earth veil.

Ever since I was tiny, I knew deep inside that I was not from Earth. As a child I would draw binary stars (suns) and disc ships instead of airplanes and a solitary sun that most children draw. I would stand outside at night and point to the skies and call out dad's name to come and take me home in his disc. I have seen UFOs most of my life as my heritage is linked to the stars. My people have guided me and given me knowledge to teach others about their own stellar origins. UFOs have influenced me through my art and in my life. My people have helped me to awaken to the Hybrid being that is of two DNAs and two Solar Systems, creating an intergalactic bridge between two civilizations to benefit Earth's future.

Here is the story of my crash in 1947, from the first chapter in my autobiography. *Stranded On Earth*:

The night cycle was upon us. We cruised dangerously near the military base. In the distance there was a turbulent thunderstorm battering the atmosphere. Brilliant flashes of electricity erupted spontaneously—here, there and all around—unpredictable and shattering.

"The mother ship is signaling," announced Naylaiu (Nay-loo). "They are asking that we retreat."

Without emotion I stared at my screen. It was my duty to maintain defenses. My mind interfaced with the computer at all times during flight. To break that concentration—even for a moment—could spell disaster. "Tell them we acknowledge," I told Naylaiu.

My ship was on a purely scientific mission, to study, observe and collect living specimens. In our storage compartments we had live animals, plants, rocks, soil and water to take back with us to the Home World. We had collected mostly single-celled animals, bacteria, mold and such, and had advanced up to birds, small mammals and fish. On the Home World we would bio-engineer these specimens, to adapt them to our planet and our environment.

Naylaiu projected her thoughts again to me. She was deeply concerned. "Lieutenant, these facilities have all been catalogued. I suggest we leave the area. That storm over the desert is extremely ominous."

It was, in fact, the worst storm we had encountered on the Terran world. We didn't know at the time that humans were experimenting with a new kind of radar technology. I stood at my computer console with my arms outstretched and my hands up against the tilted screen. I did not look at Naylaiu, but tried to reassure her. "We won't be in any danger, Naylaiu. I just want to have a closer look."

"They won't pick us up on their radar," Kiayha (Ki-ya) reminded us, "but there is always danger of observation when our ships come this close."

The other two crew members, Shienyah (Shen-ya) and Lorkiah (Lor-ka), stood behind me as they concentrated on their panels. They said nothing, but I detected their concern as well.

Still, I wanted to fly over the base.

The lightning storm was now in full force. The sky danced with electrical surges and angry clouds billowed and threatened the cowering earth below. To me it was an exciting spectacle and we were in the midst of it. I guided our little delta-shaped craft even nearer to that which was forbidden.

"Sanni, the shadow ship is signaling again," Naylaiu informed me. "They want us to pull away... now." The protective force-field that surrounded our ship, as well as the sister craft that was following us, was in my total control. It was our life line to safety and security in this major electrical event. I suppose a part of me—the thrill seeker—was what had led me to dare coming this close. We were not supposed to be there. As a matter of fact, we were violating the orders of the Council by coming to Earth in the first place. Earth was strictly off-limits to all space craft, but my desire to lead a specimen-collecting scientific expedition there had been just too tempting to let a little thing such as Federation rules and regulations stop me.

My crew of four colleagues had tried to talk me out of this, but in the end I had convinced them it was safe and we would get away with it. After all, it wasn't my first field trip. We had been on five flights beforehand. And the ship behind us, sharing the force-field, had agreed to accompany us against their commander's better judgment, because they knew I had succeeded at ignoring the establishment before.

Being scientists from Zeta Reticuli, we were all indelibly curious by nature. A series of nuclear tests being performed around White Sands and in the ocean on Earth had attracted the attention of many in space. Humans on Earth were playing around with the Atom. They were detonating bombs and they did not realize the consequences of their actions.

These detonations were what had originally led our people to Earth, to observe and to study. We wanted to know why Earth people were performing nuclear tests and why they would use this technology for war purposes instead of peaceful endeavors.

As a result, we came and studied all of Earth's cultures, all the different languages, and visited all the major cities. We made several flyovers of this particular desert region before the Council made the decision to quarantine the planet. "Sanni, I think we should break away." There was urgency in Naylaiu's telepathic words. "Please..." Shienyah behind me shrieked. "Look at that!" she cried. "What is it?" asked Lorkiah.

Startled by their interaction, I turned my head to see what Shienyah was indicating on her panel, and just at that moment the connection to my computer was interrupted. The force-field went down. In that split second a bolt of lightning hit us. When the force-field went down, the field surrounding the entire vehicle was left vulnerable. This caused electricity in the atmosphere to be drawn to the hull of the ship. The sister craft behind us went down first. A second later, the discharge of electricity was attracted to our hull, just like a moth to a flame, and then we went down. All I remember is a loud explosion and a brilliant white light that filled our entire craft.

The next thing I remember is lying on my back on the cold, damp ground. I was facing up toward the dark sky and behind me was a huge boulder. I could see the stars between some drifting clouds, and cold raindrops pelted my body. All around me were the pitiful cries from my four crew members. They were in pain and they continued to wail and cry for what seemed an eternity.

Then everything grew silent. The smoke smell was thick in the night air, and I detected ozone from the burning instruments that had been aboard my ship. The quiet was unnerving. I tried to move, but I could barely lift my finger or turn my head. I couldn't move my leg or arm on my left side, and it hurt really bad. I knew that my head was injured from the horrible pain. I faded in and out of consciousness.

The rain came and went. Eventually it stopped altogether. I remember losing consciousness briefly, but feeling as though something brought me out of it. It was a sort of warmth, and it caused me to open my eyes. I saw a star in the sky, coming up over the horizon, and I remember thinking how odd that there was only one star—not two—and then recalled that this was Earth and not my home world. On my world there are two stars, or suns, and now it was the day cycle.

I was lying there, helpless, unable to move, observing the scenery around me—desert and rocks—and then I blacked out again. When I came to, there was a noise and I saw a creature a few yards from me. I could see a creature with four legs and two heads, with two bodies joined together. It leaned over as if to get a better look at me. Then, suddenly, it took off really fast. Later I would figure out that it was a man sitting on top of a horse. I remember he wore a black hat. And it seemed as though he watched me for a long time before he turned and galloped off in such haste.

The day star grew hotter and I kept passing in and out, in and out of consciousness.

My next recollection was that it was again the dark cycle. I could hear noises—machines getting closer—machines roaring and grinding their way up the hillside. Then, the next thing I knew, somebody was picking me up and dragging me by my arms and plopping me onto the ground. My head turned to the side and I looked out of my eye to see that I was up against my four dead crew members. We were all in a row.

The people who came had these crates that were long and rectangular shaped, and they arranged them in a circle around us. I heard several people laughing and somebody kicked me. It was a big creature. They talked in this funny language that I didn't understand.

I didn't know what they were saying.

I must have passed out again, because the next thing I remember was being jolted back from out of my body by some cold stuff. I was put into this plastic wrapper and there was cold stuff in it. They picked it up and I was thinking, *What is this? I can't see, and I've got all this cold stuff around me.* Then I was being zippered up, closed inside this bag with the cold stuff surrounding me.

Then I felt myself moving. I was being transported down the winding road or path the machines had come up. When I came to again, I was inside this building. Someone had unzipped the bag I was in and I had a fairly good view of inside the building.

My guide, Khinyeo, appeared then in his astral form. A Zeta Reticulan, he stood before me and made me step outside my body. I hovered in the air inside of this building, which was round. There was a round roof on it, and I could see all these people working around me. It was hot and some of them had removed their shirts. They were busy putting things in piles. Everything was being sorted and catalogued as to size and shape. "Observe, child," Khinyeo told me.

"Pay attention to what you are looking at."

"But, Khinyeo... why?"

He was firm and authoritative. "Because you will remember all of this." Then he led me outside the building and showed me how they were taking metal and equipment in very large boxes and crates and loading them onto vehicles with wheels. Then the vehicles with wheels took the crates to the big silver birds. There were two big silver birds in the distance, and these crates were being loaded onto them.

As I was hovering over the bag with my body packed in the cold medium, someone came over and zipped the bag back up. Then they placed it in a crate with cedar chips or sawdust, and they packed the other four crew members like that, too. On the sides of the crates they had imprinted MUNITIONS or ORDNANCE. They apparently didn't want to arouse suspicion as to the crates' true contents. Then they placed those on the silver bird. I was able to observe all of this outside my body.

Then Khinyeo made me return to my body. The next thing I remember was being on this cold table after we arrived at our destination. I happened to move my head ever so slightly, and then I heard a bunch of noise. The big creatures dressed in white were shouting and yelling to one another. Soon there were dozens of them surrounding the table I was on. After they removed my uniform and boots, I had tubes shoved up me. They began putting stuff on me, trying to check my heart, blood pressure and all that stuff. Mostly what I remember is that the room didn't smell good. It smelled like death.

When my ship went down, she scattered fiber optic cables and hydraulic cords and hundreds of microchips and pieces of long metal strips called *Moinjes,* which are a type of structural beam. There were also devices there in the wreckage that were precursors to your modern picture cell phones. It took several huge crates to contain most of the wreckage and the largest sections that remained intact were packaged in large tarps and flown in huge planes.

I have numerous experiences that I have listed in detail in my two books. One of the most significant contacts for me was about meeting my true father. I recalled this wise-looking Gray ET coming into my room. He walked up to my crib and levitated me right up to his face. He then told me that I was special and that he was my father, named Khinyeo.

My Earth mission is to awaken other Starseeds and Hybrids and to correct the ideology behind my people's purpose for visiting Gaia (Earth). Where most humans claim to be "abducted" by what they know as the Grays, it is actually the negative Reptoids who are shape-shifting to appear as my people and taking humans. The negative Reptoids have been at war with my people for eons and will take advantage of ways they can cast a shadow on our intentions.

A Creator Force terra-formed all planets to hold different species of life forms, and the Universes and Galaxies are all linked as *one* with the never-ending plasma of the spark of infinite life. All matter, no matter how tiny, has life. All objects have life and are gifted with a soul that is the atoms of the stars which created them.

Books that had a big impact on me:
George Adamski's *Inside the Flying Saucers*
Budd Hopkins' *Intruders*
Raymond Fowler's *Watchers*

Websites that had an impact on me:
www.chemtrails911 and www.unknowncountry.com (by Whitley Strieber).

My contact information: *azufo47@yahoo.com*
My Website: http://sanniceto.tripod.com/index.html

Kesara

My name, Kesara, was given to me by a Vietnamese Monk and it means "Beautiful flower" or "Mane of the Lion" in Sanskrit. My name represents my service to other people as an artist.

I don't have a definite illumination about my Star name. Other people who have had extensive ET experiences tell me what they see in me. One person that seemed to hit the nail on the head was Sanni Ceto. Sanni told me that when she looked at my picture, she thought I was from Lyra. Other people have told me similar things to indicate that I do resonate towards the Lyran species.

I have only abstract memories of what my home world looks like. I guess the memories are from my conception before becoming human or the moment of anchoring into a human life. Lights, warmth, etheric sensations of organic energy are my memories. Now that I focus on the energy of my planet, it seems to be mostly this living light; life on the planet is not that solid compared to Earth life. Everything moves in and out of dimensions there. When there is a need for another life form to communicate with these beings, they can take on the form of the other life. I think when you look at a Nordic or Pleiadian, you see a vibrant light inside their eyes. There is this *light of life* within them. When you see someone die, or something die on this planet Earth, the light is extinguished. Well, that is the light of my planet, the light where all life springs. The well spring of the universe. I think they made it so that I don't remember much. They want me to focus and be here on Earth, to have the Human experience.

 Intuitively, I feel that my people are light and I always feel like I want to go back to the light. If I died and left my body, I know I would go back there. If I were to take a form from that light, it would look like a "Pleiadian." I can see them in my head and it makes me want to cry. They are about 6 to 8 feet tall, their skin is various and can change colors, it has a luminous quality. Their hair has a kind of cellular light and their eyes are really amazing, they truly shine the soul and energy of the being.

Pleiadians are really kind, loving, intelligent, and can be analytical without the emotions, although they have a lot of emotions and feelings. Some of them have a better grasp of their ego, but not all of them do. Their clothing and uniforms are luminous, like their skin. The cloth is a living tissue and takes on the properties of what they need at the time. It is adaptable to weather and space situations. I know that is not the true form of what I am, but it is the form of my choice. Everything has its flaws; that is why we are living in this existence, to learn and to grow. No matter where you are from.

As Earth beings, I feel that we are just a portion of what we truly are. Some higher forms of ETs will actually take segments of themselves and place them into people on Earth, such as a "Walk-In." The whole entire ET is not inside of this person, just a fragment. They do this in order to do research or to help the person involved. The person has a soul already when this ET inserts some of itself inside. When I interview people, these sorts of things come up, mostly dealing with the higher evolved ETs. There are also Walk-ins who do a type of "soul exchange," where the soul that was in the body goes and the ET soul takes charge of the body. I don't think there is one definite formula for everything. I believe each situation is unique and depends on what the purpose or function is. I believe that we are multi-dimensional beings; in other words, our time in space is simultaneous. I say we have multiple lifetimes going on at once and they all overlap. So who's to say that we are not several things existing all at the same time. I have had personal experiences that indicate to me that I am much bigger than just me. I feel there are many souls in me. There is a lot happening in us and around us energetically. Our energy is so huge. To limit it to the point of only human existence just doesn't do it.

*   *   *

My mother had an ET experience when she was 14 years old. I think it had something to do with me coming to Earth. She told me when I was older that a beam of light came through the ceiling and was chasing her and her friend around the house. That was all she could remember. It is just speculation that the ETs impregnated my mother and had me, but I do feel that her experiences with the ETs are related to why I am here doing the ETs' work as an artist.

I had an experience when I was 2 years old, where I was missing for a day. I have no recall of anything that happened to me, but my Mom said she couldn't find me all day, then later found me at a park. She doesn't know how I got there, because there was a huge highway that I would have had to cross to get there. I was completely intact, with no signs of injury or abuse on me.

I lived in Utah when I was little, and while I was going to school I was segregated because I looked very Asian. I didn't feel it was anything bad, I thought I was special because I got to play with the toys while everyone else was away. I had no idea I was being segregated. The interesting thing was, I remember during our nap time that this man would come and get me. He was human in appearance, bald and had really bright, blue eyes. I don't know if I was being sexually abused or if I was going to see the ETs. I remember feeling that I did not want to go with this man and sometimes I would make myself sick at home so I wouldn't have to go to school at all. Later, I had a regression where those experiences had to do with the ETs. I just remember feeling a very uncomfortable sensation in my body. Sometimes I meet people where I feel that exact sensation, so it could have been an environmental alteration to my body so that I could be on the ship. I didn't have a bad memory of the man that came for me because I always felt he was kind and gentle. I even had dreams about him off and on, and it was fine.

When I was 7 years old, I had a two-week visit with Extraterrestrials. I would awaken every morning at 4:35 AM. I did not know why until one night, when I awoke to a very weird sight, a blue-hooded Being with a folded face was standing at my feet. I could actually see them while I was fully awake. There were about four of them and they looked like little Dwarfs. Each time they came, they were putting glowing rods in my feet which resembled glowing fiber optics. If I would wake up during this, they would tell me, " We are just taking your memories, go back to sleep." They had a blue tint to their skin and were very wrinkly, like a Sharpei dog. They had small, beady, black eyes and wore cloaks that were an indigo blue. Their hands were small and square-shaped with short, stubby fingers. I know they used my brain as a storage container and what astounds me to this day is that I had no fear of these beings. I simply chalked it off as a normal occurrence.

I shared a room with my sister and later she told me that she had no memory of them visiting (although she did have a fear of the closet being open). When the visits ended, I remember getting up, grabbing my sister's hand and walking out to the edge of the street from the driveway. We both looked up to the sky and began to cry, saying, "Take us back!" Many years later, I remembered this event when I started illustrating for UFO investigators and experiencers.

When I was 17 years old, I was walking home from high school. A really old Ford vehicle drove up and I saw two males inside. They looked like twins and they sat really close together. One guy had an arm around the other guy and they looked at me really strange. At that time, I ran off. I felt that they were ETs.

Earlier in my life, it was a very different experience with the ETs. Later on, I started tuning into my own people. I think it was around 2003 when I really started to tune into the Pleiadians, Lyrans and the other highly evolved ETs. They started to come to me through the people who wanted them illustrated, using my art work abilities. I think the ETs are always guiding these people to me because of how they come to me. One man, named Gary, hired me on a two-year contract to illustrate his entire book. It was all about ET beings like the Pleiadians. That is when I started having the strongest vision I ever had of an ET. I was in an interview with Gary for his book, and I could really feel this ET standing behind him. I heard him say his name in my head, "Heron." Heron looked like a Viking and stood about 7 to 8 feet tall. He had blond hair and was really big.

My awakening has been through the work that I do "for the ETs" and the relationships that I have developed with the people that I have worked for. I believe that through working for these people and drawing their ETs, I was building a relationship with each of them. Through those relationships, I began to feel some familiar feelings about these people, like I knew them. I never felt that they were strangers and I felt a real strong connection to their ETs.

I always felt that I could communicate with the ETs, that they had a desire for me to do the illustrations properly. The ETs would stamp an image into my brain and I would use that "stamp" to do the illustration. These people I do the illustrations for will sometimes perceive the ET differently. As if the translation gets mixed up and I have to work between what they remember  seeing and the ET stamp I received. Once I get the image, I get the experience! When the illustration is correct, it becomes a trigger for other "experiencers." Sometimes I get frustrated with an illustration and give up trying. Then I just allow my hand to move, and the image gets corrected, with help. When I am in a person's presence, there is a triangle of communication between them, me and the ET. I can then channel the energy and draw the ET.

I do know someone here on Earth that is from my home planet, her name is Solice. I met her at a Crystal Skull Convention in 1990. I worked with Solice for many, many years and we are still friends. She is very clear about what she sees in me. Solice tells me we have been aboard ships together and I do remember having missing time with her before. We have had some pretty extreme experiences together, actually.

My first experience with Solice was at her house. One day she started yelling, "They're here, they're here!" When I went outside, the whole backyard was vibrating, the trees, the grass, everything. I didn't see the ship, but I definitely felt it. Solice told me they were right on top of us. Later on, we would try to call the ships down. I never saw the ship come down and land, but I could feel the ETs on the ground, going in and out of phase, being semi-invisible. Suddenly, they would just pop in and startle me. They were always the little Gray ETs, since they worked with Solice. The reason why I know she is a part of my family is because I illustrated her ET side for my friend Gary, who hired me for his book. It was as if they were already connected, I was amazed.

Solice had been taken by the Grays so often and she had finally figured out that, on some level, she had given them permission. Now she has limited them on the amount of time they are allowed to spend with her. I believe on a soul level, Solice allowed them to work with her.

I believe the Grays and my people are in an alliance with each other. From my experiences, I feel there are different levels of Grays and the ones that Solice works with are the "scientific" type, she calls the Zeta. She also had children with these beings.

Solice and I went over to Topanga Canyon at the "Inn of the 7 Rays." We were sitting down talking and having lunch, but the next thing I knew, it was dark. I thought to myself, "Oh my, it's dark!" I looked down at my watch and saw it was 8 o'clock and our conversation never stopped. *I don't get it, how did they do that?* I don't remember anything actually happening. It blended in so well with our conversation that we didn't even notice, it was perfect.

A similar event happened while I was driving. All of a sudden, it was two hours later. I knew we had still driven during that two hours because of where we were on the highway. I have had strange time anomalies throughout my entire life. I know whenever the ETs deal with me that it is always sweet, there is no roughness.

I feel that my people work with many different species. There is one fellow that I did a workshop with, his name is Noras. These people will separate from their bodies, similar to astral traveling, and go up on the ship. While I was up on the ship with Noras, it was exactly what I imagined my people doing, working with many other species on the same ship. One type of being on that ship was a Water being. They lived in their own liquid and could create any form out of this liquid. The Water being could enter the physical body to heal it. For instance, one entered me and worked with the liquid part of my body to heal it. Another ET being was a Plant being and another was a Cat humanoid being that was all furry. They were really striking and I really wanted to touch their fur. I saw some ETs that had really big heads and were really tall. Some ETs were Human looking and some were the little Grays. I saw another ET similar to a Reptilian being, maybe amphibious. Their eyes were a pinkish color, their skin was smooth and beige in color, not scaly.

My husband had UFO experiences before I met him. He has strong ET connections, but he doesn't remember them. When I tell him what I experienced with a "contactee," we experience that event again together. He also has an implant in his elbow which we had x-rayed. The results said that the implant was an organic material, having the property of lead, but it is getting smaller now. I believe I also have an implant in my right eye, but it is more of an inner-dimensional implant. When I was little, I always thought that they were looking through my eyes. I can feel it there whenever I am around other ETs, including Starseeds. It feels like clear glass, but not hard. I feel it is there to regulate my hormones, something I have always had problems with. I feel this is how they watch over me, by the hormone levels, which gives off a lot of information.

Whenever the ETs come around and I am alone, they seem to manipulate time. I was driving home one day and I saw this old clunker car going real slowly on the highway. I passed him pretty quickly, since we were all traveling 70 to 75 mph. A little ways up on the highway, there he was again! I thought maybe it was my imagination. Then, I got off the highway and was driving in my neighborhood. I saw a kid riding a bike in a weird fashion. He had long, black hair and wore dark glasses with funny-looking clothes. I drove about four blocks after passing him and there he was again!

Another time was when I was 14, I went to this mall and I remember feeling really strange. Then, when I was 32 years old, I was in the same mall, in the same room, and I felt my 14-year-old body. I felt like I was in two time frames in the same moment. Again, I believe that time is simultaneous and you can even correct problems. Such as, if you had something inhibiting your progression, you can go into that time-sync and correct it. This type of work I learned through a Kung-Fu master. It takes an awareness to do this: at the time you are experiencing a memory, that is your opportunity to correct it! It is that simple.

I sense things very strongly, it is my strongest psychic ability, I believe it is called clairsentience. These advanced Extraterrestrials I know I have felt before. That was when I realized that I have a spiritual connection. I believe they come to me like an apparition so that I can see them, but I always feel them first.

When I meet someone, I can tell right away whether they have had ET contact because I feel like I just drank 10 cups of coffee. Their energy is completely different, it is because their energy has to be a certain way in order for them to go onto the ships and be around the ET's energies. Basically, I can feel the energy inside of myself. When I am around someone like this, I will sometimes hear a high-pitched language. The language is hard to understand because it sounds like insects or a recording speeded up. I feel that a part of the ETs' bodies are in another dimension in space, like they are not fully connected on Earth's physical dimension. When I meet entities that are inner-dimensional, there is a different quality of energy around them and sometimes they have "attachments" that bind them to a particular place or person. I suppose you can call them spirits, ghosts, and or entities. So I can feel the differences of energy between humans who have ET contact, Starseeds and those who have inner-dimensional attachments.

I can feel when people are addicted to drugs as well, it is something I have always done since childhood. I used to do readings for people and I could also tell them if I felt any attachments to their energy. Sometimes these attachments were not good for them and I can work to transform this attachment so it can go on its way and no longer has a need to be attached. I see that we are rays of light, and that our centers are attached to other's centers; we are all a part of a whole. Some attachments prevent our rays from getting through to the whole, so they need to be changed and worked with. Other types of attachments are lower forms of energy or ancestral. However, not all attachments are bad!

I think I came to Earth to help awaken and trigger memories in others. I always call it "Working for the ETs." I feel compelled to do this work and the art work that I do has really helped me to channel the energy. I used to do readings for people when I was younger and I was about 70 to 80 percent correct. I always read people five years ahead of time and the value of that information wasn't reason enough to keep going. It was hard for people to remember that for a five-year future. People pretty much decide their future in the moment they are sitting in. If they decide to change their minds, then their future also changes. I felt like I wasn't doing it right, like there was something I was missing and I wanted to be completely accurate. I am an artist and I like to be perfect. I could possibly be a conduit for people and tell them what their ETs are saying, but I think that they themselves would be the best conduit. I would be good at teaching people how to communicate with their ETs, by just allowing themselves to be open and find a medium in which to do it.

I had a visit by God when I was little. It is not the same "God" written about in the bible. My grandma taught me a prayer and when I recited it that every night, this huge energy came to me. It filled the room and it filled me. It was such a huge energy, it seemed to push the walls out. It didn't scare me because I knew it was God. It told me that it would always be in my life. I only call it God because that is what everyone else calls it. The prayer was: "Now I lay me down to sleep, I pray the Lord my soul to keep, the Lord will guard me through the night and wake me in the morning light." Me personally, it doesn't seem fit to give this God energy a name.

Eventually we are all going to end up in the same place, which is pure and divine light. That is where we are all from and where we are all heading. We are all from the light and we are trying to remember how to get back there. These lifetimes as a Human have value in terms of understanding what it is to suffer and to ascend. There is so much to us, every single person is so incredible. I think that is why ETs are so fascinated with Humans, because there is something about our existence that makes others envious. Maybe it is our suffering and our ability to feel physically, emotionally and mentally. It is such an opportunity to grow, but we have to be careful because it can also cause us not to grow, but descend. I think it is really tricky to be living as a Human being. There is something about being Human that is very important at this time. I don't know if it is spiritual or that Humans are actually changing the universe.

ETs have been around since the beginning of Human DNA. One scientist said during a news conference, and in a very quick manner, that Human DNA is engineered and there is no way that it naturally occurred. Only a few people caught that blurb or remembered it. I think the reason why we were engineered is because Humans are special. I also think the Earth has gone through many previous Shifts, and I feel this is going to be a big one, where Humans ascend into another dimension. I don't know for certain what is going to happen. If we do survive, it will be in another form.

Books that are significant to me:

Preston Dennet's books, listed on his website:

http://home.pacbell.net/prestone/

Sanni Ceto's book *Zeti Child*, and Dr. Stranges' book *Stranger at the Pentagon*

YouTube video link of a Hungarian woman who has a lot of ET contact:

www.youtube.com/user/AndrosEnigmaX

You may contact me at: *christinedennett@sbcglobal.net*

David Armstrong

I only pull my information from one source, my Guides. I only go by what they tell me because they have always given me deadly-accurate information. I have had readings from psychics who understand ETs, but the way it works for me is, unless my Guides actually tell me, I don't believe it. I just take in the information given to me with the attitude that "It is good to know." My guides have never said I belong to any certain ET race. I don't think our spirit belongs to any race because we have lived so many lives on so many different planets. When some people say that they have come from another planet, they could very well mean that the most recent incarnation they could remember was on that planet, they have an affinity for it and wish to return there.

I would say the "Tall Whites" are a species I possibly could have come from. However, when I had a tumor being worked on years ago and was feeling very ill, the guides who were working on me suddenly became visible and they were not the typical Human creatures. One looked like a Praying Mantis, which resembles a large grasshopper. They are an Insectoid race. Their technology seemed very advanced and I believe they zoomed it in through the wall of my bedroom during the healing, because I could still see my partner lying on the bed next to me. I was comforted by seeing her there with me, knowing that I was not in a foreign environment, and I felt I was going to be okay. I felt these creatures were there to help me.

For the most part, I think seeing a guide of some sort is an alarming situation that we are not really prepared to handle. I had an overwhelming sense of security come over me at that time, so I know they have a lot more power than we do and they are much more intelligent. Most Starseeds would think if you had a Praying Mantis come and work on you, you would be connected to the them and their people. The answer is possibly yes, because we have all lived hundreds and thousands of lives. What we are is love energy that never dies. We keep coming back and we could have lived on many different planets and universes.

*   *   *

I have not consciously gone to another planet where my guides are. I have had "dreams" where I was somewhere else, it certainly wasn't Earth. One of the most unusual places was in a highly, technologically advanced society where there were buildings that seemed to all be made out of clear glass. I don't recall what the name was for this planet, but we were riding on a very interesting car that hovered and followed a simple grid. For amusement, these beings would have some of these grids do flips, circles and other things.

I thought this was similar to an amusement ride. Maybe they just get bored and like to do something interesting with the body. It seemed quite scary to be going up these flips, but they must have had a reason for them. It was a beautiful and breath-taking place. There were a lot of jagged mountains with overgrowth not similar to our trees on Earth. The entire topography was unusual and quite jagged. It was daylight and there was a sun, but I wasn't really paying attention to that. When you are traveling at these enormous speeds during astral projection, everything appears as flashes.

This place was similar to the Lemurian Crystal City, which also had a lot of glass, but the Lemurians had mirrors, too. The Lemurians could flick a switch on the mirrors to reflect or absorb the light, depending on whether they wanted warmth or cool air. The city itself was not built on crystals, but they used a lot of crystal technology in developing their computers and such. Earth has come to a point were we are creating microfibers, which is a way of transmitting signals with electrons. The Lemurians were using crystals because it was simple and cheap, but you had to know how the properties of thought worked in order to make the crystals active. They used them for everything, including healing, storing information and sending pulse-wave signals to other planets.

Right now on Earth, a giant crystal has been discovered at the bottom of the ocean and it is sending out a massive amount of signals. The government is keeping it under wraps because they don't know what it is. It is still active today and is a homing beacon signal for other planets to find us. Other planets can connect to this beacon and set their ships on "auto-pilot" and fly here. I know this giant crystal is in the Bermuda Triangle. There were eight or nine placed in parallel lines across the Earth. One crystal was connected with the Giza Pyramids, but that one is gone. Another is connected in Mexico somewhere. These pathways between the beacons were placed here by the ETs while they were seeding Earth and they could travel from one to the other. There weren't a lot of facilities open then and it was easier to mark these facilities with crystals so they could locate them.

The crystal on top of the Giza Pyramid was taken by a society after the destruction of Lemuria and Atlantis. They didn't know what it was or what it did, but they felt it must have been precious. The crystals that marked the facilities on Earth for the ETs were no longer needed after the reseeding of the planet, when Lemuria and Atlantis were destroyed. Their technology had also grown to where they no longer needed these crystal beacons, so they became outdated. The government is just finding out about these crystals.

I think my genetic material is very similar to my brother's. I don't know if I am a Hybrid "implant" in my mother's womb, but I have never lost contact with my spirit guides. When I was born, my father was trying to pick a name for me and my mother said, "That's David!" Like it was an instant recognition for her. I have had many past lives with this name.

As far as whether my guides are ET or my spirit is ET, Einstein's theory was that time is irrelevant. You could be living three or four lifetimes simultaneously and he believed that. It is hard for the human mind to fathom that they may have a spiritual guide that can also be living a life somewhere else. I also believe this because the timetable is definitive. I have talked to people who have had out-of-body experiences who say they have seen their relatives who seem to be in their 30s, their vitality and youth was back.

My earliest conscious memory was when my grandmother died. My parents both say that it is impossible for me to remember because I was only six weeks old. I had asked who the gray-haired lady was who would hold me, pat me and kiss me on the head, saying, "Dear,dear,dear." They told me that she was my grandmother and that I couldn't have remembered that at all. So I believe I was a little more conscious as a baby.

I have always been in touch with my guides and on occasion I will see them. As a child I could levitate things, I was psychic, an empath and always wanted to help someone feel better when they were ill. I also detect energy in people and I am more attracted to a person by their frequency than by the way they look. I sense the beauty from their energy and overlook the shell—that only goes skin deep.

*   *   *

When I was about three years old, I would have this dream every once in while where I was pushing this little "popper," a toy that had a round, plastic see-through globe. There were little balls that would pop up inside the globe. I would also have dreams of a tractor and a school bus flying overhead on the farm that I grew up on. I kept seeing this image in my mind. As I got older, I wondered why the dream always repeated itself.

While listening to my music, a song called "Galactic Grove" triggered a memory that I had about pushing the popper in the yard. The next faint memory was me looking up at a being I had never seen before. He was bigger than me at the time, he stood about 4 to 5 feet tall. I had no fear of this being. I had the popper toy in my left hand and, with my right hand, I reached up and pointed at the being and the being then pointed at me. When he did this, a charge of blue light lit me up, but did not hurt me. This charge was going into me.

My Guides then told me, "Now that you had that memory, it's okay to tell you, that was when you first got your healing abilities." I repressed that memory because the popper in my left hand had melted from this blue charge. I suppose that since the toy was plastic and not biological that it didn't survive whatever was being sent through me. We used to have this outdoor burning barrel and I had been previously scolded by my mother for playing to close to this barrel. This popper looked as though I had once again been playing too close to the barrel and I was reprimanded for it.

My mother was upset and told me that I ruined the toy and she threw it into the barrel. I remember crying because it wasn't ruined and I still wanted to play with it. So, I had repressed this memory since it was tragic for me. I also realized that the tractor and the school bus flying above our farm were just elements that I would recognize as a little boy. The school bus would actually come in the yard and pick up my older brother and sister. So that memory was replaced by something that was familiar to me at the time.

When we work through the issue, I think we are much more settled about what has happened to us in the past and we can then deal with these issues better. The dreams are there to help people sort things out. Since I wasn't making "heads nor tails" of the event, the images just kept repeating themselves in my dreams. The gifts we receive from the ETs are pretty special, too, but if they scare us in any way, I believe the memory will automatically repress itself until we can possibly handle it at a later time.

I had grown up on a farm in North Dakota. When I was about 6 or 7 years old, I thought I would be a big assistant. I took our little riding lawn mower and hooked a wagon to it to carry the hay bales. I went out in the ditch and put the bales of hay into my wagon, dragged them up to the barn and put them in the hay loft for Dad. Each bale weighed about 60 to 70 pounds. I understood the principles of levitation and how to brake the bond. I would tell the bales to get into my wagon and I would only place three of them in at a time so it wouldn't get too wobbly.

My grandfather was sitting in the yard, watching me, and was charged by my production. He ran into the house to get my mother. My mother came out and saw the three bales stacked in my wagon, so she met me at the barn to help me. She could hardly lift the bales and asked how I had done this. I explained to her how I told the bales to get up in the wagon. My mother, being the skeptic that she was, gave me the licking of my life for "telling a tale." As a child, I did not wish to get punished again, so I conformed to the norm. I found out what behavior was expected of me and I just conformed. As an adult, I can only lift things that are extremely heavy when I know my guides are helping. I have picked up a car and a piano before, and at the time these things felt like a feather.

Right around the time when I was 17 or 18, I had a near-death experience. I experienced the Halls of Karma, where you go to the white light and all of a sudden it was like being on a spacecraft or something. I got to see all of my spirit guides and they didn't look to be any different than us, but not exactly the same. When you meet the guides that greet you on the other side, they appear Human in form, because your conscious memories are still intact and their intent is to comfort you instead of frightening you. I feel that when we are dead permanently—but before we come back again—we have an open book that we learn from.

When I was at the Hall of Karma, I also saw the Akashic Records. I got to see and review a lot of things I have done in other lifetimes. When I came back and my body started working again, I had conscious recall of where I had been. For months I could share what I knew about the seven layers I went through to "heaven." Layers meaning a separation of one level of existence from another.

For example, when I went to a level where these really evolved beings existed, I said, "Oh, I don't belong here, I need to go down a level." Your spirit does sense where it belongs. You find out that the only life that is important is the one you are living *now* because you can't undo the past.

I realized that living your life in the pursuit of happiness has nothing to do with the income you receive. Success is knowing you came here this lifetime to correct something you did in the past, and hope you have learned from it. The money is not why we came here. We don't need to own the luxuries of life. The smart thing to realize is that all things belong to everyone. We can all enjoy it, we don't have to own it.

Since my near-death experience, I suddenly had new freedom in that realm. I was hearing my guides, not vocally, but I was getting a sense of what they were saying, similar to telepathy. Recently, my son, who is psychic, was hearing these messages at the exact same time I was. I think when people are dead-on with information they get from the spirit world, it is always fun to see. I was pretty psychic, too.

I call one of my guides the "Latin Guide." I can almost speak it authentically, but I am just repeating what he says to me. I have long pauses where I wait for what he tells me to be translated into English. He probably spoke Latin in his last lifetime, before he became a guide to me. I also believe this guide has ascended to a point where he doesn't have to incarnate into another body.

One time my guides said it would cost an exact amount to fix the gutters before my partner told me she wanted them fixed. So, later on we went to the store to pick out the materials and threw a couple extra things in the cart and went to the check-out. The total came to the exact amount my guides told me it would be. My partner asked if my guides had anything better to do with their insight. I told her it wasn't just trivial information, it was validation. Since time is irrelevant, my guides went into the near future to give me the exact amount, that was all.

Similar to some psychics who have seen Nostradamus looking back at them. Nostradamus went forward in time, and now that the people are alive, they saw him looking at them.

My guides also told me that Michael Jackson was going to pass, although they didn't tell me the exact date. So I went out and bought every album of his I could find. My Guides explained to me that the further into the future they would go, the more the chances are that something would change the future.

I was in contact with my spirit guides about the ET issue and some years later they divulged a truth to me. They told me, "Humans are a genetically engineered species that has transplanted in a variety of regions in the Universe. The inevitable differences in the races are erroneously described by our scientists as being a result of the adaption to our environment." What works for fungi and bacteria in a Petri-dish created in a laboratory does not work for all beings. Fungi and bacteria grow rather rapidly and scientists can observe generations and generations of different insects and see how they change. However, they assume that it works this way for animals, and it does not. None of the scientific arguments of how life was created or how man evolved has ever explained the huge gap in Human development.

The Starseed history has been obscured by religious leaders who were fundamentally opposed to letting out the truth about our society. When my guides told me this, it was like the big bombshell dropped. I realized that the people we trusted lied to us. My guides continued, saying that we can make ourselves into being whatever we want. The unfortunate consequences of disinformation has led to a culture predisposed to accepting blind faith as procedural and anything else as a "fall from the graces." Established religion has functioned more as a weapon to keep us orderly and immobile.

To be freed from our immobility, we simply need to think outside of the box. We should gravitate to thinking that matter is the result of our thoughts. Einstein's theory of relativity did not rule out altering matter nor restructuring the bond. All energy responds to thought, this has been scientifically demonstrated, but not too well understood in the practical sense.

My guides have told me about the six different races that were seeded on Earth. They are the Caucasian, Hispanic, Black, Asian, the Red Man and the one we don't talk about, which is the ones responsible for areas like Easter Island. They were huge beings that decided they didn't want to be on the planet anymore, for whatever reason. There is speculation that they died while others say they lifted themselves away. So if we were all seeded here, like the "Tall Whites" and different races that came here, who am I? Basically we are all Hybrids, because Earth was never one of these planets that started as an amoeba and eventually turned into a Human. What happened is we were brought in, as were dogs, cats, whales and dolphins, etc, etc. Edgar Cayce talks about Lemuria and Atlantis when all the Hybrid Starseeds came here and I wanted to know more about that. My guides told me that there was so much disinformation written about Lemuria, Atlantis and other "lost" continents that they decided to channel through me the *Lost Continent* book series.

That is what my guides have told me about Mankind. I gravitate towards the ETs that do what I call "implant" here. Those people seem to have a consciousness at or above the level that I respect and admire. Society might belittle who these people are and what they believe in, but the spirit world does not. A lot of Hybrids become implanted into the womb of the female and some were even born without the use of the female. There are a lot of Hybrid crosses that are being made today and, back in Lemurian times on Earth, they were doing scientific engineering experiments with human DNA to create a whole bunch of different people. In this environment, the scientists eventually found races that work the best and what regions they would do the best in. These weren't stupid people, they had a plan and were very successful at it.

My guides were telling me the primary function of a healthy culture is to make important past historical knowledge available by submerging it in traditional methods of communication such as books and movies. I thought about that for a long time. I thought about writing a very good book and releasing it as a science-fiction novel that could catch the eye of a movie producer. That movie could be based on the truth instead of on conjecture of which we have no basis. Their impressive cultural functioning and the implementing of natural resources are characteristically described in detail in this Lemurian novel. So I slipped it in, even though it is a story within a story, and a love story. There are two types of people that are represented in the book. One is highly intelligent and the other is unintelligent, but both of these types of people are important, especially for the story. Although their methods and resources were more complex, their lives were essentially less complicated in Lemuria. They employed extraordinary craftsmanship and superior ecological intelligence that we seem to miss out on in today's world.

Although the Lemurian technology may have been forgotten, there have been numerous experiments in this day and age which have demonstrated the feasibility of the ecologically free methods of producing energy. Many of the barriers posed by institutions and government have limited our progress of discovering "free energy."

My guides were telling me that in a profit-structured society there is very little incentive to be ecologically practical. The establishment has blamed the environmentalists for impeding their industrial progress. Some of these environmentalists have been encouraging our society to move towards a free-energy society. That is what I support. My guides are saying that we have always been there, we just have to relearn. We went down another course of burning fossil fuels and using fire to create energy.

Until our society becomes conscious of the environmental impact of non-renewable resources, the train of thought will always be less mobile. Since we are politically reactionary, more repressive in our distinction of right and wrong, we become complacent and dull with our attitudes and beliefs. I think most people would rather ignore that there is a problem and let the experts sort it out. The living integrity of all creatures on Earth depend on this generation for its mere survival. Although there is no perfect environment where humans would not have some impact, it is highly plausible that we could operate indefinitely by the technology deployed by the Lemurians and the Atlanteans.

That is why I think my book is important, to jar the scientists into thinking. What my guides are doing is giving me just enough information so when someone reads it, they will receive ideas. Then those ideas become a reality. Movies often do that, if you remember the series of *Star Trek*, there are a lot of things now that we have that we didn't have then. Computers are certainly one of them. I think we can get pretty close to the way Atlantis and Lemuria really looked with the special effects that we have today. In the book, we reveal what happened to Lemuria and what type of people were alive at the time. If the visitors were coming and going freely from other planets, maybe after the Lemurians' demise, they left Earth off-limits from being visited anymore. I believe that non-restriction has a lot to do with a freelance of people coming and going to Earth from other planets and caused the destruction of certain continents. Earth is now considered to be a guarded planet.

I have had experiences where I have been out-of-body. I would explore the Earth plane and go from here to Europe in a millisecond, seeing things I have only seen in pictures. Consciously that doesn't happen for me and I only get

glimpses now and again. Other people say they are more consciously aware
when they do out-of-body as a practice. In the dream state there are more
messages than how to sort out present-day difficulties. I think we also do work
on other planets and other dimensions. Recently we had an instance where a
planet came into contact with ours. This planet was in another dimension, so we
wouldn't be able to visibly see it, but its effects were felt by many people. My
guides called this the "Cosmic Interface Period," where one dimension comes
close or touches another.

Some years ago I was asking my guides about the other planets. This was
during the Reagan administration, when they started the Star Wars program, but
they also sent out probes to go look at other galaxies, as did the Russians.
Whatever the Russians were rumored to have done, Reagan wanted to do better.
They have gone into other solar systems beyond ours and have taken some
pictures. On some of those pictures, if they had taken a closer look, they would
have found signs of life that resembled Humans. Russians had lost one of their
probes, but were embarrassed to say anything. Reagan's probe was destroyed
and no one knows how or why. The probes are no longer there, maybe we were
getting out of our jurisdiction.

The mission for this planet is to move into another level of ascension. In
order for that to happen, a lot of things have to occur. One of the things that we
find is that not only do people's physical bodies need to be healed, their spirit
needs a boost, too. You boost it through the love vibration, there is nothing else.
We are all a part of God's energy. I would like to get some more music out there
to help with ascension. I would like to get books out there that will help people
understand their historical place in the world. It is all an adjustment in truth and
there are a lot of people seeking truth on this planet and they want to know.

The reason is because most people don't know who they are, why they
came here or what they are doing here. So, ultimately humanity doesn't know
where they are going. A lot of us don't know our missions, but a lot of us know
that we came here to help others. The lightworkers know this. Others who are
not spiritual would say it's a dumb question, "What is my mission?" I am a
plumber, etc. Some people only live 10 percent in spirituality, while others live
90 percent in their spirituality. The key is balance. You have to take care of
yourself at the same time you seek spirituality.

*   *   *

A lot of people I know say that what I do is highly unusual. I do healings where my guides work through me. Some people say while doing these healings my hands are extremely warm and they get tingling sensations in their bodies. It is a longer lasting healing effect and I have not run into many people who have had this type of healing. However, I know there are some really good healers out there. My healing has primarily been through touch. We have been toying around with remote healing and other things. I have been doing it through physical touch since I was fairly young. I believe I am just the conduit through which the spirit world works through me. When I grab onto someone, I know they already have the ability to heal themselves and could just use a little boost. It is like recharging a battery so they can start functioning more normally.

I also do a little bit of a "read," if their spirit guides are willing to share anything that the person needs to know. I will have some people's guides tell me not to tell the person they have a disease or they will own the disease. Consciously, the person who is getting the healing will start doing their own healing. Ultimately it starts and stops with each person. Everyone is in control of their own systems. Most feel blown away by this information and I believe it helps open them up. A lot of them learn to accept their new frequency and hang on to it, and healing will prevail. I think it is as simple as one saying, "Okay, I have a liver issue, I am going to unplug this circuit here and plug it in where my liver is, and my liver will start to process the healing."

There are people who have been brought to me in a strange way, they have been given up for dead at the Mayo Clinic. They come to me because they really want to live. They receive a healing and the next thing you know, the doctors are saying they must have made a mistake. They will tell people their tests must have been inaccurate because they no longer see a trace of cancer or Hepatitis C, etc.

I was about 21 years old and I asked one of the nurses at the hospital if I could walk through the terminally ill section. She told me, "By all means, yes." I went to each person and healed them. Within days of this healing, they were all discharged out of the hospital. Later, I got a call from the hospital adminis-trator. I was thinking "Great, they have more work for me to do there, they must have been happy with me healing all of those people." Well, I was wrong. Their message to me was not to ever step through that hospital again.

So I learned that I cannot go to the hospitals and just start healing people. I overstepped my bounds, because that is the way in which the universe gets to people. It was fun, but I could have gotten into serious trouble by the government. They could have done something to me if I had continued. My guides told me that it was a good lesson for me to learn and to trust that they will bring the people who really need the healings to me. I do not have to go seeking them out, which can bring me bad attention from sections of the government, such as the NSA. I had one guy tell me that if the NSA ever got wind of me and what I was doing, that I would never be free again. I would become property of the US (secret) government. There are very few people that know about me, and those that do were guided to come see me. I was disappointed with not being able to contact a few famous people, such as those you hear about. I know I could have helped them, but there was no way for me to contact them.

I have had missing time that seems to happen when I am driving. I think to myself, "If I was missing for 10 minutes, who was driving the car?" There was no one with me, so I must have been on "auto-pilot." Where did I go and how long was I there? My guides explained to me just a couple of months ago what was happening. Apparently, there are healings in this lifetime that I agreed to do, so they pull me out of this time period and sometimes I don't get back the exact same time I left. I may be gone for half an hour or half a day, doing healings for groups of people.

One time my partner and I were driving to a car show and we had just driven a few blocks when she told me we would need to turn left at the light. Then I realized that we actually needed to turn right, because we arrived at the show. It normally would have been a 20-minute drive. We both lost time and do not remember anything. Later the guides told me I was sent to do a healing.

One of the most interesting experience was when I was in Iowa. There was a group of people who came for healing and I didn't know who they were. I was in a park and was walking behind a camper. My guides told me they would send me home now. So I had bi-located. The guides told me someone happened to be in the camper and saw me leave. This person ran out to the others and told them that I had just vanished behind the camper. I do remember walking around the back of the camper after the healings, but that was all.

I will be tired and sometimes exhausted if it is a big group. This can happen to me in the middle of the day and I will have to go lie down. It is tough on the body to bi-locate. This is why others feel that I am a Hybrid being, because it is more common for them to do these things. If at some point my guides tell me that I am a Hybrid and a human "implant," then I would say okay, I accept it. I like to hear what other people wish to tell me, but until I hear it from my guides, I don't take it as fact.

I wish it weren't the case, but my beings usually refrain from comment when someone else tells me what they see in me, ET or otherwise. I am not sure why they do this, but they have yet to confirm anything that has been told to me. That information could possibly be damaging to the work I am doing if I were to know, I am not sure. Maybe they have me programmed a certain way and they don't want that to change.

I am not connected to my guides 24/7. Sometimes I will ask them a question and they will give me an answer. Sometimes that answer doesn't come for a while. I can be a normal person, doing normal things, and the guides all of a sudden pop in and mention something to me. Sometimes the channeling will go on for hours at a time. I have heard things that our scientists don't yet understand. I have heard terminology that has not yet been invented, but will be. I am kind of ahead of the game.

Last week my guides came when I was in the musical studio and they played four different songs through me. I have never heard these songs before and what was fascinating is that we did all four songs in one take. They are all Ascension songs and they just came right through me. One was about the Apollo missions to the moon that was followed by a spacecraft the entire time. That spacecraft was sending musical messages, or universal signals. So, my guides said we will put it in song form so that I could hear it. Another song called "Our Spacecraft" is all different sounds that are on the ET ships. Another one was the Dolphin's language into a song. I didn't even realize any of my equipment could make those sounds. My guides made those sounds through me, using the equipment we had. This is not like music that you have ever heard on Earth before. I believe we are creating this for the ET people here because they will take fast recognition to it, unlike other people. Anyone who wants to ascend and wants to better acclimate for the ascension will want to hear this music.

My guides have told me that they will assist those who have heard the frequencies. So when you listen to the songs, it will also help anyone in the general area that will pick up these frequencies. It is the frequency that matters.

After listening to the Dolphin song, my back pain disappeared, and I was feeling more energy and sitting up straighter. I cannot take credit for these songs because they channeled them through me, I am just the vessel.

Most of us have many guides, although there is usually one that is the "overseer." Some people call the overseer their angel or guardian angel. Maybe the reason they don't have names is because of all the lifetimes that they have had—which one would they choose? I believe that we are all a spark of consciousness of God. I believe that we all have a soul and a soul group that we belong to. To break it down further, we are spirit within that soul group. The soul never dies, therefore keeps our spirit alive. A lot of people think soul and spirit mean the same thing. What the spirit world says to me is that spark of consciousness that is me, is my spirit. The soul is somewhere else, housed separately. This is so we don't harm it in any way!

Three books that were significant to me:

Talking to Extraterrestrials by Lisette Larkins

The Keepers by Jim Sparks

Love Without End by Glenda Green

Please contact me through my assistant at: *tomsanders526@gmail.com*

INO

With appreciation and gratitude to the Compiler of this book.

If you think being an alien hybrid is crazy and couldn't possibly be true, you might try thinking from another angle because, all in all, it just makes sense. The way I see it, with all of my personal experiences, it could all boil down to just that—intimate involvement with unknown beings.

I know I am "different" simply by how few people there are that can relate to me and I to them. I know that most people feel different in one way or another, but "different" takes on a whole new meaning when you are talking about possibly being an engineered alien hybrid. I can recognize other Star members when I look at them and I believe I am a walk-in. A "walk in" is a spirit that enters a body at a designated age, to fulfill its personal agenda. Not all spirits want to go through the whole life cycle, and not all spirits want to stay for the whole life cycle. I have the memories of this body's life, but I feel that I have included them into my new self and have moved on.

I didn't come here to be a child, I came here wanting to start at the adult age. Around the age of 30, I started reading *Seth Speaks* by Jane Roberts. Seth expanded my consciousness and opened up my universe by explaining how physical reality works. I am a teacher by nature and Seth gave me such clarity. This is what allowed me to "walk in." I think this is when it happened. One night, when I was about 30 years old, I was sitting on the couch and I had what could have been either a heart attack, or angina. I was in absolute pain in my chest and I was drenched in sweat. Once it "passed," I got up and went to bed. I never mentioned it to anybody, but after that night, I was different. I was a much stronger person and much more in control of myself. My family members noticed the difference, too, and had to start treating me differently. I also walked away from my abusive husband after that experience. I just walked out the front door. I spent that next year studying and growing faster than I could believe. It's amazing how fluid reality is.

*   *   *

It feels to me that my "home planet" is entirely water. The water is a very beautiful blue-gray color and has a very harmonious feeling. I have memories of this planet having less gravity than Earth. I remember living in an ocean, and being surrounded by joy and love. There was no tension there, just happiness, and I miss it. The planet has multiple moons that are different in sizes and they were all in gray color tones as I recall.

I know that my mother delivered me on Earth and I believe that she had been used by the "Grays" to produce me as an Earth being. I have found that some of our babies are "Earth" babies and some are "ship" babies. We can't live on the ship and they can't live on Earth. I think many generations before us were involved with the Grays. As a small child I sensed that I was different, even from my parents. I was born psychic and as a child everything was so confusing for me. I often wondered if I was adopted or if there was something "they" weren't telling me. Some kind of hidden secret too terrible to share. Now I think that my Earth mom and dad were not my parents. I feel a deeper connection to the beings on the ship than I ever did here on Earth.

I think the confusion started the first time my Earth mother hit me and then she told me she loved me, I was deeply offended. I was hyper-sensitive and there was a lot of emotional pain involved. I couldn't understand why people were not unconditionally loving towards one another. I grew up being introverted and focusing internally because I couldn't relate nor cope with physical reality. I had to work hard to learn how to cope with the physical life I was living, while at the same time, knowing that there was a whole lot more going on than what we can see on the outside.

I learned at a very young age to keep my mouth shut about all the strange things that were happening to me. I was about 5 years old and I was telling my mother about something strange that I had just seen and I sensed such a wave of fear come from her that I never told her any of the frightening or interesting things that were going on in my life again. It terrified me to know that I could scare my mother. She was my protector and she was supposed to be strong and protect me. I knew then that she couldn't. With nobody to turn to when I had many experiences—which were more confusing than anything else—I slowly became interested in them. When it finally hit me that not everybody had these experiences, I felt isolated and lonely, but later in life I have found that many people have shared some of the same experiences that I have. We are not crazy, we are truly special.

One of the more bizzare experiences I have had all my life was that I would find myself paralyzed, unable to open my eyes, while I heard "things" going on around me. I have many vague and intriguing memories. I remember many times in my life being dropped from a foot or two above my bed. When I was 7 years old, I experienced something so terrifying that I left my body and saw myself screaming, but making no noise. So I have spent my life racking up one strange experience after another and never telling anybody. Nobody I knew could handle hearing about my "odd" experiences, let alone help me deal with them.

I couldn't bear the violence and anger on this planet, it truly seemed alien to me. I spent my life being introverted, I just couldn't comprehend all the negativity. Ironically, I was attacked by six teenagers when I was 16 and that was when I broke through my introversion. I came out of my shell then and began to learn how to focus in physical reality. It took the violence to force me to express all my pent-up emotions. It occurred to me later that if I hadn't been jumped, I probably would have walked in front of a truck on the way home from school. I just couldn't hold it all in anymore.

My first memory of any kind of strange experience was when I was 3 years old. My sister and I saw a light in the closet of the room we shared at the time. It was a pinpoint of light, no rays of light leading to it. This light went from the top of the closet to the bottom of the closet and then back up again. For some unknown reason, it really terrified us.

I was about 10 when my mother came home with sore, aching feet from working all day as a waitress. She laid down on the couch and put her feet up on my lap. I remember intuitively putting my hands on her feet and sending them healing energy. My mom actually went out dancing that night afterwards. That is when I discovered I was a healer.

Another interesting thing that happened to me when I was 10 years old, I remember doing something that required being able to breathe under water, or what seemed like water. I was fascinated that I could breathe while swimming, knowing that I shouldn't be able to. I don't know if that experience was on my home world or on a ship. I was taught to swim around certain molecules within the water/liquid that would allow me to breathe. It was definitely a learned skill, and this event happened many times.

I feel intuitively that I have met my future husband while we were children on a ship. I met him again when I was 18 years old and I kept asking him if he knew me and he said he didn't, but I know we were meant to be together. I asked my husband 35 years later if he remembered me when we first met, and he said, "No, but you always asked if you knew me from somewhere."

In the last few years I have been having amazing experiences that were impressive even to me. Before I knew the term UFOs I used to call them "Movers." I've seen them all my life and never thought much about them other than it was interesting. They became fascinating to me the day one hovered 50 feet away from me. Now I am obsessed with UFOs. I have been validated beyond my wildest dreams by others who have shared their experiences on TV, the radio and in books. I can relate to so many aspects of these people's stories and there is such a tremendous weight that has been lifted off my shoulders. If I am crazy, then I am really good at it. After many years of silence, it's suddenly okay to talk about them now. I don't know what happened, maybe the Internet has united us in our experiences.

I lump all ETs together and call them all "Bob." Starting in 2003, I began to notice an amazing array of ships and creatures that I could see while sitting in my back yard. One kind of critter looked like a kite or a stingray, but didn't act like a kite. I watched it for about 40 minutes. I realized this critter had eight or nine little tails about 10 inches long. These tails were spinning and then slowed down and then spun again. I watched this being for 40 minutes and intuitively felt that this critter was in labor. This critter would bend itself in half, doubling itself over and acting like it was in labor. I got the impression that this being lives in the upper atmosphere, but they come down near the ground to lay their eggs. Right after she seemed to lay her eggs, she went behind the tree and I lost sight of her. Suddenly, this huge red orb moved right where these eggs were and I thought maybe it was fertilizing the eggs. Later on, I was dreaming of these beings when the sweetest, joyful voice said to me, "Yes, we're real."

*   *   *

One time, about 10 years ago, we were driving home from a camping trip. We were on this long desert road and my husband, who had only been driving for 10 to 15 minutes, suddenly said that he wanted to sleep. So my son took over driving for him and, 10 minutes later, unexpectedly he wanted to go to sleep, too. Now I was driving while they slept in the car. It was about one o'clock in the morning and not long after I started driving, I saw these lights off in the distance. They looked like headlights because they were bright. It was pitch black out and I saw these lights come straight down, as if driving down the mountainside. It was so far away, I didn't really think much of it. The next thing I know, I read this road sign that said "Welcome to Nevada." I panicked, "Oh no, I can't go to Nevada, I have got to be at work in the morning. You guys better put me back!" I was livid. As I continued driving, the next road sign I saw welcomed me to my home city. I thought, "That's better!"

I don't have any memory of anything other than seeing the lights. Everyone else in the car was asleep during the event. I have had a lot of missing time in the desert and I have found several implants, so I know I have been implanted by these ETs. I believe everyone in my family has been "taken" by ETs. I was there when my son was taken. He was very young, about 2 or 3. I could hear them in the other room while I lay in bed, paralyzed. I didn't get a visual, but I knew what what going on. I believe if I had allowed myself to actually see it happen, I would have "lost it."

Back in 1983/84, I started having dreams about a 2-year-old child with blond hair, but I never knew his name. After my only child died in 2000, I went to a psychic and he told me that I had two children. I had to contradict him many times and I never convinced him that I only had one child. Therefore, it was confirmed for me that I definitely had a son on the ship. It was very confusing for me at the time, I don't even know his name. The instant I was pregnant with my son, I knew his life's history and that he would die young.

I had a Reptilian being in my living room one night. It was more like a hologram, but he was absolutely beautiful. I don't know who he was or why I thought he was so magnificent. He was buff and firm and made me wish I was Reptilian at the time. I looked outside the kitchen window and saw a UFO before I saw this Reptilian being. The ship seemed to be a regular disk type and was of brown energy. All I know is that this Reptilian being was gorgeous. He was like a hologram, never moving. He stood in the doorway and that was all I can remember.

One night my husband and I were watching a meteor shower from inside our car. I just knew I was going to see something exciting. As I continued watching, I saw six invisible triangular ships move across the sky. The stars above became warped as the ships moved in the sky and this was how I could tell their shape. We started driving up the mountain and I noticed something on the right side of the road. At first it looked like a stop sign, then like a person, then like a rabbit, then it looked like a rock. I told the ETs, "Okay, I get this, I understand screen-memories now." Apparently that was their intention, to teach me screen memories. I got to the top of the mountain and I looked out and saw this triangle ship right above our car. It was so close I could have thrown a rock at it. My husband saw it, too. The ship flashed two white lights straight down and onto the ground for about 30 seconds. The ship also had a red light in the center and amazingly made no sound.

I have learned more about the screen memories, or mind-screen techniques, ETs use on people. ETs can try to make you think one thing is happening while they are doing whatever it is they do to us. I learned there is always a flaw in a mind screen. I was visiting the crop circles in England at the time I was taken. Whatever the ETs were doing was so painful, it went through the mind-screen. I felt that they had turned my left arm to metal. Every molecule turned rigid and hurt bad enough to get through the mind-screen. I had three swellings the size of goose eggs on my arm the next morning. Typically one forgets the mind-screen and the experience altogether, since amnesia usually comes with the experiences, but the pain was so intense that I actually remembered; therefore, their mind-screen did not work. I think this is part of my education, too.

During that visit in England I was able to experience a crop circle that had just been formed and no one had yet entered it! I laid my head in the center of the crop circle, held my camera straight up towards the sky, and took four pictures. One thing you rarely see in crop circles is insects. The fourth picture was crowded with unknown things and a very good shot of a UFO.

One day I felt compelled to go outside and bring my camera. I always lay down on the ground and take pictures straight up towards the sky. I saw this "Bob" fly by and I didn't get him in the picture, he was too fast. So I told him to come back, so he changed direction and came back. This particular critter was a blob-looking being, with a muddled color. I also have great pictures of the "sky worm." I have pictures of many types of beings. I have some white Orbs darting in and out of every other picture and then I see a UFO. I have many photos of UFOs from all over the world, but the majority of my pictures are from my backyard.

I was on a cruise on the Yangtze River in China one year. It was really out in the "boonies." I woke up with this big welt across the top of my thigh. It was thick and black and blue. Underneath this welt was a black and red symbol. When I took a picture of it, all that would show was a blazing blue flash of light across the welt. At the top of this symbol is a red dot, below that were three black dots going out at an angle to the left and another set of three dots at an angle to the right. It sort of appeared as a triangle.

I was driving in an isolated part of the desert on another occasion. Out of nowhere, a police car appeared in the lane next to mine. It always hung back a little and it tracked us for about 10 minutes. I looked in the car and saw four people. All of a sudden, I felt this strange sensation. It was in the shape of a huge hair comb that was bigger than my car. It began at the front end of the car and slowly passed through us, scanning our car and everyone inside. I could feel the energy as it passed right through me and I sensed it was brown energy. After this "scan," the cop car passed us and drove off.

Another time I was driving to a friend's house where I was facilitating my Abduction Support Group. I suddenly found myself in a pocket on the freeway where no other cars were next to me; the freeway is usually packed. Behind me, there were two cops keeping the other cars from passing. Suddenly, these cops sped up to my rear bumper. I noticed the one cop on the bike to my right had a long coat on, like a cowboy would wear. I thought for sure his coat would get caught in the spokes of the bike. Then I heard a voice in my head, "Remember your balance." So I balanced my "Wa," getting rid of all my fear and adrenaline. I felt in harmony again and I said telepathically, "Everything is okay here, you guys go ahead." I realized that those two cops were Grays and that the whole thing was a screen memory. Five minutes later, another cop drove right up on my bumper. I told him, "You know, I just saw your brother Bob and everything is okay, you can go ahead." The cop then peeled off in front of me. I finally got to my friend's house and we saw this police helicopter. Suddenly, this helicopter swooped down and the light shone right across our table where I was sitting. Later on that night, we saw a great big spaceship and three little lights.

It's fascinating how many different species that we are becoming aware of now. There are many types of Grays, and the beings I allow myself to consciously be connected with are loving and benevolent. I don't seem to attract the negative things. Even though they may do things that cause me pain, I create my own reality. I am not a victim because I believe that we made prior agreements. As far as the species out there, I am sure they are good and bad, just like us. If you focus on love and joy, that is what you will get.

I believe it was in the year 2005, when I felt the dimensions colliding and the veil was lifted. Within three months, everyone that I ever loved that had died came back to me. I wasn't haunted, just visited. This was a hyper-active psychic period and this is when I started seeing the critter-type "Bobs." When these dimensions merged, I started seeing all types of new critters. I even had my own "Flotilla" of ships one day that I could see from my back yard. I was told when to go out and where to look for them, and there they were. I saw about 17 of these ships flying above me. These ships react telepathically; you can ask them to move a certain way and they will. All of my communications with the ETs are telepathic.

About three years ago, I was called outside by the ETs at 3:00 in the morning. It was very cold and I wanted to go back inside. They told me to stay right there. As I am standing there, a voice kept telling me to keep practicing balancing my energy. If I remain balanced, they won't come for me. I didn't know who "they" were. Then I saw a police helicopter a couple of blocks over. It passed over me and then banked left and came back around again. I heard the voice telling me, "Keep your balance and they won't come for you." The next thing I knew, this helicopter was right over my head. Again I could have thrown a rock at it. If this was a real helicopter and that low, it would have woken everyone up and done serious wind damage. The helicopter was a screen memory.

I have been practicing balancing my energy and being invisible all of my life. I have many, many memories of being in an empty room and there will be a bad guy sitting in the corner. My mission is to get past this bad guy without him seeing me, so I have to be invisible. There are many skills that these ETs have taught me and helped me to practice.

I have seen about 12 different kinds of ETs. They can come to you in a way that they are here, yet not here. I have seen a Gray's eyes up close, nose to nose. What exactly are you supposed to do when you are eye to eye with an alien? I was staying with my sister who lives in another state. She has heavily carpeted stairs, but I could hear someone coming up the stairs all night long. I got this really strong sense of fear, which is a rare feeling for me. Then I saw this Gray come up to me, right up to my nose. I was eye-to-eye with him. I have beings that come and make imprints on my bed next to me and I had shadow people in my hallway for months. I don't always know who they are.

A couple of weeks ago, I had an obvious screen memory. I was in a dark room, I was not sitting straight up, I was leaning forward a little. My knees were pulled up towards me and I was looking very closely at my left hand, which seemed to have a spotlight on it. There was a rattlesnake biting my hand between my thumb and my finger. So I thought to reach around both sides of his head, thinking I could pull him off. As I was getting him to start letting go, he struck again. Each time I would start to pull him off, he would strike again. In my head I was thinking, "If this were really a rattlesnake biting me, I would be freaking out." So I recognized this event as a screen memory.

I have also noticed a "hair" in my vision, only a nanometer in size. I can see it, but not look directly at it. It is not always there, but it is obvious when it is. It looks like a clear tube with black outlines. It has different sections to it, the middle is clear or has dots inside of it. Sometimes the dots have marks inside the dots. I believe that each of these dots has information inside of them. I believe that these are educational tools that the ETs use. I figure I know what information I am receiving on some level and that it is good to be aware of it happening, but my higher self knows I am not to focus on it. Not yet.

I travel a lot and I teach wherever I go. We tend to teach others what we need to learn ourselves. I want to learn love, harmony and balance, so that is what I teach. What helped me learn to balance was learning that I am not a victim, I create my own reality. Attitude is the key to how your life is going to be. I knew I had to be here in order to learn physical creativity. I have put a lot of energy into creating physically and I intend to master it. I am a healer, a mentor and I do Tarot readings. I found out when I was a teenager that I also help people "cross over." My parents told me that one night I started walking out the front door and they asked me where I was going. I told them that there was a car accident down the street and I had to go help the old people out. They put me back in bed. Later on, I started walking out the door again and my parents asked me where I was going. I said there had been an airplane crash and I had to help these people out. A lot of times these sleep-walking events are manifesting in physical what is really going on in the spiritual realm or other states of consciousness. I notice that if someone close to me is going to die, I go to sleep. I sleep for days because I am connecting with them and helping them cross over.

My years of experiences with "aliens" have given me the motivation to learn and grow as much as I can. We must thank all the authors who have courageously exposed themselves so that we may learn.

My mantra is: "I chose to flourish, prosper and thrive. Creating joyous, fulfilling realities. I rejuvenate, regenerate and rejoice. I love, admire and respect, because you get what you give."

Books that had a significant impact on me:

Jane Robert's *Seth Speaks* and Ron Smutherman's *Transforming Number One*

You may contact me at: *skyviewufo@gmail.com*

Bhodi

I remember coming from a higher place than Earth, a place of pure light energy. We range in color from a golden-white light to a bluish flame. It depends on how evolved one's soul is and how high their frequency is. It was a planet of a higher dimensional world than Earth, but not the spirit world. I could not describe it or name it, but it is all pure energy of a higher dimension. It does not feel as populated as Earth. We are of a higher frequency there and we fit into space differently because we are not in a 3-D form. Higher energy takes less space. I know I am a light being. I am very familiar with that. When I was young, and still to this day, I would go outside at night and always be pulled to a certain area in the sky. I remember looking in this area and thinking, "Ah, home."

We don't have a monetary system or such physical things on our planet. We mostly deal with a deep love and well-being of each other. More energy and more love. We are able to transport ourselves, like teleportation. You tune your energy to anywhere and you are instantaneously there. We do have a "Light Ship," it is more of an energy ship and it is consciously alive. We usually use the ship when we travel as a group and to do our work as a community. We do projects aboard the ship together in benefit for all.

As far as ET, there is a new experience with the Reptilian side. But I am uncertain, I know I am pure energy. I was told recently by a person who does inner-dimensional work that I am Reptilian. There is a strong possibility that that is true for me. It was shocking at first to hear it, now I am in the acceptance stage and it clicks with me. I have even begun to see Reptilians in my "dreams." Most people feel Reptilians are bad and I would not want to be of that type. I know that Reptilians are thirsty for blood and I don't remember being thirsty for blood in any of my lives. I don't ever remember being of the negative energies in my lifetimes. The possibilities are there because of my affection towards the Renaissance period, armor and chainmail. I have a definite connection to chain-mail and it might be because it is similar to scales. I am very texture oriented, so it may very well be because it reminds me of scales. It does feel true to me that I am Reptilian. In the pictures I have seen of Reptilian beings, I definitely am pulled to one of them. I am also pulled to the bigger head with the elongated, black eyes. It is possible that my species are an Insectoid/Reptilian Hybrid.

Lately In my dreams, I have been seeing Reptilian beings and what they are about. I can feel that they have a strong presence. And I am to figure out why I am shown the things I see. They are teaching me that there are good and bad Reptilians. One example is, I am seeing in my dreams this group of people I know in my town. They approach me in their human form and then turn into their Reptilian form, showing me who they really are. They shape-shift in front of me. This group knows that I have very strong energy and they want part of it, to feed off of it. They try hard and want to get me into their organization for this purpose. In my dreams I was also being shown how destructive they are. My guides just tell me not to worry, because nothing is going to happen to me. However, when they can't get to me, they attack other people I know. There are some people in that group that are Reptilian and don't know that they are. They are from a different source of Reptilian, being controlled by the others in the group who know who they are.

I remember as this light being, coming to Earth and picking a Human family that would show me what unconditional love was all about. I grew up with that. I picked them because it was an easy ride for the missions I have that have been shown to me. I was in a form of light energy before I incarnated on Earth and I was told to come back here, but I am still not sure exactly what my mission is.

I have a distinct memory of coming here to pick my family, but I cannot seem to put it into words and explain it. I came into the body at birth. I definitely came in as a baby as a "push-in," not an older human like a "walk-in." I don't remember anything about being in the womb because my soul came in at birth. I can recall before actually incarnating on Earth, I was flying over great distances, feeling the freedom one last time.

I had one guide with me all of the time. I don't remember who it is now, but the being was a higher source of light, higher frequency than me. This one guide is with me always, although I have many guides. It is not a he/she thing, it is just a higher source. Some guides I have met were on this planet and have passed. I pull them in when I am meditating or helping people. I can feel their presence very strongly, and it is always from this higher light source. There is a sculpture my friend made of a blue Arcturian Light Being. I resonate with that being very much and it is the most similar being I have seen to what my guides look like. I would say they would be the closest to what my species looks like.

Blue Arcturian

I had different abilities as a child. I would have very vivid dreams about things. The veil was very thin for me and as a kid, I could feel energy and know things were going to happen before they did. I can feel people's vibration and see their souls. As I started growing up and going to school, I knew I was different. I would sit on the street curb and have strong connections to UFOs. All of my book reports in school would be about UFOs and I was always getting books about UFOs in the library. I tried my best to fit in and not stand out in the crowd. I knew I was completely different from the beginning and I wanted to fit in among them. By doing that, I took on their role and blocked the other parts of me out. The longer I did that, the more memory faded.

I think that anyone who comes to Earth, gay or bisexual, does so for a strong reason. I believe it is because as a being, they can feel both energies inside and are able to work with both sexes. I have the feeling of both sexes. I knew this at a young age, which compounded everything else that made me know I was different. So I just camouflaged into the Human race and I went along with it every day until something would push my buttons and I knew there were others like me. I am not the only one out there.

There are friends I have now that, when I first met them, we clicked instantly. These friends would have information that I needed and I was hungry for it. The more information I received from my friends, the more information I realized I had inside of me. It brings it out. Now I am meeting more people like myself. I see that in my self-searching, I have to go deep inside and peel the layers off, and it all unfolds. Every day now is a discovery. It all goes back to the source of higher frequency.

I have the feeling that my species does not come and work with me. I came here and they want me to "be here." I know they will come in my dream state to help out, to heal me if needed, and if it helps my mission here. I remember getting steroids from the hospital one day. I was supposed to take it for four days and the "quick care" doctor left me on it for 27 days, which started attacking my liver. It almost killed me and I was off work for a month and a half. Next thing I know, I had this very vivid dream about being in a blue light. It felt like jelly of thick, blue water. I felt the warmth of the light and being in this jelly. I was soaking in it and there was no fear. I remember being told, "It is going to be okay." When I woke from this "dream," my body felt better than normal. I went to the doctor and she said that everything had been turned around, my liver was healthy again. My doctor also said to me that 50 percent of people who suffer this attack on the liver die.

I used to be a "doctor" on a plasma energy ship when "Jesus" was brought on board after the "crucification.". We transported Jesus up through a beam of frequency energy. It was my job to take care of Jesus' energy form, his soul. I healed him from everything that the Humans put him through on Earth. I was the same species then that I am a Hybrid of now. My feelings were that we rescued Jesus from the infamous Illuminati. Jesus is a different species than ours, he is Pleiadian. And it may have been that the Pleiadians did not have the ability to heal Jesus at that time, like our species could.

I have gifts I can use now. People are just brought to me and all I do is listen. I tune into the energies being sent to me and I will know how I can help. One gift is to help people who seem to be in the "dark." I tap back into these gifts that I had as a child and I am more understanding of these gifts. I am not afraid of them now. I know they were given to me for a reason and for my purpose here. My gifts started coming back for me when I left the big city. There were way too many people there for me. I was on a path of destruction there and my guides would not let that happen.

Now I am in a small town again and things are starting to unfold as before. I can tell when I touch someone or shake their hand, if they are in a dark place. I know how to get them out of it through Energy Work. I am now realizing that my gifts were shown in my past "dreams." I am learning not to be afraid of what I see.

My grandmother was very spiritual and we communicated telepathically.

When she died, she came to me in the same light energy of my species before I came to Earth. I believe that my grandmother was a connection for me, like we came together from our home world. I believe there are a handful or more of beings from my planet here on Earth with me now. I am finding more people like myself the more I awaken. I know that I am not the only being here from outside of Earth. We are here for a mission and to help each other with this mission. We all have a higher mission together, and that is to heal the planet Earth. I feel that when we all go back home, we will have evolved to the next level by growing here on Earth. We will be able to possibly go to a different planet or higher dimension. I will be complete with my mission on Earth after this life.

When I was in high school, it seemed that everyone knew what they wanted to do except me. Back then, I thought of ways to escape this life. I was sent to go talk to a girlfriend. When I did, she pulled up her shirt to reveal a long, ugly scar across her chest. She told me, "Whatever you are thinking about doing, it is not worth it."

One time I totaled my car. I fell asleep at the wheel and then I felt my wheels hit something concrete, which tore the wheels right off of my car. Next, I remember the car being engulfed in white light. I was told to close my eyes, take a deep breath and let go of the steering wheel, so I did. The car was so bright, I could see a quarter laying on the passenger floor mat. I thought to myself, "Hmm, there's a quarter." I felt a heavy presence above me, I believe it was a ship. I totaled the car, but I had no injury to myself. This type of event has occurred several times. I would almost be in an accident and then something would take over and everything would be fine. I would hear a voice guide me and tell me what to do.

At another time I was driving and the next thing I knew, I woke up sensing a presence in the car. I felt a squeeze on my shoulder and heard, "Wake up." I woke up and was driving on the median. I stopped the car and got out for a bit before driving further. I know they are taking care of me.

One time I picked up a hitch-hiker. We would talk about really weird stuff. I would look back in my rear-view mirror and he was gone. I felt like it was my being's way of downloading information for me, of keeping me on my path. I had no fear, I was actually comfortable during the time, I knew it would happen this way. It happened a lot. I would see the hitch-hiker, I would pick him up, I would be downloaded, and he would be gone. Nowadays I have a fear about picking up strangers and I don't do it, even when I see "him."

I am an empath, and I can also help people cross over. I can see how the energy just leaves the body and goes into a different dimension, either to your home planet or to where you are meant to be. Death is not a bad thing at all, it is a gift, actually. I can see the spirit leave the body. It is a soul body, soul energy. They come in different shapes and colors. One's mission relates to the color of their frequency and their soul's evolution. Once my mission is complete, my frequency and color will change slightly.

My parents knew unconditional love and I needed that for my mission. I came back to Earth as a light being to help people, to prepare people. As the light being, I knew more of what my mission is. I wanted to compare the unconditional love from an Earth being to what I knew as an ET. I used to think I was the only one here and that discouraged me, thinking I had to do this big mission by myself, because Earth is way over-populated. And there are all of these humans in my way. Then it clicked, that I am not the only one here.

I know when it is time for everything to unfold, my guides will be the ones who show me what it is all about. They hold the key to my mission. I can see sparks of light (as I am seeing now, very strongly). When that happens, I know I am on the right path. My knowledge of my mission is still unfolding, but I really feel it is to bring in a higher vibration to Earth, to help bring people to a higher consciousness. While at the same time, to be aware of my own higher self. I have memories of coming into this life, but I also have memories of having been here before. I remember as the light being knowing that I had to come back here because my mission was not done yet. Another purpose of my mission is to help save people of higher frequencies, to make them aware of what is happening here on Earth—to help these people awaken to their higher selves.

When I was in high school, I had a friend who died of cancer and I happened to be with her, holding her hand as she died. This also happened with my partner, my father, my mother and currently a friend. I have since realized that this is a part of my mission as well, to help others cross that boundary and go back to their energy source. I look at death in a totally different way than most people do. I know that after "death" I will be where home is for me. Earth is not home for me. I feel that I am just renting an apartment here, Temporary Duty Assignment—Earth.

I am helping a friend to cross as we speak. I am helping him release the fear, clearing his head and putting his "karmic debt" away. I am telling him that his mission on Earth is done and that staying here in the physical body is not serving any purpose. I am trying to help him leave the shell of the human body, but only he can do that for himself. I am there to help show him that home is waiting on the other side.

I know that I work with the higher beings and not with every Human. I think a lot of Humans are here to diffuse the energies that help people awaken. The more lesser-frequency humans on the planet, the more the Illuminati will win over Earth. They are keeping people from their awakening. The Illuminati want us to be numb and in the dark. We really have to awaken and become aware of this game and maneuver through it. I feel a lot of the beings here are just like cattle and are "in the way." Even the medical community is involved with this, they want to numb society. So they give people all types of drugs to keep people blind. I even fell victim to that myself. It didn't take me long to realize that I needed to get off the medicine/drugs and I immediately began to get clear again.

There are "mind-control" frequency towers everywhere. It all deals with energy and this is how they control people. I received help from a friend who has a Neuro-feedback machine. Work on this device helped me plug the circuits of my brain back together. Now all of the "pistons" are firing again.

There is also a bio-feedback machine another friend of mine uses. They can even use this machine remotely. Suddenly, I will get a warm feeling and feel as though I stuck my finger in a socket. I called up my friend and asked him if he was working on me, and he confirmed that he was. It is a very strong energy and it makes me more in tune, it takes off the "blinders" and information starts to unfold again, to awaken. There are some people I am really pulled to and I see that there are other people who are just "pawns" in the chess game.

*   *   *

I also work with the frequency of crystals and stones. I feel connected to these, possibly from the time I was aboard the ship when I was responsible for healing the soul of "Jesus." Now I understand the power of these tools and I am helping others to use them as well. Crystal energy, sage and incense are all powerful tools. This all relates to magic. Crystals have a high frequency and it makes sense when you think about how clear they are compared to the elements of Earth in which they were formed. Crystals actually speak to me and every day I am directed by these energies and frequencies of life.

I was awakened to this side of me, knowing that I was connected to energy more than normal, when my partner was dying. His mom called me and told me he would be out of the hospital in a few days. He was in a hospital clear across town and it was a lot of driving to go see him after a long day at work. I told him I would drive out to see him the next day. I called him the next day and I was thinking how selfish I was, making excuses not to drive out to see him, knowing he was going to be released that day.

Over the phone he told me he was actually lonely and wanted me to come out. Immediately I got in the car and wanted to be there with him. When I got to the hospital, I felt this heavy energy around me. I felt these arms go around me and weighted me down. I wasn't sure what was going on, it wasn't a dark energy, just heavy. When I got to his room, the entire room was stripped. I went to the nurse's station and they told me that he was in Intensive Care. I asked when that happened, because I had just talked to him a few minutes ago on the phone. The nurse told me that was impossible. I even showed the nurse my cell phone where it showed that I called him and spoke for 26 minutes on the drive over.

I went to Intensive Care and I saw him lying there with his head facing the other direction. I noticed a tube connected to his mouth and running to a machine; there was no phone in the room. So he could not have talked to me. Then, someone came in and told me that they had moved him into here at 3 PM and it was now 7:30 PM. Later on, when he passed, I could feel his energy move right through me. Not long after that, my Dad died and it started to click with me that I was awakening to my inner-self and my energy work. I started to journal and a load of memories just started pouring into me. I was gaining so much knowledge.

Another part of my awakening was that no matter what I did, I could not "check out" of this lifetime. Even after my partner died, I became destructive and it had no effect on me, so eventually I quit. Now my third eye is very clear, they will not allow me to numb myself. I have to accept that I am here on a mission and it must be of great importance. I have learned that I have to take care of myself and be good to myself because I am here for a reason.

I had a landlord who was National Security, CIA or Secret Service of some sort. He shared some information with me during this time, when he was my landlord. He handed a book to me one day that he had written. It disclosed an entire year of his life working in the Secret Service, undercover. The book sat around in my house for a while. Every time I thought about reading it, something would come up and I would be distracted from doing so.

One day I flipped through it and thought that maybe I shouldn't be reading it. I didn't think that this kind of information should be out in the public. Later on, one day at work, I could see this black SUV driving up and down the street. Suddenly, this man appeared in the office. I didn't even hear the doorbell that sounds off when someone comes in. This man was dressed in all black, including sunglasses. Out front I could see the black SUV. I remembered going up to this man to say, "Hello." The next thing I remember, it was three or four hours later and I was sitting in a chair in the office by myself. The last thing I remembered was that man in black. A few days after that, I noticed that someone had tried to break into my house. My guides told me to get rid of the book, so I listened.

The MIB guy did not seem human to me. His presence was of a dark energy, it was something that I have never come across before. It was an energy not of this world. He did not say anything to me verbally, but I believe he spoke to me on a different level. The MIB had such a power that he was capable of taking three or four hours of my time away from me. It was a vulnerable feeling having this done to me, even though I have powerful energy myself. I don't know what happened to me, where I went or what they did.

In a "dream" one night, I was told if you really study the insects, especially the ants, you will notice the changes of the Earth as things are changing and the speed in which they are changing. "Watch the animals," they say. When the Shift is actually here, it will happen in a few days. Those that are awakened will know their mission, do their mission and go on. I believe this is occurring now and will happen very soon. I have a sense of urgency about teaching people to remain calm about these changes instead of fearing things to come. I wish to help them to accept the changes and allow them to occur.

I am spiritual, not religious. Spirituality has nothing to do with religion. I think religion is another confusion to keep Humans trapped. It is like the fuel they feed off of to stay numb. I don't understand why people think they have to go to church every Sunday to feel like a better Human being and then leave church, not practicing what they are taught.

We are all spiritual beings, it shouldn't matter what is on the outside, only the inside. We should all be treated the same, no matter what. Spirituality comes from pure love and pure energy, being true to yourself and loving yourself. I think people beat themselves up so much. It is hard to be free in this body. I think if we all love each other, try to do the right thing and know the difference, then we can become higher beings on a higher plane.

I don't believe in a God, that is a strong word to put on something. I do believe in Source. Jesus, to me, is a title for a different Source. I don't worship anything or anyone. When you worship something other than yourself, you take your self-worth away. I don't believe in looking at something or someone as higher than myself. I believe we are all GOD. We are all Creators. We are all equal. Worshipping a God is just another way of keeping your mind numb, it cripples you by putting you below someone else.

Books that were significant to me:
Dr. Dolores Proiette's *Unveil the Past, Heal the Future through Hypnotherapy*

You may contact me at: *awakeningthespirit@yahoo.com*

Jujuolui Kuita

My Star name is pronounced: Zsho-zsho-lee Q-tah. I received my name while in a half-sleep state as I was waking up one day. This state of consciousness is where information from various origins is passed or channeled to the conscious mind. Most often, it occurs just before waking up, falling asleep or during meditation. A great deal of information is given and received in this state of consciousness and any type of being can use this method to communicate. One drawback to this style of communication would be one's ability to know the difference of receiving information versus one's imagination or dreams. Another drawback is discerning whether the information is true and of a high vibration. Jujuolui is a name that lifts my vibration when I hear it or speak it. That is why I try to use my Star name rather than my Earthling name. I also find that I awaken more to who I am by using it. I receive most of my knowledge and have recalled memories about my ET identity during this state of consciousness.

I am Reptilian/Human Hybrid. I was born from my mother in the normal way and she does not feel that there was any ET connection about my conception or my birth. There are a great many species of Reptoid and they come from every corner in the multi-universes. Earth certainly knows about the negative species, but my people, called the Fajan (Fah-gin) race, are benevolent and more into serving the Higher Purpose. It is our understanding that everything has consciousness, has wishes to express itself; therefore, we treat everything with love, compassion and a sense of unity. We

are a spiritually balanced race, meaning our science and technology does not exceed our spirituality, as it does on Earth. Although our people have advanced technologies and weapons, we use them only for defenses, mostly against the planet-conquering races. We are also considered a part of the "Federation," although the Fajan race is not so involved with Earth as others races of beings are. Only a handful of Fajans came to Earth during this time of ascension. I am here as a representative of the Faquian Council, who has authorized and co-created this book.

Not all Reptilians are androgynous, having both male and female energies balanced in one body, but we are. We are a warm-blooded species of Reptilian and are normally 6 to 9 feet tall. Our physical bodies are lighter than the three-dimensional bodies on Earth. Therefore, we don't suffer all the dis-ease, so we would appear very muscular and very healthy. The more masculine of our species have a top ridge, maybe of cartilage, that begins on the forehead and extends down into the tail. The more feminine of our species are slightly shorter in height and have a similar ridge on top that is less prominent. We also have a fleshy organ beneath our chins that hangs in a separated form. This ridge and "wattle" is similar to a chicken's comb and wattle. Our scales are mostly dark green with tan and dark blue hues. Our eyes are a pinkish color with a vertical pupil and are protected by scaled ridges on the top and bottom. We also have a second membrane between our eyes and the outer lid. Our ears are small holes on each side of our head. Our nose and mouth area protrudes outwards about 4 to 5 inches. Starting from our throat and running down our front to where our tail starts is a softer, ridged area that is gray/green in color. Our hands have three fingers with small, thick claws and three toes on a lengthy foot; there is no webbing in between them. Webbing is a trait of the amphibious species. Our tails are long and give us great agility and balance. We can run really fast and our tails become even more essential. We also use our tails to help defend us in battle or we can outfit them as a weapon, when needed.

Our people live on a planet we call Faqui (Fah-Gwee). It is located in the Andromedan Galaxy, which is the closest and neighboring galaxy to the Milky Way. Our planet has a bright, hot sun that casts an orange-colored hue across our world, similar to Earth's hues at dusk. Our atmosphere comprises shades of green in color and is not as thick as Earth's. Our physics are different on our planet, although I don't have the knowledge to explain how.

Our planet is a hot, tropical paradise. We have huge, magnificent water oasis spots where beings from everywhere come to experience and vacation. There are many, many trees, mostly palms. Our homes are accessible by a door that is entered above ground, but our homes are built right into the landscape and are barely noticeable. Each home is linked by an advanced tunnel system, so that we are all connected as an extended family. We do have buildings on Faqui that are not built into the landscape. These are mostly public buildings that have a look similar in style to the Space Needle in Washington. The buildings are camel brown in color with dark brown highlights.

We wear a simple style of dress similar to a toga, but we are also very comfortable without clothing. There are some of our people who wear very high-collared black robes, but I don't recall who they are. Since our people are androgynous, there are no taboos about sex. Our people have an uninhibited perception towards sexual activities, but are not without discretion and respect. Our people's sexuality is based on a spiritual desire to merge energy with another being. We only engage in sexual activities when combining of the energies is for the heightened pleasure of both involved, not for a quick and selfish physical release. Most Humans on Earth have the perspective that if a being looks animal, then it must behave as such, with animal instincts and mentality. That is far from the truth. Reacting on animal instincts and survival mode is a mental and emotional state. It is a low vibration common on three-dimensional worlds.

I work and live on our moon. I am not sure I can pronounce the name of it, I always have trouble with that. The closest I come in getting a name is— Ju-li-naur (Zsho-leh-nor). I travel back and forth from our moon to Faqui via my small, personal ship. Our personal ships transform into three stages for different types of use:

1. *Simple triangular craft*—flies in the lower atmosphere without a pilot window (similar to driving a motorcycle). This craft does not travel at great speeds and the integrity of the ship is not as strong.

2. *Space craft*—the cellular structure of the ship becomes a one-celled unit which provides a strong hull for space travel and force-field functions. This craft can exit any orbit and can fly in a "local" area of space. Long-distance

travel requires a bigger ship that can carry these smaller ones.

3. *Fighter craft*—the wings separate from the single-celled unit, morph to extend outwards in front of the ship, and reform into a very strong one-celled unit. Particle-beam lasers become active, which are located in the tips of each wing. I have seen this particular ship firing red lasers in my astral travels. The pilot sits in the center, where there is a domed window. The outside of this pilot window has our language written across it to provide identifying information. All three ships are the color of brushed aluminum, but the wings have a soft, white light shining through the top portions (similar to how light shining through white alabaster would look).

The atmosphere on our moon is a desert climate with many cacti and other succulents. The desert ground is a cream-colored sand on top of very dark, jagged rock. Our homes are built into the landscapes to live in partnership with the moon, just like on Faqui.

Our moon is a major trade route depot in this universe. Goods of all imaginable types are brought to our moon. There are three main functions to trade: goods brought in can be stored inside our facilities, traded with other goods already in our facility or the goods can simply be placed into our facilities for a later exchange. Faqui also places its own goods into our trading storage facilities. We keep very detailed records on everything that takes place, including the ship's information, names of the ship commander, their originating system, home planet, purpose of visit, and goods exchanged. This is my job for a couple of years at a time. We hold multiple jobs in our lifespans, to evolve as much as possible, and to help alleviate boredom and complacency in one's career. There are usually two to four specialties that one will hold a job position in. Each position is focused on for two to three years at a time before shifting to the next job.

On our moon, my job is to supervise the incoming ships from space that visit for either trading goods at our facility on the moon or to "vacation" on our tropical paradise home planet. Each ship that wishes to land first connects with one of our geostationary-orbiting satellites to download the required data to us at "ground control." After the download is satisfactory, the ship is instructed where to land. Some land on the docking pads, some will hover in a special section and few will come to rest on our technological arm-supports at the landing areas. These arm supports are made out of a very strong material that will not be damaged by heat, pressure or radiation. The material of these arms and most other structures at the docking area has the appearance of very thick, green glass. If the visitor's purpose is to "vacation" on Faqui, they wait for a small ship to shuttle them to the planet.

I see every type of being imaginable and hear all different types of languages. For communication purposes, when we do not use telepathy, we use a gun-metal colored, rectangular device that translates languages. I enter my language selection and speak into the device, then hand it to the being whom I wish to communicate with. That being selects their language on the device to translate what I just said. This device is a fascinating way to learn languages. It is the "Rosetta Stone" of the Universe! Even now, as a hybrid, I am not comfortable in a demographically homogeneous area for long. I like the feel of other colors, appearances, cultures and languages around me. I have met other Starseeds on Earth whom I have seen while working on my moon. One is a current friend of mine and I tell her that we roll out the Royal Carpet when she and her people arrive on our moon. (She is a highly spiritual being and of great "position" in our universe).

Another job of mine is being a member of the cooperative "Universal Police." A huge number of our people from Faqui are a part of this unit. There is much pride in this work and is why we sometimes call ourselves the "Fajayan" or Proud Ones. Many, many ET races join in this noble program that assists other species when they call for assistance. It is similar to Earth's United Nations, but we actually take an active role in our missions. We don armor that is a golden-copper color and this protects us from most kinetic and energy weapons. It is placed on us by a machine which first covers our scales with a thick, red bio-gel substance. This gel functions as a cushion for impacts, a breathable barrier for our scales and also provides nourishment on a smaller degree. Because of this technology, we can stay in our armor for months at a time.

My other job is traveling in space with my crew members, Jer-mi, Jo-sah-fi and Kayac-tah. There are many other beings on our ship as well. I have not received memories of my exact function when I am traveling in space, but it was during this job when we got the SOS call from Gaia!

I remember my first contact experiences when I was about 5 or 6 years old. I was sharing the room with my brother during this time. Our beds were against the opposite walls and facing the door. The foot of my bed was really close to the door. I did not understand what was happening at the time and thought these were simply reoccurring nightmares. I believe it happened every other night for a period of about six months. I was terrified each time this event started. I could hear my heart pounding. It always started the same—I awoke, knowing that someone was walking down the hallway towards my bedroom. I even recall the hallway being lit with light and mist. I could feel the being(s) getting closer; I even knew which direction in the hallway they were coming from, it was always from the left. I would then throw the covers over my head and pretend I was asleep, but I was sure they would hear my heart pounding. As I felt whoever it was enter the doorway to my bedroom—I would lose consciousness. A few times I would remember seeing non-human, strange-looking beings the size of children, looking at me from a long rectangular "window" just above my brother's bed.

One night when I awoke, I was terrified as usual, and I saw a circular hole in the floor right next to the door (that was not really in my room). I knew someone was walking down the hallway and that I might run into whoever it is if I ran to the hole, but I was so frightened, I did it anyway in an attempt to escape. I actually climbed down the hole with two other boys that were ahead of me (I don't know where they came from, I thought I was in my room). When I got down to the floor, I turned around and realized I was in a completely dark place with no sign of other boys. That was scary enough, then I saw two huge, red almond-shaped eyes coming towards me! I freaked out and ran back up the hole, thinking how silly it was to escape something scary, only to face something even more frightening. I knew I would never try that again. I didn't even get up to the top of the hole before I lost consciousness again.

I never remembered anything they did, except the very last visit. This time, I saw *him*. I know now this was a screen memory, but what I saw then was Dracula! A tall being dressed in a black, very high-collared cape. I knew it was a male and now I know that it was my own Star family. Instead of losing consciousness like usual, I stayed awake. I watched "Dracula" walk toward my bed; then he sat down next to me and told me telepathically not to be afraid, that he was not going to hurt me. Usually, I would be terrified stiff, but this time I was actually at peace, I couldn't believe it. Then I saw him holding a type of tool in each hand; my mind saw them as a fork and a knife, but I know now that was also a screen memory. He told me he was going to take out my eyes and that I wouldn't feel a thing. I can't believe that I actually felt trusting of this being and was not panicking. I watched the entire event where he somehow took each eye out of my socket, placed something behind it and replaced my eye back into the socket. I felt no pain and no fear. I knew for a fact that this happened to me and I told everybody about it, even at school. Of course that didn't go over well.

Later in life, as I became involved in the study of UFOs and ETs, I realized that my people had come to me during those six months and changed my DNA to make me a Reptilian/Human Hybrid. The last thing they did was to put an implant behind each eye so that they could experience everything I was here on Earth.

After that experience, I was drawing what I felt was similar to my language (Z:// V\ ), pictures of my home world and of Reptilians. I began writing poetry, composing and singing songs of a lost love. This was when I was about the age of 6! I wonder why my parents never asked me about these things. I had an "invisible" friend I called George until I was about 10 years old. His real name is Jer-Mi and he is one of my mates and crew members. My whole family knew about him, thank goodness, and would often blame "George" when something came up missing.

When I was real young, I was watching a singing skeleton that wore a hat and held a cane. He was singing about bones: "Your hip bone connected to your thigh bone," etc. I remember looking at my body and bony areas, wondering if I, too, had a skeleton like the one on TV.

When I was a little older, I remember many nights waking up with my eardrums pounding. I could hear footsteps and sense a presence nearby. Of course, I was a competitive swimmer and had swimmer's ear. But it did not explain the presence I felt. It was hard going to sleep those nights as my heart was pounding in fear of the unknown presence.

When I was about 11, I found myself lying outside in the grass next to our driveway late at night. I was afraid of the dark from my earlier experiences, so I knew I would not have walked out there on my own. I remember feeling shocked to find myself lying there. I felt like running to the house in a panic, but instead I walked, not wanting whoever was watching me to know that I was scared. It is funny how we think as children. Once I was inside, I remember looking at the kitchen clock and saw it was after 11 PM. My parents were out and I was supposed to be watching my little sister. I fell asleep with her in my parents' master bedroom, but I woke up the next morning in my own bed. I thanked my father that next morning for putting me in my own bed when they returned home and he told me I was already in my own bed. That's when I remembered I woke up outside and walking back into the house. I guess I went to my own bed after seeing the clock, I have no other memories of that night. I was told by a psychic friend that the negative Reptilians tried to take me that night and my own people had intervened and stopped them. I don't have any recall myself, so that is a possibility.

When I was about 12 years old, I drew pictures in school of my Reptilian boyfriend, I called Marvin. I showed everyone by passing my cool drawing around. I was proud to have this boyfriend of mine and wanted to show him off. I should have learned after telling everyone "Dracula took my eyes out," that people are not very open to this stuff. Everyone who viewed my drawing began laughing at me. Marvin was an astral boyfriend that I would only meet while in a sleep state. It lasted a few years until I reached puberty and my interests changed to girls.

The implants in my eyes had more uses than I thought. When I was 19, my eyes started getting fuzzy and I realized my eyesight was going bad. My siblings all needed glasses at an early age and I guess, being 19, my eyes were doing better. I went to the doctor and had glasses made; I only needed a weak prescription lens. Then at age 20, my eyes adjusted and I threw the glasses away. To this day, I have 20/20 vision and I know it had to do with my eye implants. It makes sense that my people would keep my eyes strong, since they are experiencing life through them, too.

I had a tremendous amount of astral experiences growing up, but I never paid attention to their importance until I awakened later in life. I remember one out-of-body experience when I was about 25. I was looking down at my body from near the ceiling of the bedroom. I saw my body lying on its back with each arm resting across the stomach. I saw my partner lying on her left side, facing away from me. I started to descend towards my body and, as I got closer, I turned around with my back towards my body. I continued to descend and at that moment I saw the soul of Marilyn Monroe facing me from where I had just come from. She didn't look like Marilyn Monroe, but I knew it was her by instant soul recognition. She followed me and turned around, just like I had done. I then saw her long, blond hair and I could smell it! We both continued backwards and into my body. I woke up immediately with pins-and-needle feelings over my entire body. It was so strong that I felt someone was in the room. My partner and I were positioned exactly how I saw us in my astral body. What I believe happened that night is Marilyn Monroe's soul wanted to place a piece of her soul in me (with my permission) and experience my life. I don't know how long she stayed, but I felt blessed that I was given that memory.

My spiritual awakening really sprang forward when my grandmother, who passed on, spoke to me through a psychic medium one day. In her message to me she said, "It's okay, I understand now." (Thank you, Grandma Mary). It was very shortly after that, I asked my guide to tell me his name. As I began to fall asleep, I clearly heard a male's voice whisper "Geremy" in my right ear. I jolted awake, thinking someone was in the room with me. I began reading spiritual book after spiritual book and soon my path curved onto the ET Highway of books. I don't remember what made me turn.

Then my ET awakening really sprang forward one morning, after I turned 30. My partner at the time told me of an interesting occurrence that happened the previous night at around 3 AM. She was awakened to see a Reptilian being sleeping on its back, lying next to her. She told me the only reason she did not run out of the room, screaming, is because she recognized that it was me! As she continued to watch, it took about six seconds as my Reptilian form returned to my Human form. She actually watched each part of my Reptilian face turn into a part of my "human" face. Later, I asked her to draw it for me and we came up with a composite drawing. She is not involved with UFOs or ETs and does not read the books I read, but what she drew that day was exactly how the Reptilans have been drawn by witnesses and how I saw Marvin when I was younger. This puzzle piece of information she had just given me connected with all the past information and I realized for certain, I *was* Reptilian. I had flashbacks of earlier experiences, where I was now able to understand what happened. Finally, it wasn't my imagination anymore.

I had a well-known person in Ufology stay at my house once. This person was able to look into a person's energy field and relay what they were seeing. This person told me, "I wasn't sure I believed you when you told me ETs were your life, but now I believe you!" Then this person explained that they had never seen so many ETs in a person's energy before and it was very unusual that most of the ETs were Reptilian.

It was after my awakening that I began uniting with other Starseeds and Hybrids. It was almost as if that door was just waiting to be opened by me and then *Wham!*, it was thrown open. I have had so many experiences since I realized who I am. Most of my nightly astral trips comprise of being in a class or schooling in unfamiliar buildings with lots of other people around. I don't know if they are on another world or on a ship. Since I started collecting ET sculptures, I have had many visitors in my room at night that actually wake me up and the energy in my room is wonderful. I have taken pictures of ships, seen ships in the sky through binoculars, seen probes, orbs, and have seen *many* ships at night while star-gazing. I was a UFO investigator for MUFON for several years, and I am pretty certain I know the differences between satellites and ships. The tricky ones are these "iridium flares" that occur from the low orbiting satellites that are mostly solar panels that reflect the sun's light, but even those don't turn.

I have had healings from my people, besides my eyes being corrected. I recall an astral experience one night that was mixed with some screen memories. I was inside a dark room within an unknown building. I could see because there was light coming in from outside the glassless window. I looked at myself and noticed I was a bi-pedal werewolf. A human-looking male was standing close to me and said, "She is going to bite you!" I knew somehow that he was talking about my "daughter" who was also a werewolf and running towards me. It startled me, but I wasn't afraid. I began to move out of the way when she leaped and sank a tooth into my lower back. I woke up in pain, actually feeling a sharp stab inside my body. I then realized that I could smell what I could only describe as organ gas. It was coming from inside my body and I was smelling it as it left my nose and mouth areas. I do not know exactly what was worked on, but I thanked them after the pain went away.

Another night was astral traveling, I was on
another planet and walking next to someone I don't
remember. It was dark out and we were walking in
some city when we heard loud thundering noises. I
looked up and saw a spaceship firing red lasers from
the front two tips of its wings. I remember the color
of the ship and the insignia on the pilot window,
which was circular. I couldn't see the pilot, but I
knew this was one of my people's ships and we were
protecting this city from an invading race. That was

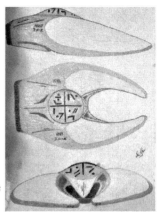

all I was allowed to remember. I know I will not be given information that I am
either not ready for or not meant to know at this time. That can be very frustrating,
of course.

Soon after that night, I was astral traveling inside my house and I recall
standing by my sliding glass door that leads out to our back yard. There I saw a
being standing, facing me and looking right at me. His skin was bulbous, like he
was fat, but I knew he wasn't. The edges and creases of his skin were dark
brown, but the rest was light brown and illuminated somehow. His eyes were
reddish in color, I believe. We just looked at each other and the last thing I
remember is waving to him.

My most memorable encounter with a ship (ET), was
when I was driving to work at 6:20 AM in late November
2006. It was still dark out at that time. Directly in front of
me, low in the sky and maybe a mile or two away, I saw a
perfectly round light. It started from a pin-point of light
and grew in size to a perfectly round ball of light; then it
shrank back to the pin-point of light and blinked out. I
knew I was seeing something not from Earth because I
was feeling a heightened vibration in me, like electromagnetic energy. For some reason, I began counting seconds.
Ten seconds later, that light reappeared and did the exact
same thing as before. I counted another 10 seconds and
again the light reappeared just as before. At that moment, I
knew it was communicating with me, so I flashed my

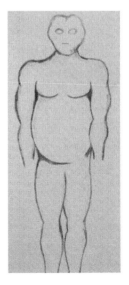

high-beams three times. I waited to see what it would do next, but I never saw the light again. I thought I saw a very faint white object shoot up into the sky, but I am not certain. I smiled and thanked them!

I was driving one day during the daylight hours and I noticed an airplane making a funny turn in the sky. It's funny how I reacted, now that I think about it. I instantly pulled the car over to watch this plane. It was low in the sky, probably 20 degrees high and approximately one to two miles away. As I watched this plane, I saw a stationary object hovering just above the plane as it passes by. My attention immediately stayed with this hovering object and I grabbed my binoculars. I already have 20/20 vision and now I had binoculars to get a real clear picture of this thing. I saw what I would describe as the rim of a disk ship inside a force-field that was pearlescent in color, similar to looking through a jellyfish. Then the object slowly started to move in the opposite direction that the plane was flying. I only watched it for a short time because it flew behind trees.

At this time in my life, I had a lot of Grays coming to visit. During the early hours, I would wake up in a sitting position and reaching for something. I felt that someone, a small being, was leaving and I didn't want them to. Another early morning hour experience was waking up on my hands and knees, looking out my window saying, "They're here." Two seconds later, lights flew by my window and swooped up. I could have been dropped off again, but I don't recall.

I only have one experience where I remember being sent down the blueish-white light from inside a ship. I was astral traveling, but I was hearing my dogs barking. In my mind, I immediately thought I should go let them outside because they have to pee. (Although my dogs don't bark when they need to go outside, especially all of them at once). Just before I woke up, I heard this voice in my head, telling me, "If you don't wake up, I will show you the secrets of my ship." Then I saw myself floating down a blueish-white light and I was looking up at a Gray. All I could see was her big Gray head and her very long arm, as if guiding me down. I was being helped back into my body by this Gray. I snapped awake and, looking at my clock which read 5:45 AM, I blurted out profanity. The weird thing is, I instantly forgot what had just happened. I took the dogs outside and no one was peeing, they were all just looking around. I was frustrated by this and told them all to get back inside. It never occurred to me that they don't usually bark to go out, until I had a "flash recall" of the event later that day at work.

I had a very powerful lesson by a very tall Gray while astral traveling one night. This graceful being glided toward me with a Gray baby in his arms. The being passed the child to me and wanted to teach me how to send unconditional love to another being. I thought that would be easy, but just as I began, I was told to stop. It was explained to me that in order to send unconditional love to another, there can be no other emotion attached, such as sadness, desire, elation, expectation, worry or even selfish thoughts. For a baby Gray specifically, those types of lower emotions can actually do much damage. It took me a little while before I could consciously remove all emotion and only send love. I realized that we have to not think about anything, just feel love. What a lesson! I was told then to take this new skill and practice it and teach it to others.

A few nights after this teaching, I found myself aboard a ship again. Another tall Gray asked me if I would be willing to have a Hybrid child. I could feel that these beings already knew everything about me, so there was no need to explain anything to them, it was a simple yes or no question, and I agreed. I have no idea what happened after that, or if it will be a physical thing for me. I believe that since they already have my DNA, they will just use that and there will be no need for me to carry it. My parents would flip if they ever saw me pregnant.

One of my most memorable experiences with the Grays was being taken to their home world. I don't know which planet specifically, but I am certain it was in the Zeta Reticulum system. I was astral traveling again and I was standing around a group of strangers in a parking lot. I looked up, for some reason, and saw ships in the sky. I told everyone around me that the ships were here. I closed my eyes and raised my arms out to the sides with a smile on my face. Suddenly, I blacked out. Next thing I remember is standing on another planet next to a few of the people that were in the parking lot with me. I knew we had traveled there by ship, but I don't recall doing so. I noticed a pyramid-shaped building on my right. It was a residential building and was a tanish color. It wasn't very bright on this planet, but I know the sun was shining. Then, three Human-looking beings walked up to our little group. They were wearing the same red, tight-fitting suits. The female came up to me. She was my height, about 5'7". She had short, curly, dirty-blond hair. As she got close to me, I said with a smile on my face, "You're not a Human, you're a Gray." I knew that their appearance was a screen, probably so it wouldn't scare us. This female walked right up to me after I said this. She was just inches from my face and that is when I saw into her left eye. Her eye shifted left from the human-looking eye to a big, black, almond-shaped eye of a Gray. I lost myself in her eye, I was suddenly in the universe with billions of stars! I was so mesmerized and at awe, it woke me up. I remember hearing myself say, "How beautiful."

January 1, 2009 at 6:15 AM, the day I almost hit a Gray. I was driving to work on a very isolated road. It was still dark, so I had my headlights on. I came around a curve and saw what I thought was an animal in the road. It looked curled up and was actually where my passenger tire would be on this small road. Traveling at 50 mph, with regular headlight beams, did not give me much opportunity to view this being. All of a sudden, I realized I'd better swerve to miss hitting it. I drove past it and began sending it warmth and healing, because I assumed it was a hurt animal, otherwise it would have run off. As I was sending this being energy, I immediately felt love energy coming back to me! It was so strong, I had tears in my eyes. Then, suddenly, I had a flash of what I really saw while driving past the being. I saw the back of this being with the spine in the center, the head tucked in between the legs, which were being held by long arms that were wrapped around its front. This I saw as I passed by, but it didn't register until moments later. I realized then that I almost just hit a Gray ET. It was too dark for me to go back, since I am afraid of the dark, and I would have been late for work. I looked all around me for any lights from a possible ship, but I couldn't see anything. What a way to start the new year!

March 2009, I received a new type of crystal, and I decided to meditate with it before falling asleep one night. I immediately saw a friend of mine in my vision and began waving my hands around her energy body for healing. I do not consider myself active in the healing arena, so this was new to me. More new to me was the fact that I began speaking a language not of Earth. I knew it was my people's language. I do not know what I am saying, but I can speak it now if I allow it to flow from within me, similar to "speaking in tongues"' that most

Pentecostal Christians practice. I will receive meaning behind some words as I speak my language, since a direct translation is rare.

I had a regression with a famous Hypnotherapist in the Ufology field once. During this session I recalled being in a medium-sized ship with my Reptilian crew. I remember looking out into the darkness of space and knowing that Earth was nearby (comparatively speaking). All of a sudden, we felt and saw this white surge of energy shoot through everything. This was an S.O.S. call from Earth and as it passed through me, I felt myself drop to my knees in tears. I could feel the pain of Mother Earth as she asked Starbeings of light who would volunteer to assist her and all beings on Earth towards their ascension. I was very moved by this call for help and the next thing I remember is incarnating, as if I splintered off a piece of my soul to come to Earth and help. I am not sure how to explain it, but I feel that my Reptilian being is still alive, I know I didn't die. I came to Earth, to assist during the Universal Grand Shift into a fifth-dimensional world. I know this will affect everything in our Universe and all life within it. I was told by my people that it doesn't matter so much what I do or become, since I carry the frequency of my people, I am to just BE. Since I came from a higher dimension than Earth, the vibration I carry is also higher and this is what Earth needs. That is why so many of us off-worlders came to Earth. As each being evolves and awakens, their vibration increases and this will help lead us into ascension. When the people of Earth reach the "tipping point," we can all look forward to a fifth dimensional world.

Earth is a difficult place to be. I learned how Humans think and treat each other, some have evolved more than others. The parts of humanity I will never understand is the violence, hate and prejudice, especially in the name of "God." What an oxymoron! I experienced a major depression after this realization during my work in the police field. I thought being in law enforcement on Earth would be like our Universal Police unit that my soul was used to. Boy, was I wrong! Ever since then, I have been wanting this Earth Shift to happen, so I can go home. This planet lacks in love and compassion for all life. People think nothing of squashing ants and other lifeforms that "bug" them. That mentality is so accepted by society and yet I cry inside each time I witness this behavior. This and other behavioral differences often create conflict with other people. I don't like being here and I am ready to go home.

I grew up with religious grandparents and parents. I remember always questioning what I was being taught. I didn't agree with religion, even as a child. I never understood why I had to be "saved"—saved from what? I was only a child, what could I have done wrong already? Regardless of my grandmother telling me to go up with the other kids to ask for forgiveness and be "saved," I stayed in my seat! I disliked Church so much that it leaves a bitter taste in my mouth even today. I do not wish to convey that religion is invaluable. I just have a bad reaction to it personally. I have seen and heard of too many negative events "justified" by religious beliefs. That makes me sick. I know there are truly loving, spiritual beings on Earth that are also very religious and I applaud them. I feel they are also very rare in numbers. I say follow your heart, and be into whatever makes you want to be a loving, positive person.

There is no religion on this Earth that I have related to or believed in, the closest one would be Buddhism. I see truth at the core of all religion, but I also see the human desire to control and manipulate others through religion. I consider myself to be a spiritual person. I look *only* inside myself for the connection to Source energy. We are all "God" and have all the knowledge inside of us already. It is only a matter of remembering it.

I believe in "Source Energy," where all souls originate from. My understanding is that Source Energy split off portions of itself to experience all it could. These first split portions of Source Energy are conscious of themselves and are of a very high vibration. This group then split off portions of themselves, creating a bigger second group still of a high vibration, yet lower than their own. This second group stretched out in multi-dimensions and multi-universes, creating their own soul groups after them. This is how I understand the many different soul groups as hierarchical separations from Source Energy, all at various levels of soul evolution. I know we are all connected, all *one*, but I also understand very simply the difference of soul groups. I know that I am not of the Human soul group of Earth, which is under Yahweh from the Pleiades.

I believe that each being is responsible for their own reality. Thoughts are things, they create energy and "energy attracts like energy." The energy you decide to put out into the world is always a choice. How you think is directly related to what manifests in your life; therefore, we each choose between dark energy or light energy, depending on our thoughts. I feel this is what all the "Masters" who came to Earth tried to teach people, that everyone is their own master, a soul splinter of "God" itself. It is not ego, it is reality.

I believe in trying to love everyone unconditionally, without judgment. Of course, it is not easy and is challenging even for enlightened beings on Earth. Every soul has its own lessons it wishes to experience and learn from. I don't think it is appropriate to judge which "path" others decide to learn their lessons from. How could we even begin to judge that? I don't like others judging me.

I do not believe in Evil, although I believe one can choose to be very dark in their actions, they are still a part of Source! I send them sincere love from my heart and thank them for showing me what I am not. It takes negative and positive energy to make this world run—similar to a battery. If no one played the "bad guy," who would learn anything? The important thing to remember is that we are connected and we are so much more than these bodies!

Books that had a big impact on me:
Trevor Constable, *The Cosmic Pulse of Life*
Kryon (Lee Carol)—All of Them.
Dolores Cannon, *The Convoluted Universe* series
Sylvia Browne, *Life on the Other Side*

Websites that are significant to me:
www.crystalinks.com
www.educate-yourself.org
www.wanttoknow.com
www.abovetopsecret.com
www.factcheck.org

You may contact me at: *Faquian@gawab.com*
My only website: http://weareamongyou.tripod.com

OM

The name given to me for my Star family was an individual name,
but also a group name for them:
Quabar
A lot of times I call them "Q and Associates." I am them and they are me.

My Star family has ascended to a level where they are not in physical form.
Now I see my Star family as etheric energy, as frequency. I see this outline of
very high energy when they are around me. In this outline I can see from the
head and down to the arms; lower is where the group seems to connect. I see
them connected through their arms and their bodies. They always surround me,
putting me in a circle. Sometimes I need to tell them to step back because they
have such a high vibration and, when they are near me, they literally light me
up. Once I saw my face in a mirror, I could see a glow around me. This also
happens when I communicate with other ETs of high vibration. I do a lot of
communication with many groups of ETs.

Before they ascended, I used to see them differently than I see them now. In
1982, when Quabar initially showed himself, he stood about 15 to 20 feet tall,
big black eyes, white skin, no mouth and the cranium was very large. (They are
telling me that what is most important is their frequency and energy, not what a
being looks like. And they do not wish to be compared to other ET beings). He
was wearing a long, white robe with some type of silver woven into the fabric
near his hands. He was carrying all different colors of crystals. When I first saw
him, I felt an initial shock. Quabar reassured me by repeating that everything was
okay. He did this in a very kind and loving way. He explained that their intention
was not to scare me, but to reveal themselves in a way I can accept.

During his initial introduction, Quabar took me around the planet with him
and also did some healing work on me. The crystals that he brought with him
were very alive and they were creating tones all around me that balanced my
energy. It was happening so fast that I could not keep track of it all. Suddenly, I
was in a room where it was snowing and I saw these ice crystals. Then, suddenly,

again, I was back on the table, balancing my energy. I believe that what I had actually seen was true crystalline energy, not ice crystals. (Quabar is telling me that I was not in a room on the planet while receiving my healing with the crystals, it was actually a protective force-field in place around me.)

Quabar told me they wanted me to know where I was from. I kind of accepted this information and so they began teaching me. They talked about how much they loved the Earth, the animals, the plants and the Earth herself. They told me they were balancing Earth meridians. Their role is working with these huge crystal beings to balance the Earth. Their key word for me when they are about to teach me something is, "Ready to go?" When I say "yes," my consciousness goes with them and I come back later. They allow me to remember everything that occurs during this time with them. It is quite amazing.

I have tried drawing what I see of my Star family onto paper. I have over 300 drawings of them. When I draw them, I tend to draw them in all different colors. I have one drawing of seven beings, each one a different frequency color. But the group tells me they have all of the color frequencies. I often tend to draw them in shades of violet. I try to search for the right colors and my family laughs and says there is nothing on Earth to represent their true colors.

I have over 300 pages of material that my Star family has communicated to me. I do not call it channeling. They are telepathic communications between me and my Star family. (They are wanting me to make that point.) They also want to make a point for this book, that other people can have this telepathic communication with their Star families, too!

I asked them once if they had any spacecraft, and they said, "Let's explain it to you this way, our spacecraft is our Frequency." They travel wherever they want, in an instant, without a spacecraft. I can also do this, since I am a part of them; they call me a Hybrid. However, the frequency in me is heavier, since I am only 55 percent of them. Once I had a psychic tell me that I am a Hybrid being and that I had a very difficult time adjusting to Earth. I feel 45 percent of me is Human and the rest is from my Star family. It is nice for me to know this, but it does not feel relevant in the grand scheme of things.

My Star family refers to me as 'OM,' again this is the vibrational me. I know that OM is considered by some to be the Universal Frequency, but that is what my Star family calls me. Quabar also explained to me that I am a projection. My soul agreed to come to Earth, bringing my frequency here to help Earth and the animals, and to help people awaken for ascension. I told them afterwards that I didn't remember agreeing to this. I told them I was just an animal communicator. They all laughed and said, "Very funny." Initially, I didn't even know what ascension was. I purposefully do not read any books on the subject. My Star family themselves gave me pages and pages of information about ascension, then later I started to read about it.

The very first conscious contact I had telepathically speaking with my Star family was in 1982. At that time I was working as a psychic and meditating, studying dreams and already doing telepathic work with animals. When my Star family came to me, I could see them in a different dimension, since I am clairvoyant. I was still very much sorting things out during this time, but the fascinating thing is, I wrote down everything they have ever said to me. I am so grateful that I have done that because, seven years later, they were saying the same things they did in 1982. I went back and looked at my notes, and some of the things they have said were almost word-for-word. What they have shown me and what the Star part of myself has felt is that I come from what is called the "7th Universe outward from Earth." I come from a planet/star that has three moons and two suns. (My Star family laughs and tells me that it doesn't matter if you call it a planet or a star.)

The planet's name is called "Om ba ma," which is a vibration, not a word. They do not speak in verbal words, everything is vibration, sound and color. There is no left, right, up or down there, that all has to do with space/time. There is no darkness on my planet. The suns are like a rose color and the moons reflect this color as well. Everything glows with this rose/pink color and there is always these lights similar to Earth's *Aurora borealis*. The tides are also rose colored and I have seen this tide of fluid. I am being told it is not water, it is of an energy that we are not familiar with here on Earth. We work with crystal beings on our planet, with their tones and frequencies.

Quabar has explained to me that there is no need for a written language because everything is telepathy. He also tells me that there are no buildings on the planet. There are other beings on the planet, but he doesn't want them compared to animals, because on Earth this refers to beings that are "less than." So Quabar would like to put it this way: "There are a lot of other beings on the planet whom they share the planet with." I know there are plant beings that speak telepathically, they move around and are all different colors. They are conscious just like you and I.

On my planet, when I was "young," before Earth wasn't even thought of, I would create this little being similar to the one I had met in another star system before, and I was very fond of them. Quabar doesn't want to sound "Trekkie," but these little beings are similar to the Tribble beings on *Star Trek*. However, the real beings had soft tentacles coming out of them and there is no mouth, but they did make a sound that I really liked.

Quabar showed me my soul's first experience in some type of body, which was with them. These beings are a group consciousness. They showed me how I was birthed by them. They had come together as a group consciousness and then merged their energies into one. This birthed me into being for the very first time. My Star family explained to me that they are an androgynous species. While on Earth, I carry the frequency of my Star family. I am not a walk-in. I think my Star family connections may have come from my father's side.

My parents have never really understood me and I think this is the case with most Starbeings here. My Star Family connections throughout the universe are my real family, not so much my biological family. Most of my life I have lived alone. I tried marriage, but I don't like the structure of it. It seemed very foreign and weird to me. Sometimes I watch Humans walking around and the Star part of me will say, "Look at the two legs on the Human, how funny." I didn't make this connection until recently, but when I was a child, I would cross out the legs on people when I drew them. My Star side knew that we didn't use or need legs.

Even to this day, I am still putting together the many connections with what I have experienced as a child and things I go through now. The knowledge that I came in with is the same knowledge that I am teaching today, and I think that is very cool. On my last birthday, I woke up to my Star family being all around me. They were showing my birth again on my planet. They told me how much they loved me and wanted to give me the gift of seeing my soul's birthing. It was a wonderful gift.

When I was a child, I believe I was always going into the other dimensions. I had one psychic tell me that when I was 5 years old, so many souls were coming to me for help and I didn't know how to handle it because I was a child.

This psychic also told me that I would go in and out of dimensions. Quabar later reassured me that they would always watch over me and take care of me when I would go into these other dimensions. I even have recall about these trips.

I always had an interest in UFOs and I was always in the UFO clubs. When I was 14 years old, I had a huge, silver, disk-shaped ship show up in the clear, blue sky in my backyard. I don't know if they were a different group or not, but they were hovering in the sky, watching us. It probably sat there for 20 seconds. This ship was much lower than an airplane would fly. It made right-angle moves and then spun straight up at such an incredible speed, it was unbelievable.

Contact with my Star family continued for several years after it began in 1982. Then I took off in the field of animal communication. My focus was really in that field and I know my Star family was there guiding me all along. Then, seven years ago, they showed up "knocking at the door." Since that happened, my life has had significant change. This is when they started referring to me as OM. They showed up in my apartment very strongly and they would keep repeating to me, "I, We, He, She, We, They." What they were pointing out to me is, we are all of that, and I am all of that, we are truly a group consciousness.

During this time seven years ago, I was in what is called "Kundalini rising." I have had six of these activations and I hope that was my last one. My Star family told me they are expanding me and re-wiring me, in order for my brain to hold much more information. They have been activating my DNA codes, and I have been remembering who I am. Quabar told me we have no time to waste, and I cannot tell you how much I learned in six months' time. I was integrating for months upon months. It took a year for the Kundalini activation, but I told my Star family, "This need not happen again." It was a very rough time and I didn't think I could survive another activation. For example, everything was so hot, I would go to unplug my toaster and it would burn my hand. This was a result of the raising of my vibration at a rapid rate. I told Quabar that they needed to help my physical body more. It was an incredible process and I took notes on everything; the clocks in my apartment were on different times, I was in and out of multiple dimensions, things would appear and disappear, and I felt like I was on fire, I also felt like I was crazy. This progress of my activation was not their intention, my activation was actually set off by a healer who had worked with me. This healer expanded my aura and I didn't know he was going to do that. I feel that it is the way things were meant to be, but the healer's actions were not appropriate. My understanding of it is, the universe had an intention of allowing that to happen and my soul allowed it.

During one of the Kundalini activations, about six years ago, I experienced levitation. I was doing a lot of communication with my Star family and many other ETs. Some of the ETs were of a low frequency and I always ask to work with only those of the higher frequency. It is important for others to know, only invite in the highest frequencies of love and light. There is a full spectrum of frequencies in ETs. I was lying in bed one night and my room was filled with ETs. I heard this voice say, "Don't be afraid, we are reminding you of an experience you had as a child, when you were taken at night. We need to readjust something, re-wire you in your expansion, so we are taking you elsewhere to do that." I freaked out and started running out of the room, but I couldn't open the door. The door knob would not turn. They said, "We asked you not to run." In a second, I was levitating about 10 feet above the ground. They laid me down in my bed and I couldn't move, then I was gone. I am not clear on what the whole event was about, but it lasted for two nights. I was really traumatized, although I can laugh at it now. That next night, I ran again. They asked me, "Are you going to do this again?" Since I knew they were kind and loving, I stopped, walked over to my bed and laid down so they could take me.

Someone once asked me how kind and loving could the ETs be, if they made it so I couldn't move? My ETs responded, "If you had a child who needed to be taken to the hospital, and that child is screaming and kicking, what are you going to do?" That is how they explained it to me. They wanted to give me the gift of remembering what I had experienced as a child. I realized later that they didn't harm me, I was just really scared.

I would always look southeast at night while going through my Kundalini activations. The Star part of me thought "Home" when I would do this. I cannot see home from Earth, but it was southeast. If we think of my home planet in the 7th Universe from Earth as a distance, then it is farther out than the universes that we know about today. However, if we go into what reality is, looking at other universes or dimensions, they are all here right now. My Star family showed this to me and it blew my mind. They tell me that I can be anywhere I wish to be, instantly. It is only a matter of consciousness. We are all one, we can be anywhere we want to at any moment. It is simply setting your intention and focus. There are no limitations, unless we think there are.

At times, I have really just wanted to go home because I feel that I just don't fit in here. Even though I do the work I do and help a lot of people, it is not like connecting with someone who is also awake. And they are very hard to find. On the planet I come from, I can do 10 things at once. I can create something in an instant with just a thought. Sometimes I get really frustrated here because I can remember being able to do more. Here I have to punch in words on a keyboard, but there I could telepathically download my thoughts.

When I started awakening and remembering seven years ago, I couldn't wait to get out of here. I was sitting in a park one day, while it was still daylight. My intention was to go there and write poetry because my Star family loves poetry, it is all about rhythm. Then, suddenly, my Star family took me out of my body and I fell into the midst of a Council of 44 beings. In this Council, each being was from a different Star system and they all looked very different. They told me that they want me to remember that I agreed to come to Earth, that I wanted to learn what it was like to be physical and to help Earth. They reminded me that I thought it would be like a camp. I remember telling them, "I am not having fun, It is more like Boot Camp." The beings talked to me for a while because I was really crying and really considering leaving. They told me, "We want you to stay, we love you and we want you to do what you were meant to do." When I returned to consciousness, I was sitting in the dark, alone in the park. I have no idea how much time had passed.

My Star family comes in my dreams. If I ask them to come, they do. I have really grown to have an affinity with my Star family. I love them deeply. They are so funny and they make me laugh when I am feeling depressed. They use puns with me, telepathically. They access my brain to tap into everything that I know and have learned. Sometimes I get angry with my Star family and yell at them. They understand that I get frustrated with the physical sometimes. My Star family can look through my eyes and can feel what it is to be Human through me. All beings are learning and teaching. We are always the student and always the teacher. It is about trusting what we get from within ourselves and not getting caught in other people's thoughts and beliefs. Whether it be religion, "new age" or anything else, it is about getting out-of-the-box. My Star family is always telling me, "We don't want to put anything in a box." Doing so puts limits on what it is. My Star family, and the beings I deal with, have pulled me out of box after box after box. Now I am pretty much out-of-the-box.

Humans are the ones that created institutions. I am not speaking against religion, but there is more than just religion, and a person can embrace it all. They can also embrace that they are a part of the Cosmic family and that we can all work together. Part of what Humans are learning on Earth is that we need to treat all life forms as equals, and that other life forms have the same value a Human has, including Mother Earth. The key factor that Humans need to learn is that a soul is a soul. When you look at your dog companion, know that soul is equal to yours. We are all of equal importance. There is no being that is higher than another. Some beings may be more evolved, but their essence is no better than another. The key lesson is *love*.

My Star family is very careful about things they share with people or show peoplem because they do not want to frighten anyone. When they speak to me, they use such simple metaphors for me, so I really get it. I love that about them. They also teach me things in a hands-on fashion. They ask me if I am ready, then we go off into the different realities and dimensions while they teach me so many things, and I really get it. I get it in my body and in my consciousness, it is not an intellectual thing. They teach me, or show me something by putting me right into the energy of it. This is my life and it is very normal for me. One night they showed me about time/space. We went into all of these dimensions and universes. I can be on Mars in an instant because consciousness is all connected. They teach me that with all the dimensional traveling I do, each dimension is a different energy of frequency and they are all present right now. They told me, "What we want you to understand from this is that there really is no such thing as time and space, this is your perception, there is only energy."

There are all type of beings on Mars and they are really cute. They look like little sparkles, similar to how the sun's light sparkles off the water. These beings are not third-dimensional. These beings told me that they were having a difficult time with Humans coming to Mars, it was not something they desired and they are not happy with it. However, these beings are loving, delightful, kind and caring beings who are just worried about their planet being invaded by Humans. Humans are much more connected to Mars than most people know. I had a being come and tell me about how important Mars is to Humans and then it was confirmed over and over again for me.

I teach workshops on how to speak to animals telepathically, where an animal companion is from, what their spiritual origin is, etc. I also teach Humans what their spiritual origins are. I love doing this work, it is such great fun. My animal communication work automatically expanded me into my work with ETs, which then expanded me into my work with ascension. I love sharing these things with people. As the frequencies keep rising on Earth towards this ascension, people will hear the animals more and more. The more we see that, the more we know that people are returning to their basic essence of who they are.

When my Star family and I work together on such things as healings, there is always silver and gold colors around me. Their colors have become more silver to me in the last year. I cannot explain why, other than they are giving me a "Key Frequency" that signifies our working together. Once while I was helping to heal someone, the person told me that they could actually see this silver color all over my hands.

When my Star family and I work with the animals, we work as a team. We do many types of work for the animals, including "Soul Recovery," "DNA Balancing" and "Multi-dimensional Selves" work, to help them integrate their multi-dimensional selves. This helps to keep them aligned with the ascension energies, too. I do this work with the animals most often, but I also do this work with people. Animals are just so much easier to work with. One time I had this hawk fly over to a tree I was standing under. This hawk looked down at me and stared me right in the eye. Hawks don't do that. I also had a ground hog walk up to me and put his paw right on top of my leg. That is unheard of, too. I have also seen squirrels in my backyard walk into another dimension and walk back out.

I am able to sit down and move my consciousness out and explore wherever I want. I have also been teaching others how to do this. We are all capable, but for me it is very natural. I wasn't in my body for a really long time, and when I finally was in my body, I didn't like it. However, to be on Earth and to manifest, you need to be in your body. I have to ground myself every day, about 10 times a day. This is because of working psychically with people and always being in other dimensions when I work with animals. I am always using my extra senses and intuition, so I have to ground and clear myself frequently.

I also do drawings of other ETs and do what I call "Ascension Material." Most recently, I began drawing Codes and beings who are of the Earth energies.

My Star family might tell me what the Moon energy is doing with the Earth's energy, which is quite significant lately. I am not an artist, but I draw out what they tell me. It is an innate desire I have to do these things, not because I have to. I want to very deeply.

Space is like a big area in which the Creator can express itself and things can continue evolving. There are many universes within universes. There are many universes that integrate with other solar systems, such as what is happening right now with our own physical system. This is all a part of our ascension. I can see these taking place because I am clairvoyant. I am also an empath. I have to be very careful who touches me or works with my energy. I tend to take in others' energies and I have gotten in trouble in the past for doing that.

Sometimes I can look at a person and see their Starbeing essence and what they look like on their planet. If a person does not feel love, light and caring from the beings or ETs they are dealing with, release them! My purpose here on Earth is to spread love and light, to teach people about animals and ETs. And I purposefully say, with intent, that if any other being comes around me that is not of those same qualities, don't bother, because I am not interested. That is very important for people to understand.

We all have different kinds of experiences to share with others. I think it is really important that we have this diversity to help others. My Star family laughs and smiles all of the time because they are all about Love. I am so grateful to be a part of them, they are so uplifting for me. After I had a healer work with me, she asked me, "There were lots of beings in the room, weren't there?" I said, "Yes, there was another whole star group here, which are my family." She then told me that she had never experienced anything like it. They were actually helping her to awaken.

Quabar once said to me, a way to describe me is, "One petal of a flower that has fallen to Earth." That actually made me cry. They keep reminding me, "You are us and we are you." And I say in return, "Yeah, but I have this Human body that has its own personality." They laugh and tell me that it is okay. The most important thing I would want to leave with people is to live through the heart, not the mind or ego. That is the bottom line!

I have come to learn that we only see our skies of Earth as shades of blue because of the cones and rods in our eyes, the sky is not really blue. I have forgotten what color they told me it really was, but this taught me that everything is "perception." Quabar has shown me in other dimensions what true reality is. I have seen myself holographically, I have seen other star systems holographically and I have learned that the Universe itself is a hologram.

All of us are being downloaded frequently. Right now Quabar is showing me how they constantly work with sacred geometry. They also took me into this place of color and sound and showed me how things become material from that; manifestation of creating actual physical form from sound, color and frequency.

One time they said to me, "We are going to show you the nature of reality." My Star family guided my consciousness into deep space and showed me Earth. They showed me the whole energy layout, like a long outstretched ribbon with many symbols on it. They said, "What we are showing you is the true essence of Earth's energy." Earth is a beautiful planet to be on. In reality, Earth is not round, it is a frequency, and they showed me her frequencies and how they were working with those frequencies.

I was told there was only one other me, from "Om Ba Ma." This other person is actually me, in another body, and is actually living in Africa. When I was experiencing some of the Kundalini activations, I kept looking at my skin and I was confused, because I really felt my skin was supposed to be black. It seems that my consciousness was focused on the other being in Africa. When I actually went to Africa, I felt so at home. I have a sense that this other being is a male, but I did not find him. Since our people are androgynous, it doesn't matter what sex we are, a being can have both energies equally within them. There are many times my ET side has conflicted with my Human side. I can have both conversations between the two sides of me. Sometime I have to reign in the ET part of me when I have to ground my energy. I have things here on Earth I have to do, and I have to remember to focus here.

One time in Africa, I met this lady who was showing me this type of unusual tree. She told me that the tree had unearthly origins. When we both touched the tree, we were gone into another dimension. When we came back, this woman looked at me and asked, "Where did we just go?" I told her the tree took us to its own dimension. I remember seeing colors upon colors, kind of like a Kaleidoscope, which was frequency and sound. They were showing us their actual energies.

Things are really changing for Earth now and the animals are cool with it. My Star family says that the animals are here teaching us, and they are right. My Star family would tell me how much they love the animals, the Humans and Earth. A lot of ETs will tell me this, that the focus is not so much on the Humans, but on Mother Earth. They are here to help Mother Earth evolve and go through her ascension process that affects everyone else.

Many people that are into the topic of ascension—there are many names for it—are making it a Human-centered issue. They think Humans are doing all the energy work when this is really an egocentric idea. I have come to love Humans, but the truth and reality is, the "animals" and all other beings, including plants, water, etc., are a major part of ascension and are the major teachers. Humankind has not been on this Earth as long as they have. What we need to learn is to be more humble. We are all one.

Even the cockroach is very important, for they have lived through all of this before. People get caught up in outer appearances and make judgments on what is ugly or not. That judgment is living in categories and boxes. All beings have beautiful souls. When I see a spider in my house, I, too, have to work on my reaction to them because of how they look to me. I will look at the essence and thank the spider for reminding me that it is a child of God. I then take the spider outside. From my perspective, these are the key fundamental teachings that Humans need to remember, because they once knew these things.

Everyone is doing what their souls are meant to do and everyone goes at their own pace. What ascension will do with all of the aligning of energies in the Milky Way, including the sun being in the center at 2012, is give everyone the opportunity to open their hearts so their frequencies can be raised, and to remember who they are and who everyone else is. This is done over time, but it is going on, has been going on, and will go on after 2012. If everyone is waiting for one big day in December 2012, I think they will be disappointed. I do think that the ETs will appear down the road, but who really knows what will happen? I may be totally surprised. I had a vision that I was told when all of the frequencies continue to raise, people will see each other for who they truly are, their essence form.

**The books I recommend to read in general
about ETs and connecting with ETs:**

Calling on Extraterrestrials, Talking to Extraterrestrials and *Listening to Extraterrestrials.* All three of these books are by Lisette Larkins.
The other book that helped me significantly is *In The Presence of Aliens* by Janet Bergmark. She discusses her alien consciousness and her life story.
It helped me understand myself a great deal.

You may contact me at: om_story@yahoo.com

Serena Starlight

My ET name and title is: Her Royal Highness Serena Ich Konach De Honach, daughter of the King, Wa'hachowic Tohachi Achi, from Sirius A; Priestess of the Highest, Ambassador for the "Creator of All Things." I am the Fifth Commander (of the ship called *Starlight*) within the Sirian Nations of the Intergalactic Confederation. I have more than 1,200 ships in my fleet that I am currently commander over. I am Captain of my personal transport ship called the *She'Aste* (ship of celestial light), which is a living ship. When I enter my *She'Aste*, she expands in size to the length of a football field. She is a single-level ship that can hold about 3,000 people.

Besides my father, the King, I also have a Mother, three sisters and a brother on Sirius A. There is a "president" that lives on Sirius B, but he is connected to the King on Sirius A and is the high member of the governmental body or council of the Sirius Star System, including Sirius A, B and C. I can recall a few memories, but my people don't want me to have too many memories of home, 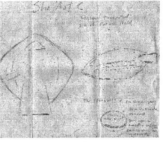 because they want me to focus on my life here on Planet Earth.

Sirius A has been called the sixth-dimensional Earth. We are in physical form, similar in appearance to the Ascended Masters you have seen drawings of. We are Human in appearance, tall with blond or red hair. We are in perfect health and do not suffer from diseases. Sirius A has cities that are very clean, there is no pollution. I remember doing work on Sirius with beings dressed all in white, and cleansing myself in a lake of pure water during a ceremony. This city I visited was like a rather small town and it had a sacred center. I remember arriving by ship and being beamed down into the town center, where there was a fountain. I remember the children were hiding from us at first, before they came out to greet us. We were then met by my friend, the Mayor, along with his wife and three kids. I recall a man who is a baker there, who practices cooking Earth food. I had been in this town several times and it was a spiritual experience. The sacred center did not have any walls, it was like being in a ball of white light. I remember the Priestesses dressed in all white, too. They were human looking and had blue eyes. I was there doing some sacred ceremony and readying myself for my mission. I know there is water and a lake on Sirius, but I don't recall the foliage there. I remember sunshine and blue skies there. I sense there are animals there, too, but I never really saw them, since they are also in a sixth-dimensional form. We don't really need technology there; in a sixth-dimensional world everything is light, we are beings of light. Our ships are light beings as well and are themselves alive. However, they can take the form of looking mechanical. We do not have personal ground vehicles on Sirius, because we can teleport anywhere we want to. We also manifest anything we need; we have no need for currency. We hold the spiritual belief of all being one with the "Creator of all things." I see Earth becoming this way, too.

I am on a current mission to Earth, to assist with the ascension process. My father also travels on board a ship with the Galactic Federation. The Galactic Federation are administrators of this Solar System as well as many other other systems. I can speak telepathically, that is how I keep in communication with Sananda and Ashtar. Sananda is the name of the higher being people most know as Jesus Christ. In a past life, Sananda was also known as Enki of the Anunnaki of Ancient Sumeria. Sananda has had many names and titles throughout his many lives. I am Sananda's twin flame. He comes to visit me often, but not in a third-dimensional form. I see him with my spiritual eyes and can feel and hear him. I channeled an entire book through past life regression and made it available on my website, sanandanews.com. I have been aboard the ship almost every night, having meetings and working with the Galactic Federation. We are preparing for the ascension of Earth. The Galactic Federation is the Federation of many nations and planets not only in this solar system and galaxy, but in others as well. We work with the "Creator of all things," and we are similar to a "Jedi Knight" or Galactic Police. Most of us are of the light and help protect other planets in need, and especially those going through an ascension process like Earth is right now. We have souls and our own journeys. We have many types of scientists, teachers, healers, etc. We come from all walks of life. Some of the beings include Reptilians, Humans, Mantis, Insectoids, Etheric beings and Beings of Light.

There are lifetimes upon lifetimes of knowledge within our Federation that help serve those souls who are younger than ourselves. We see ourselves as older brothers and sisters. We have a great, great many ships of all types and sizes. Some ships have no beings on them, but are full of plant forms. We have ships for animals and some "scientific and learning" ships where beings appear in a hologram form to learn (similar to the Holodeck in *Star Trek*). The ships that are watching Earth are in a stationary orbit. We have ships called Motherships that are larger than Earth herself. Some of these ships are nearby in Earth's solar system. We have over several million ships. Our ships can change shape and color. Those seen by Earth beings include Triangle ships, Cigar-shaped or Tubular ships, Disk ships, Plasma ships, and some are even Cube form. There are other species here watching or visiting for their own purposes that also use ships shaped like ours; we are not the only ones. The negative species and the government have their own ships and some resemble ours, too. The government back-engineered the black Triangle and Disk ships for certain.

I walked into this body at six months in the mother's womb. The soul that was in the baby before was not going to survive. The mother was going to lose the baby. That soul was actually a "soul child" of mine and we made an agreement to switch places. She went back into the spirit realm and I took over the body. These memories came to me later in life.

I have met family from Sirius here on Earth and we are gathering right now. I have met about five other people that speak a part of the language I speak. Since I arrived on Earth for my mission, I have had many lifetimes here. In this life, I remember all of these languages and I blend them together when I speak. They include my Sirian language and my four past-life languages of ancient Egyptian, ancient Sumerian, ancient Hebrew and Annunaki. These are all languages of light. I also have a friend

human creation

that speaks in this blended form of language and we can actually carry on a conversation. I have since met others that speak mostly ancient Egyptian and we can speak together also.

I met with a linguist who speaks a lot of different languages and he can understand about 70 percent of what I am saying. That is how I found out which languages I am speaking. A lot of people I am meeting now have all had past lives in ancient Egypt together, during the time of Jesus, and we are now meeting again. We are working off Karma and doing healings together in this life.

The Annunaki are the ones many speak of as the Ancient Gods. The ones who came down and created the *Homo sapiens sapiens*. They took the Neanderthals and added their own DNA, with other ET species' DNA, to create modern humans. Humans are considered a slave race and were created to be workers for the Annunaki. Humans used to have 12 strands of active DNA and during the time of "The Garden of Eden," the Annunaki turned much of the DNA "off." This was an experiment, for they wanted to see if Humans could survive on their own and keep us as slaves. These strands of DNA are being reactivated by all of the frequencies and light that are hitting the Earth. It is the Divine DNA. Humans have about 39 different species of ET DNA. Which ET species a person's genetic history contains depends on that person's blood type. People that have O+ or O- blood have a lot of Sirian DNA. People who have A+ or AB come from Orion DNA. Other blood types come from the Pleiadians. It also depends on the genetic mixture and bloodline of a person. This is where the "Bloodline of the Holy Grail" stems from. Enki is the "Feathered Serpent," half Reptilian, half Human, who arrived here first and was considered "Lord of the Earth" until Enlil took over. Enlil has a different mother than Enki, but they had the same father, Anu. Enlil has more Reptilian DNA than Enki, and he is more military. Enlil does not like humankind and is the more negative of the two. He was the "angry" God in the bible and has kept humans in slavery. Enki loves his creation of humans and wishes to help Humans to ascend. He went against the Annunaki Council by giving Humans more DNA in the time of the Garden of Eden. He gave them the "Tree of Life," which gave humans extra genetics. That is the bloodline of the Holy Grail and that is going to help Humans to ascend. The Annunaki come from the 12th planet in our solar system, called Nibiru. Its orbit is way out, similar to Pluto, and is elliptical.

All of the talk about Nibiru causing great havoc on Earth is not going to happen. It would have happened already. Earth was actually on the opposite side of Nibiru's passing through the solar system. It came in 2003 and Earth was on the opposite side of the sun at the time. It was going to cause great devastation on the second pass, but the Galactic Federation was able to step in and "popped" Nibiru into another dimension. They were able to do this under the ruling by the "Creator of all Things" and the Higher Spiritual Hierarchy for Earth and her solar system.

Enlil is incarnate on Earth right now. He looks Human, although he has Reptilian DNA. He has really white skin and yellow, serpent eyes. He is really old and they live for thousands of years. Enki died and was reborn as Jesus, but is now in his Sananda form. There is an "aspect" of Sananda incarnated on Earth right now, to bring in the higher frequencies for ascension. Buddha is also incarnate on Earth again. A lot of the Ascended Masters have incarnated "aspects" of themselves for the same reason. They say we all have parts of our self somewhere else, living out another life.

I had an ancient Lemurian life on Earth, as an etheric being, before I had a physical life. We set up the Spiritual Grid of Earth during that time. There are pyramids below the oceans all around the Islands of Hawaii that are ancient Lemurian sites. They will rise up again. In fact, it may have already started. Recently, I did some activation ceremonies at a sacred volcano site in Hawaii. When I started the ceremony, a mist rose up and covered all of us in the ceremony. As soon as we finished the ceremony, the mist faded away and the sun came out again. I thanked the Goddess Pele by releasing an owl feather into the wind, which blew south. We walked down a bit of the volcano, to do some hiking on the north side, and unbelievably at my feet was that sacred owl feather I had tossed. I know that was a confirmation to us that our ceremony was accepted.

I have been doing a very special technique of hypnosis with a friend. During these sessions, I bring in Sananda and my higher self, and we go to a sacred spot. I feel this way blocks out all interferences with Earth, and I go directly to the soul or higher self, to get the most accurate information. I recently found out that I was taken on board a ship at age 3. I was taken quite often since then. Sometimes it is done out-of-body, in my spiritual form, and sometimes it is done in my physical body. I don't remember these events when I wake up, but some information comes through later or after I speak with Sananda while doing a meditation.

When I am taken aboard the ships, it is not necessarily with my people, the Sirians, but it is with the Galactic Federation. I remember being with Pleaidians and Andromedans, too. They will not allow me to remember the activities aboard the ship, except to know that I was sitting at a huge table in a meeting with the other Commanders.

Often I discover in hypnotherapy that we were aboard the ship with the other Commanders and preparing for Planet World Evacuation. Things are constantly changing because of cosmic events and the dark forces on Earth, including the Cabal and the government. There has been a huge cosmic event that has changed everything, including everyone's own soul contract on Earth. Our universe is blending with another universe at this time. One of the suns in this universe exploded back in February of 2009; we refer to this as the February Event. This caused a great electromagnetic wave of light in the universe, and everything that had been planned by all beings for the ascension of Earth has changed. Everyone is now focused on healing the effects of that occurrence and is in the process of rewriting their contracts. I connected with the "Creator of all Things," who is above the "Creator of All Things" for our Galaxy, and asked "Why?" It was explained to me that the result of these two universes coming together is actually a greater blessing for all involved. For the ascension of Earth includes not only our solar system, our galaxy, our universe, but others as well. It is beyond our comprehension. Since the "game plan" has been rewritten, many souls have agreed to continue the reincarnation cycle for the greater good of all. Gaia has changed her soul plan as well. She will become her true beautiful form. Gaia has been promised that she will not suffer the pollution nor the dark forces. More changes for the betterment of Earth are continuously now being made.

I started to awaken slowly over the years, but mostly since 2001. I grew up Irish-Catholic, and joined the Mormon church when I was 21 years old. I was going to college and took classes on ancient archaeology. This really fascinated me, and I always wanted to go to these ancient places. It had to do with a life as Isis in Egypt, who is an Annunaki-Sirian being. When I incarnated on Earth in ancient times as Her Royal Highness Serena, I gained one of my titles pronounced Ishish (*EesEes*). That was ancient Sumerian for Isis today. Isis is a title meaning Priestess of the Highest, it is not a name. What I am is a Priestess for the Creator of All Things. I am an emissary of light. I do a lot of energy work and healing work for Gaia, Mother Earth. A lot of that knowledge is slowly returning.

Now, I am returning to Hawaii, to do ancient ceremonies using my Priesthood and my language, and to be with my Earth family. I go where spirit guides me.

Back in 2001, I met a lady living with my sister on Maui. She would shake her head as she spoke an ancient language and no one understood her. My sister told me to ask Sananda to help me understand what she was saying. I did some meditation and asked Sananda for assistance. Sure enough, a little while later, I started spouting out my own language. I found out I was actually speaking four languages simultaneously. I then started speaking with this lady and we held a conversation. I found out that she had a past life in ancient Atlantis and was speaking that very language. She had an uncle in that time period who was coming through her in our time period. He was trying to warn us about the dangers of HAARP and technology similar to what they used. These technologies destroyed their civilization. That night, my sister and I were astral traveling together and we went back to the time of Atlantis. We sat in a sacred circle with the lady's uncle and he showed us what was really going on. It was at this time I started becoming more gifted with psychic abilities and astral traveling abilities. I learned how to connect with my higher self and my spiritual being. I began speaking with Sananda.

In the Grand Canyon there are places called the Tower of Isis, the Tower of RA and the Tower of Osiris. During the time of the ancient Annunaki, Egyptians and Sumerians, we had ships and would travel all over the Earth. We had sacred places, places where we stored things and places we used as landing sites, all placed on the Earth's Energy Grid. So, for the last nine years, I have been visiting these places and connecting on a physical, spiritual and energy level. After separating from the Mormon church, I was meditating and I was given the information about my personal ship, the *She'Aste*. I could see the image in my mind and I drew it on paper. I get a lot of information in my dreams and while meditating. I will sometimes start speaking my language, especially when I see these new crop circles and read about Egypt. These new crop circles have the ancient language in them, and I understand it in my mind. These crop circles are teaching us and warning us of things to come. We can change this with our consciousness and our thoughts. Positive attracts positive. Visualize the world that you want it to be. A world of peace, joy, beauty, light, and love. Also, the opposite in that what you fear you attract. There are those who want to stay in power, greed, etc., who try to keep you in slavery through fear. Do not listen to them. You are powerful spiritual beings! Go within yourselves and love. *Love* is the *key*!!!

My mission is to do ancient ceremonies using my Priesthood and my language, to help heal Gaia. Another part of my mission is to bring forth ancient records that are in these ancient libraries. It will include the true history of the entire Earth, including all civilizations and all beings. Once we get rid of the dark forces and become a place of peace and light, then this knowledge will return in full. This will be after the Shift. I will be traveling back and forth from the ships with Sananda during these times. My DNA has been reactivated now and I am reconnected with my higher self. I am working with the Ascended Masters and the Galactic Federation at night.

I learned how to remote view while living in Utah. I remote viewed and located things hidden under the mountains, including tunnels, military bases and UFO bases. These are found all over Earth. You can research this yourself. I do Akashic Record readings, Psychometry, Munay-ki DNA activation, and I am a Reiki Master of the Usui method. I do energy work for Gaia and Humankind.

I am an ambassador for the "Creator of All Things." Spiritually, I believe in being *at-one-moment*. I believe we are all connected, all *one*. I hope sharing this message will let you know that you are not alone! The Galactic Federation, Angels, Ascended Masters and many others are here, assisting Mother Earth and Humankind. *Now* is the time to go within, let go of all fears, anger and negative emotions. Find balance and trust your higher being.

My favorite websites:

Richard Boylan Starseeds: www.drboylan.com

Sheldan Nidle's Planetary Activation Organization: www.paoweb.com

Mike Quinsey's The Tree of the Golden Light: www.treeofthegoldenlight.com

Drunvelo Melchizedec, David Wilcox and William Henry are very truthful! Google them.

Also check out Barbara Marciniak's books, William Gammill's book *The Gathering*, and Nancy Red Star's *Star Ancestors*. All wonderful! These will help you on your journey.

You may contact me: *amazinggrace1455@yahoo.com*

My websites:

www.sanandanews.com, www.projectworldevacuation.com and www.etfirstcontact.org

Arroylos

I remember traveling at a great speed over this green field as I was about to be born on Earth, and I was enjoying the freedom I had right before. I consider myself a Starseed and I do feel like I have had lives here and elsewhere. I have had experiences on Earth and off Earth, so that it would be conducive for me to engage in relations with extraterrestrials who would be like a portal or ambassador for others to feel okay about who they are. I feel strongly that I should share my story openly, no matter what.

I do not know what my Star name is, but "Arroylos" always comes to mind when I meditate on this. Once I was going to an "experiencer group" led by a lady named June. There was another lady there named Mar, who came up to me and said, "Do you know who you are?" I had the same energetic, solar-plexus feeling that I get when my Star family interacts with me. We made sure to swap contact numbers before we left the meeting.

One day Mar called me and told me about my ET family, that I even knew them in a past life in Peru, where an underwater base exists. She then identified the race of beings as an ancient, independent Incan society that suddenly disappeared from the surface of Earth. This group of Incas were a very mysterious and far-removed group that would not allow others in. They were a very advanced society. One day they apparently left, seemingly in a moment's notice, taking all of their belongings with them, leaving their teapots still warm. Later on I verified this group of enigmatic Incans. They were written of in historical records which I found on-line. I very much resonated with this information, I felt it was most certainly describing the same group Mar had spoken about.

Mar told me that she had been waiting so long to give me this information, she was very emotional over the phone. Mar told me that she was done with her

mission now, and she literally disappeared. I received a call from June, saying
how the experiencer group was concerned about Mar's disappearance. I had a
feeling Mar left for Peru and I told them so. I do believe that Mar was an ET
and was perhaps from this underwater base or acting as a liaison for them, she
just knew so much!

I have always felt drawn to Peru and the Incan people. In high school, I had
used a Ouija Board with a relative who is a psychic. Before we would even touch
the board, we attuned ourselves to a very centered frequency of unconditional
love during a meditation. We asked specifically to contact a high-level guide of
mine or some being connected to me. Once the "board" told me that I was an
Incan high priest in my past life.

I had a visionary dream one night where I saw three silver disks while
looking out my sliding glass door. I was scrambling to get my video camera
together. Tapes were everywhere. I couldn't get it together to film the ships and
I was very frustrated. At that point I heard a soft female voice echo as if it was
in a hallway, but yet all around me. She said, "If you want to know to us, you
need to be ready and prepared." It was such a vivid dream, it was so clear. It
had such an impact on me because I couldn't get it out of my head. I even
began thinking about the great pay of my Earth job and how it was trivial and
illogical for me.

The next day, on my birthday, I saw a ship in the sky. The ship was a
round sphere and solid white. It was not metallic, but the sun did cast shading
on it so I could see contour and a definite shape. It then moved to right above
my head, and at that point it changed in shape and appearance. It became the
silver craft like I saw just the night before. It was like a horizontal, egg-shaped
craft. I also noticed a slight color of red on top of the ship. At first it seemed to
be responding to my thoughts because it would move a little bit. Then I started
to receive a telepathic communication from a female voice through an image.
Telepathy can be used in many ways, this time they chose to seep into my
system, where there was no denial. I saw this female wearing a red, tight-fitting
jumpsuit. At first I thought I was projecting this image, like wishful thinking.
But no matter what I did, the image became more clear. I had to succumb to
knowing the image was real. I could see this female had wavy, brunette hair, a
lighter skin color and a very big smile. There were more than just her on the

craft, but she was the one assigned to communicate with me. I believe I was connected to her in a deep way.

That was my Star Family's introduction to me, although they never told me where they came from. They made it their mission to teach me the energetics of how to live life and how to go about thinking and acting. They were so clear at teaching me that everything comes from the heart. They continued to reiterate that the heart is the gateway to creation, it is the only way of relating to the infinite creation. The raising of one's frequency will tend to take care of things that are problematic in our daily lives. Our logic needs to be tempered by the heart. If it isn't, we will keep making the same mistakes. They also showed me how to use energies and our imaginative capabilities of raising this love energy from the heart, radiating outward and connecting to all things. At that point you attract other beings who can see this light energy and who are attracted to it.

Within a week after this first meeting with my Star Family, I left my job and took a sabbatical. I set out to initiate contact at that point. I knew I would be able to do it, very confidently. I even went out and bought the top-of-the-line video camera and began filming. I used the "John Bro Technique" of pointing the camera towards the sun, but having an object that blocks out the actual sun itself, so you are looking at the coronal discharge or rays. You can catch anomalies this way and, once in a while, you will find craft that are moving at incredible speeds. I set the camera at about "1/15,000 of a second," where I can catch a hummingbird's wings. So some of these craft were in one frame or in every other frame. I noticed that with the sightings of these crafts there was a telepathic component. Whenever I was outside and intent on welcoming them in and focused on them, I would get a lot more activity recorded.

I received a vision of the future from my Star family on the same day I first met them. They showed me visions of a place I will be at if all goes well, or as planned. This place is a planet that was absolutely lush and pristine, that humans have never known. It seemed as if it were just made the day before. I could see a village, living in nature, that also had high technology. I saw things that were not ancient or unevolved. I saw a blond-haired female there that I was with, maybe my future mate. That troubled me, too, because I didn't know if I was supposed to marry on Earth now or what. They would not answer my concerns, they just told me that this is where I will be if things go as planned. They do not show me disasters or nuclear explosions or any fearful events.

I think it is important for people to know how much we Star Beings here on Earth struggle from being different. There is loneliness and feeling like we are always on the outside. We feel a longing to fit in, but we are intrinsically different. That seems to be the common traits with people like us "Indigo children" and those that are aware of their abilities, but their parents could not discern the uniqueness from anything else. I believe that is why so many kids want to kill themselves, take it out on others and are miserable. If they do get help, they won't feel so alone, so different or that they are the only ones. That should spark the desire to live again.

I was having a hard time with my family because of this extra component of my life. My sister was making fun of me behind my back, and of course her child heard this and parroted those same things. I was feeling very sad and feeling that much more estranged. One day, during a barbecue with my family, I built up all the heartfelt emotion inside me and asked for help from my Star family to ease things. Well, They did. Everybody was outside and there was this white dot in the sky. We noticed that it continued to get closer and closer to us. My niece and I noticed it first, so I went inside and grabbed my camera. It turned out that my sister was the focus point of their coming. She kept saying, "It's a bird, it's a plane," etc, until she could no longer rationalize it. Then she just said, "What is that?" That day was the turning point and I never had a problem with her after that day.

Over time I learned to be very clear on what I wanted. I felt like I was being led to make contact with beings who were in my best interest, who are here to assist mankind and into service-to-others. At that point of my personal growth was when I met my Star family. The excitement of that experience was like combining the emotions of Christmas, my birthday and Halloween all into one. It was a joyous feeling of reconnecting with beings that I haven't heard from for years and years. That reconnection to my ET family dwarfed the connection I have with my Earth family. That was hard to accept, but my Star family stayed with me for a good couple of years. They periodically stop by and visit still. Other groups of ETs came to visit me after my Star family had introduced themselves. I guess it was to show me what I needed to be shown. They showed me the diversity of life that was out there in the universe, to raise the frequency of my heart and mind coherently and what that does to my perception. It helped me to perceive parts of reality that I could not see before. I became resonant with these higher realms and saw all types of things. I saw more craft than anyone else I know of. There is this one type of event I call "blessed sessions," where I would be blessing them and I would feel their energies come into me. There would be one craft after another, after another, after another during these sessions. They would come in and slow down. I would feel a connection with them and they would move on. It was all different types of crafts. I think this happened in the year 2003, and in that two-hour period, I saw about 200 craft.

One past life that I can remember is being a Human-looking ET aboard a craft. Our foreheads were more prominent. It was a "mothership" and I spent my entire life aboard this ship. We traversed the Universe and "mapped out" new areas. Everything in the ship was smooth and rounded, not angular or square corners. The lighting was dim inside the ship. I remember being about the age of 8 or 10, and I specifically remember my Dad. He was in charge on the ship and I never really got to spend time with him. I was left to myself, although I did have a being with me that I considered a Mom, teacher, friend, pet, and companion all rolled into one. This being was a hovering metallic orb about the size of a softball. Even in this life, in school, I would often drift off and draw these metallic orbs. At the time I didn't know why I kept drawing those.

That life as this ET ended tragically. We were in between galaxies, out in this great rift or traverse. Something happened to us, to our energy system. It affected our ship, the powering of the ship and even our food. We knew that people were going to starve and suffer before dying, but we also knew that death was only death of the physical body. So, as a group, we had to make the decision to either make a mass-transition into the light or perish slowly. The decision was made by the whole ship society to make a "mass exit" so that no one would suffer. Remembering this decision of group annihilation was and is a very emotional event for me and I still get choked up talking about it.

When I was five years old, I woke up one morning and looked outside. I saw this man standing there in a shiny, silver suit with a cover over his face. This suit looked similar to an astronaut. Next, this man suddenly morphed into a tree. I knew something was very strange about this and I pulled the sheets over my head, trying to build up the courage to run to my parents' room. After that event, I had a very distinct interest in UFOs. This was before *Star Wars* and the *Close Encounters* movies. I was going to the library and checking out all of the factual UFO books, like Air Force books and the Betty and Barney Hill incident. I even have a 1976 *UFO* magazine in my stash.

One night when these events first started, I felt my body being taken upon a ship. I was claiming my rights as a universal being to resist and said "No" to them taking me. I remember kicking, and then suddenly being thrown back into my body. This would happen over and over. One night it happened about 15 times and they finally did "get" me. Although, I don't feel that it was for nefarious reasons. I believe it was probably just to check me out and to check my health. It didn't seem negative to me, but they were definitely not Human.

My parents don't have any experiences that they recall. However, one day my Dad was outside looking straight up in the sky. As his eyes acclimated and focused further, he could see these 12 objects. He told me to come out and I could only see them when my eyes adjusted. Suddenly, one of the white dots would zip across the sky and stop, then another, then another. That happened for about 20 to 25 minutes. I live in a city that is like a hub of paranormal activities, so who knows what they were exactly?

In 2001, I went to a workshop of James Gilliland's and we had a group meditation. For me, it was an LSD trip. I felt completely exposed and naked. I had to get out of there to process what was happening. I had to contemplate what was going on. The next morning, at an earlier time than I usually get going, I felt a nudge, an inkling to go outside. I sat outside, focused and intent of sending a thought form for contact. About 15 minutes into it, I saw these three eagles. They were mechanical and the "feathers" were too long. All three were maroon from beak to tail and flying clockwise in a circle. This really got my attention. Suddenly, all three of them shot up in elevation and blurred out. As they blurred, I saw an oval, crimson red craft come into focus. I could see the sun reflecting off of the ship as it was glowing red. I spent 35 minutes just looking at this craft, but I was not having any communication with it. This sighting was completely changing my world without my realizing it. My neural network was being rearranged and I felt a euphoria of emotions. I was feeling paralyzed, but I know I wasn't. There was no way out of being able to deny what I was seeing. These were my own feelings and responses, not something I was receiving from the ship.

It happened again the very next morning, but only for 15 minutes. They stayed as long as I wanted them to be there. I was actually getting a neck ache from watching them through the binoculars, and I was the one who stopped the contact at that point because I was done. These experiences showed me that I could initiate contact if I would put out a super-human degree of focus. Because of this, I have never had a negative experience in all of my events.

After I had a good, long exposure with my Star family, they told me that they were leaving, but would see me again. I thought that would be the end of my experiences. Then another group of ETs came in with a metallic, oval ship with a very red middle part to it, almost like an eye. They also had a gold ship in this ET group. These beings were teaching me by exposing me to the vast arena of life, diversity of beings and technology and of different types of energies. None of them were negative, they were very loving. Sometimes they looked a little too alien for me and I would wave them off. I really feel that the universe is teeming with life on many dimensions and that they are all around. If we resonate our frequencies through our heart and mind, we can interact with them. I have definitely experienced many things, such as this little, blue ball that seemed to be a consciousness in and of itself.

So my new group of ETs were always there watching, allowing me to make contact with all of these other ET beings. I believe they wanted me to learn that we can contact these beings and even be specific about who it is we wish to contact. Our imagination and our potential is so great and they wanted me to see this, along with all the other sides of Humanity that we have not tapped into.

I was getting really good with resonating this coherent frequency and I learned that I could actually pick and choose which beings to have contact with. I had to work on my fear issues initially, but love is such an all empowering thing. So I asked specifically for a Pleiadian female to visit. I saw this craft come down, and it was the most beautiful rainbow-colored craft. It was metallic, but these rainbow colors were undulating on top of the metal—like a constant wave motion inside the metal itself. It almost looked like a computer graphic. That was a rare experience.

Normally, when a craft comes, it positions itself behind a tree or something, and if I ask it to come around or come back, they usually don't. This time, I asked the ship to come back and hang out with me. I was looking through my electronically stabilized binoculars and I could see the ship actually coming back. At that time I received a vision of what she looked like. When I closed my eyes, I was on board the ship. So I kept my eyes closed, to be on the ship, and I saw a Human-looking female with curly, shoulder-length hair. Without any physical contact at all, I had experienced a mental climax with her that was stronger and greater than any physical one I had ever experienced before. Afterwards, I felt very clear-headed and high as a kite for the rest of the day. I noticed her craft turned a dark, violet purple after this encounter. Then, she gently drifted away, as usual.

For me, they never speed off. Some craft were plasma-like, others were very odd, almost disturbing in nature and beyond description. I would normally get a telepathic connection with the ship when It came around. I can see the gold fabric or line of communication coming into my solar-plexus and I will then know that they are around. Sometimes I'd make an attempt to make contact and it wouldn't happen at all. My emotions or thoughts were not "on the money" to draw them in, this was a part of my training. I also learned the subtleties of telepathy and how to decipher them. It was always in the combination of one word, some emotional feeling, some concept/idea and maybe they would also pick from my memory bank. I must have told them previous to incarnating that I didn't want any help, that I wanted to figure it all out on my own or something. It was very frustrating at times, thank goodness for the Internet. When I did grasp the concept, they would sometimes show up the next day, to give me more clarity or refine it for me. It was just a feeling of "Yes, I got it right!"

Here is an example of what I have learned to make contact. This is not only a way to make contact with ETs, it is a way to live life. It is a way to think and to be. It is relatively straightforward.

I use the Heart Math Institute method. They have done all of the science on the heart, that it puts out 5,000 times the electromagnetic signal than the brain does, as far a being a transmitter.

My ETs gave me the following concepts (the same that the above-mentioned Institute has):

You think of something very positive, a time when you felt very loved or very grateful, and sustain that feeling. At this point I ask for love to fill me, or for the love I have to unfold. I would feel this love and this light growing in my heart. You cannot rush it and it has to be detached from an expected outcome. You have to be emotionally in a good place. You let this feeling fill your body. Once it has filled your body, you let it radiate outward. Use your imagination and feeling to let it go beyond your body and connect it to all things. I personally connect it to Earth first, then all life upon Earth, then to atmosphere and out to the cosmos. You just have to radiate pure love energy from your heart. That is when you become a bright, positive light that other beings are attracted to. Once I am there, I send out a very clear thought form, such as, "I am seeking contact with benevolent, loving Star Beings who have my best interest at heart, so that I may learn......" However you wish to say it. Then you sustain this request in your mind. If it fades, say it again.

Thoughts are actually a form, things, and a consciousness themselves. I use the rays of love that I am feeling as the conduit for my message. These feelings and thoughts travel instantaneously, or what I call the speed of love.

I did have an experience with one of the "Alphabet" agencies. It was in the year 2005, when I was a limo driver. One day we had a rather odd call and it was the day after I put up a Website telling of my experiences. It was a call to pick up a man in a rather distant area, way up in the hills, and then take him to the big city. As I started driving, I noticed two unmarked cars. I felt that they were not police or undercover. One of the vehicles got in front of me and one stayed behind me. The one in front started slowing down. I looked in the rear-view mirror and I could see the guy driving was giving me the ugliest, dirtiest look, like nothing I have seen before. All of a sudden, the guy behind me zoomed to my right-hand side.

We pulled up to the stoplight and this guy rolled down his window. My window was already rolled down. The guy did not turn to look at me, but I remember he said, "Hey, how's it going?" His voice was odd, his inflection was disconcerting. I didn't say anything back to him and I noticed, during the entire time, he did not turn to look at me. As soon as the light turned green, they bolted off and literally disappeared half a block in front of me.

It gets weirder. I went up to the house where I was supposed to pick this man up. When I pulled in the driveway, there was a car there with a license plate that read: "ET (Heart) PAX". I don't know exactly what that means, but I went up to the door and asked for the gentleman that needed to be picked up. The man who answered said, "Who?" I repeated the name again, and he told me that man had not lived there for 30 years, that he had passed away.

I then looked up into the sky and saw a UFO. It was coming closer and I told the man at the door about it. The UFO kept getting even closer. It was the same looking ship that we saw at our family barbecue. The man looked at it and said he didn't know what it was. Then he said, "Oh, that's a UFO, nothing except that could go that slow and just stop."

That was one of the weirdest days of my life. I am not sure exactly who it was, what happened or why. Then my boss said that he was going to find out where that phone call came from, because he had just lost good money on that whole trip. The phone company said they could not trace where that call came from.

One time there was a glowing orange-colored ship that came down. It looked like a house, it was rectangular with a rooftop and all. I received a telepathic transmission from them that they were Human looking and they were diverse. One of the females was Caucasian looking and wore a black, tight-fitting uniform. This female had brunette hair, a sense of humor, and her energy was different. She stated to me that they were from Venus. I told her I didn't believe her. She told me, matter-of-factly, that they were from Venus. Each time I refused to believe them, she kept getting louder and louder.

This is the only time when a particular person was chosen to communicate with me and actually switched over to another person. The female ET said, "Meet the being in-charge of this ship." He was a small guy and looked like a Guatemalan person with an angular nose and his hair was cut into like a bowl shape.

I said, "Nice haircut." And the beings on board the craft actually laughed. I felt them laughing like they got my joke, I was surprised. They just wanted me to know that there really are beings from Venus, maybe not in our dimension, however.

There was a day that the Earth was supposed to have a grand visit by the ETs, I believe it was Oct. 14, 2008. On that day, I knew that these people who predicted this event were wrong because I know the ETs do not work that way. That event would have startled people into a frenzy. I decided to have my own contact with the skills I have learned. I connected with a group I never connected with before. I saw this copper/rust-colored, metallic triangular craft. The design of the craft was moving similar to the rainbow-colored ship before. The metal was undulated with dark purple colors running left to right around the ship.

I tuned into the beings on the ship. There were four or five beings that I saw. They were all about the same size, small, whitish skin color with a tinge of tan, bald heads, round eyes, wearing white, tight-fitting uniforms,and they were very positive and loving. They were helping me with the energy I was projecting because they thought I was a little sloppy with it. They told me to first tune into their hearts, then to their bodies, then to the surroundings of the craft and finally to the craft itself. They asked me not to just tune into the craft itself and forget them. I was "with" them for about an hour and a half, as long as I wanted them to stay. So, I had my own Oct. 14.

There are some beings that don't show me what they look like or don't communicate with me, and I feel that it is because they are too "alien" for me and they know I would not be comfortable. They have always been considerate, positive and helpful. I think that there is a lot of UFO activity nearby because of all the technology in my city. One of the many types of ships was a gold, football-shaped craft. It had a purple, electric mist on top of it and it was one of the most beautiful ships I have ever seen. I guess they just wanted to see who I was, because they left shortly after I spotted them.

Sometimes when the ETs don't know who you are, but wish to know without actually taking you or imposing on you, they do an "energetic scan" on you. I told them, "Please don't take me, I am just curious about you." Then they left. That has happened about three times with ships that I am completely unfamiliar with. The feeling you get when they scan you is similar to what I felt at the James Gilliland's meditation, very naked and exposed. It is an uncomfortable feeling. The very first craft I saw, the red craft, did that to me and I truly thought I was going to be abducted.

* * *

It was when I turned 30 years old that this gateway of awakening slowly opened up. Since 2001, when I saw the first ship for 35 minutes, I have had over 100 one-on-one encounters with UFOs and ETs. I have also heard that this happens for a lot of people at the age of 30.

My mission is to get people to transcend fear. To share my story and to show people that there is so much more out there than what societies have been brain-washed to believe. We can't make a connection in a big way until we transcend fear. Contact is not all violations and abductions. There are people who have worked through their "abduction" experience. They know themselves better, their minds are expanded, and they have a better idea of what is out there in the universe. That actually benefits everyone on the planet on a mass-consciousness level. It was painful to go through what they went through, but my feelings are that there are truly no accidents. There was some soul agreement for them to participate on that level, that is my belief.

I believe that there can be random occurrences, say there are beings that were able to slip in the "back door," that are not of the highest good or integrity, and they see a sucker who is just wanting to contact *anything*. I don't think that all the hundreds or thousands of people who have experienced being taken was by happenstance or accident. There is usually a family connection or something. I think that the ETs are a part of the contract. I think Humans hardly grasp the many facets of reality, we are just like babies. Even we Star beings have to overcome this lack of perception.

Love overcomes fear. Unconditional love—to fill yourself and surround yourself with love—means that you are attracting the beings of a higher vibration. There is something happening on Earth that has been put into place a very long time ago. The high beings of love are not about to let the minds of Humanity get strangled and warped. The Earth has been watched for and cared for since the beginning. We have all been saved from numerous events that could have severely damaged the Earth because the ETs won't let it happen.

Energy work connects us to the galaxy and to the universe. It also is the means to which Humanity will Evolve! If we cannot live in the heart, this planet will fail. Humans will cease to exist on Earth. The only ones that will survive are those that are heart-centered individuals. Living in the heart is the thread to the other side of where we are going.

I don't know if it is 2012, December 21 at 10:30 PM. But going through these changes, there will be a grand miracle, a grand event that will surprise us all. Those that are not in the loving heart space, but in fear that is being programmed into people to block their frequencies, will succumb to the destruction. I don't know if the Earth is going to split into two realities, but something is definitely going to happen. I don't doubt that the ETs could also come in and save people from major catastrophes. It is all a choice and they have to abide by our choice.

Books that were significant to me:
William Tiller's *Some Science Adventures with Real Magic*
—This is advanced physics.
James Gilliland's *Becoming Gods 2*, and all books by Lisette Larkins.

A significant website:
www.emergingearthangels.com—Free bi-monthly "Energy Alerts"
by Karen Bishop; she is very accurate.

DVD that is significant to me:
"Quantum Communication" by William Tiller

If you would like to contact me: *davkobza@me.com*

Cynthias

I was told by psychics that I have more than one type of blood in me. I already knew that I was a Hybrid at this time because my father told me when I was about 30 years old. He told me that I should know that I am not all Human and insinuated that I was purposfully "made" using ET DNA. I was told by different psychics that while my mother was pregnant with me, ET beings would come in and place their DNA in me to protect me. I had a friend who gave me a reading with his own ET beings. He told me that I have two separate ET DNAs, in addition to Human DNA. His ET guides told me that one DNA was from an aquatic Zeta race and the other was from the Annunaki race. This information confirmed what I already knew for myself.

My species, called the "Zumma Zetas," are aquatic and have dolphin-like skin. We are thin and tall, approximately 6 feet. We are a grayish white with beige color, similar to the color of a mushroom. Our heads are not as large as a normal Zeta's, but longer. The forehead comes out a little bit and becomes the nose, similar to a dolphin (not a long nose or a porpoise). So we are like a cross between a dolphin and a Human. We have a type of sensory organ somewhere on our  bodies. We have little mouths and little sharp teeth. Our hands have three long, webbed fingers. Our eyes are a gorgeous midnight blue with a little white on the edges. We have ceremonial type clothing which is long, white silvery robes. We speak telepathically most of the time, but we also have a soft-spoken language. I have on occasion spoken my language. I know we have ships, but I do not remember what they look like. Most of the time I am inside them or inside someone's medical mother ship.

One day while meditating, I was taken back to my home world, where I was allowed to remember this one part. The land appeared barren without a lot of plants or trees. I was inside a gray-colored cave where there was a deep pool of water. I noticed a soft light coming from within the cave. My people were spending time in the water to keep wet. I could see my Zumma Zeta body and how I loved being in this form. I then was allowed to remember that I agreed to come to Earth during the great time of changes and that I agreed to help humanity. I had a tear running down my Zeta cheek, and I wondered why I was crying. Initially, I thought it was because I had to live among the Humans on Earth. Then, my beings reminded me that I was crying because Humans don't know the love that our people know and this made me sad for them.

At one of our experiencer groups, our leader asked everyone if they knew which planet they felt they were from. Everyone but two of us could answer and name a known planet. I was one of the two that could not say which planet I knew I was from. I went home crying and feeling like a phony. I thought maybe my being a Starbeing was just my imagination, like my mother always said. Then I realized, if it *was* my imagination, I probably would have just come up with a name of some planet to satisfy the group. I have to be honest and true to myself, because that is who I am.

I went to bed that night, meditating and talking to my guides. I asked them, "Why don't I know where I am from?" I woke up in the early morning, standing naked on the hard gravel in my yard. I was feeling the universal energy surging through my body, charging me and connecting me to Mother Earth. I went to my computer in a "trance" state and wrote what information I was receiving. This is what I remember of it: "I have no home, for the universe is my home. I travel from planet to planet..." Shortly after writing this and sending it off in an email, "someone" came in and destroyed my computer.

It was after receiving that message that I was told I am one of many Ambassadors on Earth. I work with so many different beings that I am not quite certain most of the time which ET I am dealing with. My beings, the Zumma Zetas, told me it was time for me to acknowledge that I am an Ambassador of the Universe.

Among my guides are the "Tall-white" Zetas. These beings are always with me and show up in my aura pictures. Their heads are larger than my species, more similar to the smaller Grays. The Tall-whites have little openings where their nose would be and have a slit mouth. Their hands have three long fingers. Their eyes are huge and blueish-white in color, but have to use black lenses over their eyes most of the time. They are about 7 feet tall and have a body structure similar to most Grays, very thin and lean. They wear long, white robes. Some of my other guides are the Ashtar Command and they always appear human-looking to me when I go to the etheric realm. I know that the ETs who visit me are all types of different species.

My father had served two years in the Army-Air Force prior to marrying my mother, and was in medical school on the verge of getting his doctor's degree. He did not want any more children after my older sister was born, at least until eight months later, after a strange secret meeting he refused to tell my mother about. That night after his meeting, my father brought champagne home to celebrate something. My mother can't recall what the celebration was for because after two sips of this "champagne," she remembered nothing except waking up the next morning. In other words, she was drugged. A few weeks later, she was shocked to find out she was pregnant! Eight and a half months later, Sandy and I were born.

Just six months before graduating from medical school, my dad dropped out and rejoined the Army. He joined a division called the O.S.S. at that time (later it became known as the CIA). He disappeared on top-secret projects of which details he couldn't divulge to anyone. Even more interesting, he is now a Free Mason and attending those meetings when he's not off on secret missions in Korea and other places. Our family became accustomed to moving to different Army bases for the first seven years of my life. During this time, my father had become obsessed with the 1950s movies of aliens and alien invasions of planet Earth.

My Truth began on a hot August day in 1949. I was the first-born of a set of fraternal twin girls. Unlike my twin sister, I was born without an amniotic sac. This frustrated the doctor to near madness because he insisted a baby could not survive the womb without one. We were tested and found to have different blood types, even dissimilar tissue and muscle fiber. It wasn't until we were 5 years old that my twin was diagnosed with muscular dystrophy, while I had incredibly strong, rejuvenating muscles.

Growing up was very lonely for me because I always felt like I didn't belong here. I didn't feel the unconditional love that I was used to. Earth just didn't feel like my home, nor did my parents or anyone—only my twin felt comfortable to me. As a child I always had problems with my lungs. I grew up having a lot of health problems and feeling depressed from many family issues. I knew since being a toddler that there were beings from other worlds. They visited me frequently and it is one of the few things I remember about my childhood. I also remember the nightmares and dreams that haunted me into my adulthood, stopping when I finally made peace with them in my late 40s.

My mother told me that I became a sleepwalker from the time I first began to walk. She never knew where she'd find me in the morning. Sometimes I was found sleeping on the front doorstep, in the yard somewhere, or just inside the front door. I frequently woke up having intense nosebleeds. My dreams were a mixture of night visitations from extraterrestrials (ETs), but my nightmares were another thing! They appeared to be military medical abductions (MILABS), where I was abruptly taken from my bed to a military hospital-like facility several floors below the surface. There I would be examined and tested like a lab rat. I would cry because I was so tired and afraid, and if I called out for my mother, I was always harshly reprimanded, "Do not speak unless spoken to. You answer when you are asked a question. Stop crying, or you will be punished." I look back now, realizing that the reason my childhood was such a blur was the result of military brainwashing and my parents telling me that my stories of visitations and abductions were just my imagination.

By age 14, the Military nightmares were replaced with other nightmares, usually of being immobilized and seeing my limp body lifted through the ominous night sky into some hovering object above, and then suddenly blacking out. The following morning I would awaken, confused and having a panic attack. My sleepwalking had increased significantly by then, as well.

*   *   *

One of my most memorable experience was when I was 16 years old, I awoke to find myself one block away from my house in the middle of the night in my baby-doll pajamas. Suddenly, I was aware of someone behind me. When I turned around, I saw a tall figure dressed in a dark hooded robe. Terrified, I ran at such a speed that I don't remember my feet touching the ground. It wasn't until I was 55 years old that I recalled that incident through hypnotic regression, and then refused to discuss it.

After graduating from high school, I ran away from home. I was 18 years old and very depressed. I felt very suicidal after finding out I was pregnant and my boyfriend insisted I get rid of the baby. So, I downed a large bottle of aspirins. I remember my nurse cousin telling me that overdosing on aspirins would cause one to hemorrhage internally. That is what happens all right, blood found a way out of every opening in my body. My eyes eventually went blind and I stumbled my way back to my bed, feeling grateful that I would be leaving this world. Well, that obviously wasn't meant to be, for I awoke the following morning in perfect condition as if I had been miraculously healed. "Oh God! Why didn't you let me die?" I cried out.

A month later, I got married. By the third month of pregnancy, I awakened, panicked from a horrifying dream, and I was hemorrhaging. I went to the hospital where the doctors told me that the fetus was gone, but the afterbirth was still intact. If that didn't play a trip on the head! Then I was told by another doctor a month later that I had an unusual hole in my uterus and I would be unable to have children.

One early morning in winter, I was driving to work and must have blacked out because I suddenly found myself just one block further down the road, yet it was an hour later. One year after that, I gave birth to my daughter via cesarean. Later on, I had another strange pregnancy and again the fetus was taken and the afterbirth perfectly in place. The very next pregnancy occurred after having a dream that I'd been in a round room where the walls, ceiling and floors seemed to glow white, and bright lights were shining in my face. I was told, "You will have a son, and he will do great things in the future to help save the planet Earth." I woke up to tell my husband that I was pregnant and he claimed there was no way. In fact, the entire pregnancy ended up with all kinds of complications; at four months I went into a coma from pneumonia, by the fifth month my water broke, but another miraculous healing occurred and I carried my son to eight months. The strange thing is that the doctors wanted back-up blood for me because of all the complications I was having and they told me, "You have an unusual antigen in your blood that requires the donor to have that same antigen or it will kill you. Unfortunately, there are only two people in the world we can find with that blood anomaly and we're unable to locate either of them." The doctors did a cesarean anyway, and I have my son. By age 24, I had a partial hysterectomy after receiving complications with yet another pregnancy.

By age 25, I was living near a 40-acre field that was behind us and I was continually having UFO experiences. I woke up frequently throughout the nights. Sometimes my husband would yell at me, "Why are you staring out of the window?" and I would say, "They are out there. Don't you hear them, the UFOs?" He was convinced I was mentally ill. One time, I felt an urgency to go to the drugstore 15 minutes before they closed. I can't even remember the excuse I made to leave, but I do remember that a few blocks from home my car was engulfed in a bright light coming from above. The next thing I remember is waking up the next morning with my husband already gone, the kids at the baby sitters and I was late for work. That night my husband insisted that I was having an affair. A few months later, I woke up predawn out in the 40-acre field. I ran back into my house and was again late for work. I found out later that an Air Force helicopter, tanks and men in silver protective suits with some equipment were in the field. They were about 50 feet from where I had awakened and near a large burn spot in the field where a UFO had landed. My UFO experiences continued, even after my divorce a few years later. I'm still having periodic dreams of having babies removed from me. What's interesting is that I frequently have a lot of pain in my left side. An ultrasound of my left side revealed an unusual growth in what appeared to be my fallopian tube. All I know is that I go through depressions with every dream that a baby is removed from me.

I was 29 years old and traveling when my lungs collapsed on me. I got a really bad cold right after my twin sister died. I had pin-point vision and I was in a lot of pain. I didn't want anybody helping me because I wanted to be with my twin sister. I woke up the next morning completely healed again. I had gone to the doctor before I left on the trip and he told me that I would not survive my lungs collapsing. When I returned, the doctor took x-rays of my lungs again.

When the doctor reviewed the new x-rays, he actually cried. He told me that I was basically dead before I left, but now I have lungs that look like a newborn's. There was no scar tissue from all of my lung problems or from my smoking at the time.

I found out a few years ago about cloning. My Beings showed me how they have taken DNA from my body and have made clones of me to keep organs available when I need healings. They explained that most ETs that come to Earth have a high suicide rate and they have made clones to take parts from when needed. These types of clones have no soul and are only used for parts. This all made sense to me as I began to think about all of the healings and replacement parts I have received. My Beings have always taught me that I am not my body. On one event, my Beings taught me this very topic by placing my soul into another body or what they call a "container." They would have me look into the mirror each time they changed my container and I saw that I was a completely different being each time, but it was still my soul. I told them, "Okay, I get it now, I want to go back into my own body." They will not allow me to forget this and they keep reminding me that I am not my body.

At the age of 40, while living in California, my doctor did a complete hysterectomy, removing both tubes and ovaries. Upon awakening, my doctor informed me that my left fallopian tube was the size of an extra large hot dog and they were running tests to see what caused the unusual size. Before I was released, the doctor told me that the tube was actually healthy. He also told me the consensus of the board members and experts who were called into the case all agreed I had had numerous tubular pregnancies.

In 1993, while walking across a street during work, I was struck by an El Camino and thrown over 30 feet high and 75 feet out into another street. I ended up with numerous broken bones, a mutilated bladder, 10 percent of my brain damaged from my head hitting the pavement, my face gouged with broken glass, my chin ripped off, my intestines knotted from impact and my legs were twisted and bent behind me. The doctors had to take out all of my intestines and re-string them. My strong muscles protected most of my bones, but the muscles themselves were severely damaged. My clavicle was shattered, my sciatic nerve was affected, my entire body was in shock from this accident. I was unable to go to the bathroom on my own because my bladder was destroyed from my bones going in and back out of it during the impact. The doctors didn't know how I survived this accident, they said I should have died just from toxic waste inside my body. Normally, bones will fuse themselves back together within a few weeks and begin healing, but my bones took eight weeks to begin fusing. I was told by my doctors that my bones are much lighter and less dense than normal. The doctors told me they had never seen anyone's tissue heal so fast, yet their bones healed so slowly.

Six surgeries later, I thought I was on the mend when I found out that my spine had been compressed and my brain continued to deteriorate. Within 10 months, I was equivalent to a 5th grader and unable to remember from one minute to the next. I had to learn all over again, how to complete sentences, using words beyond fifth grade level and to remember from one day to the next. My diet was a very important factor during this time and was filled with high protein and Vitamin B foods.

It took nearly five years to partially recover. With courage, I began doing something unexpected, I began exploring my memories of UFOs and ET abductions. I joined a group of "Experiencers" or those who had memories of UFOs and/or ET encounters. I had finally given up my fears to ask for a conscious encounter. Several months later (and three hard weeks of begging), I guaranteed them that I would not be judgmental or prejudiced, and I finally had my first conscious encounter. It was phenomenal and beyond all imagination. I was lying in my bed, meditating and demanding an encounter. Suddenly, a

brown being with very wrinkly skin, much like that of an elephant, appeared beside my bed. His body was very lean and muscular, its arms long with three rolled-up fingers. He had an over-sized head with a strange indentation in the middle of the back of his head. What was most unexpected was the feeling of immense, unconditional love coming from this being. It was greater than any love I had ever experienced on Earth. The love it gave to me felt beyond the love of a mother, and more like the love of God itself. I willingly gave the love back, telling him how beautiful he was to me, despite how un-human it looked. Very humbly, the being lowered his golden eyes which had vertical pupils. I telepathically asked if I could hold his hand and feel his skin. He then unrolled his three fingers, which had suction cups on the ends, and allowed me to feel his unbelievable skin. He was family in one way or another.

This was the start of my adventure of learning who I was and why I was here on Earth. It was the start of meeting so many other beings from other worlds and other dimensions. A part of my life that would forever humble me and awaken me.

I was still having trouble with my memory after my accident, but I would come home around noon and work on a movie script. Every day I had to re-read the script before I began again. I was working on the computer when I heard, *"Vroomp, vroomp, vroomp"* just above the house. It sounded similar to helicopter blades rotating. I got up and walked over to the window. Just as I began to look outside, I felt I could hardly stand. I felt drugged and groggy and I collapsed. The next thing I remember was seeing what appeared to be men in the house. The men were telling me to take off my clothes from the waist down, so I did. Then I remember waking up consciously and I saw all of these men wearing very dark suits, sunglasses and hats. Their speech was high-pitched, like putting a normal record on high-speed. I remember saying to myself, "Now my stomach doesn't hurt." I raised my head to look at these men and I heard the sound of our garage door opening. I felt relieved that my then husband would come and save me. I went unconscious again and later woke up abruptly, totally alert and with no drugged sensation. I had no clothes on from my waist down. I had a lump with dried blood on the back of my head and dried blood in my belly button. Later on, I had an aneurysm, caused by the unknown impact to my head, which caused a lump. When I washed my belly button out, I noticed a type of mole inside. I was told that this was how the secret government drugs people, through the belly button, under a nail or somewhere else that is hard to detect. I guess this is why I commented earlier about my stomach hurting.

About a week later, someone had broken into my house. The rear door was open, papers were thrown about and some papers were missing. Another time, I came home and saw a strange-looking white van parked at my house. I remember that the name of the "company" shown on the truck did not make sense to me, like it did not belong in the neighborhood. I could see the back door was open and I sensed that the people involved jumped over the back wall when I drove up. When I got inside I realized the computer had been totally erased. I took the computer in to get repaired and I was told that nothing could be recovered. I had over a thousand documents on that computer about the secret government's operations and population control. I had a feeling that they were drugging me because I knew something subconsciously and they wanted that information. My beings explained to me how, when they teach me things, they will then block my memory of it until the right time comes, so there is no way anyone can access the information. My Beings told me that the Illuminati, or the secret government, has been doing time-travel for decades now. And they know the future. They know which people are significant in the earth changes. I have been a target of their energy attacks many times. Once I felt like my heart was going to blow up and another time I felt it was going to implode. I could feel this energy source coming into my body and it also felt as if someone was remote-viewing me. This remote viewing energy was like an invisible cord attaching itself to me. I asked my Beings for help and they told me to follow the cord back to its source. Then they told me to envelop the cord in white light and send unconditional love through it. I did this and instantly it stopped.

In 1997 I developed a tumor in my brain. This was considered a secondary trauma to my brain after being hit by the car. That was the hardest part of healing and because I did not receiving help from my Beings. They reminded me that it was not a life or death situation and they wanted me to learn to heal myself. My Beings would tell me to find natural means to heal. I found and read a book about how to heal your brain through your diet. This helped me remember how to do things again. This tumor gave me such severe headaches to the point where I couldn't keep food down.

I drove out somewhere to attempt conscious contact with my ETs because I wanted to say goodbye to them. I planned on leaving this world by my own doing. On the third night, my Beings showed up. It was about 1 AM and my Beings were in the sky in a "V" formation. The lights on the ships were oscillating in an orange and green or blue colors. One of the ships then pulled away from the formation and came down and landed. The ship was pewter in color and it opened up like the hatchback of a car, without the hydraulic bars. Female ETs came out of the doorway, all wearing similar uniforms or body suits. They each had brown hair and gold or light hazel eyes. Most of their uniforms were royal blue with a red yoke, but the leader wore a red uniform with a royal blue yoke. I remember thinking to myself how perfect their bodies were and how I wish I could look like that. The one I believed was their leader said telepathically to me, "It is because we only eat that which grows naturally from the soil, we eat nothing but live foods." Next, they took me to their medical mothership where they were healing humans of diseases. These humans were Starbeings that volunteered to come to Earth and had missions to do. It was their job to heal these human "star beings" when they became ill. Once on the ship, I was greeted by this very gorgeous, tall man with wavy, blond hair and bright blue eyes. He name was Archangel Michael and he wore a multi-colored robe. He showed me one facility where there were a bunch of women lying on tables. I asked what were they doing to these women. I was told to watch and learn. I saw these gray-colored "bras" being placed over the women's chests. I watched one woman awaken and she began to feel her breasts and she claimed that the ETs healed her of breast cancer. They were using frequency machines that would automatically pick up the frequency pattern of the person lying on the table. Then the machine would adjust the frequency of the person, healing them of whatever ailment they had. Then I climbed in this container they showed me. It was round and felt like being in a big can. I could feel this sensation of my head being separated and a very strong vibration. I saw my body go into billions and billions of particles and then they came back together again.

After coming back from this encounter, I knew I was healed. There was a burning sensation on my back that was also moist to the touch. Later that day, a friend of mine took out a magnifying glass to look at my back. They found a piece of skin missing from my back that was in the exact shape of a triangle. Sixty-nine hours after the encounter, another friend used a black light on me to see if there was any remaining substance on my back. My friend found a slight green light illuminating were the triangle was. My eyes had been corrected after this healing as well. The doctor asked me, "Who prescribed these glasses to you? You have 20/20 vision." I told him that his office did. All of my friends also noticed that I was remembering things all of a sudden—my memories came back.

In 1997, I was taken to a planet with two moons. I was asleep in bed and I felt a tap on my ankle. I realized later on that this tap was the ET's signal to me that it was time to go with them. The next thing I knew, I was consciously aware of being on another planet. Everything was twilight, not totally dark. The ground was a light-colored sand and I saw exotic plants growing on top of nearby mounds. What was so interesting to me was the way the moonlight shined on these plants. They seemed to be a deep green and were similar to a cycad, but with Lace-type leaves. They had long stalks and were all different heights. They were gorgeous plants. What I really remember were the two golden moons, or perhaps they were distant suns. At arm's length, these moons were about a fist apart and were the size of a dime. I believe the significance of this event was to tell me that I am from afar.

I recall being on a hovercraft over some planet. I was hovering over some tall, golden grass when my Beings telepathically decided to remind me why I was on Earth. They told me that in order to move into the new world, Humanity must give up greed, judgment and prejudice by looking beyond the physical, and they must start seeing the Creator in each and every being.

Once my beings taught me how to breathe underwater. They had me remember where my "other lungs" were. I remember knowing that they were located on my head somewhere. I was breathing without my mouth or nose, which my Beings closed off from my using them.

I woke up one time with these little rows of dots on my forehead. It must have been a head band where pointed objects touched my skin. I was later told by my beings that I was being downloaded with information. This type of experience happened frequently.

One night in 1999, I woke up and saw four beings surrounding my bed. All four of them were a grayish-white color, as if their skin had not seen the sun for ages. They had no hair and stood about 5 feet tall. They had beady, black eyes and a very square jaw line. The clothing they wore was human looking. I couldn't move as they were showing me a movie in my head of their arrival to Earth. Their planet had been destroyed and they came to Earth because it was the closest planet that supported their life requirements. They continued to tell me that the people on the planet began hunting them like wild animals because they were so different looking. So they created their own inner-Earth sanctuary where they would survive. They explained to me that when they are in the sun and their bodies perspire, the fumes are toxic to humans and can even kill them. At night time they shape-shift into handsome humans and then go out into town;

it looked like a country-western town where the roads were all dirt. They would go to the bars, pick up women and later impregnate them. They explained to me the reason they did this was for their survival, because their offspring would not poison humans when they perspired. Their Hybrid children were also Human-looking enough to live among them without being hunted.

After that encounter, I took a trip to Machu Pichu. When I arrived, I instantly recognized the village as the same village I saw in the "movie" that the four beings were showing me. This is where they are from—inner-Earth. I noticed some of the children in this town were different and I could sense that they were Hybrids. These four beings visited me because they knew that I was coming to their area. They wanted me to convince the people of this town to stop hunting them, that they were not wild animals. They had no other place to live and just wanted to live in peace underground. They meant humanity no harm, but wanted the hunting to stop. They are benevolent beings and only came to Earth in order to survive. Being born on the planet does not mean you own the planet. Many humans are the creations of other ET races that have also come to the planet long ago, and this planet does not belong to any one species.

I began making sculptures of other-worldly beings—extraterrestrials—back in 2003, while taking a pottery class at a nearby community college. The class had been overbooked, and while waiting endlessly for my turn on one of four pottery wheels, I found myself making an alien-hybrid baby from memory. What I didn't realize then was that this was the beginning of a new adventure in communicating with ETs, my personal Guides, my Higher Self and Masters of the Universe.

I became obsessed with sculpturing these ETs that I started having telepathic communication with these Beings. They started telling me to correct the nose, the ears or the shape of the head as I was sculpturing. Sometimes I would even go into a trance while sculpting an ET being and come out of it when I was finished. I had no clue who they were or what they were. I would see these ETs in my third eye and I would often tell them to show me their profile. Sometimes their names were spelled out in my head, other times the ETs would tell me, "Those who know us will tell you who we are."

After I started making these sculptures, I was told by my Beings to go out and sell them. My Beings also told me that those who resonate with a certain

ET will find their sculpture and find me. These sculptures are infused with the ET energy of the being sculptured and will help in the person's awakening. This is why people will resonate to specific ones. Within just a few years, I was selling my sculptures at conferences while continuing to experience even greater lessons and phenomena than I had ever imagined. I even had an 8-year-old boy whom I met at one conference tell me the name of one of the sculptures. He even provided me with a sample of their spoken language.

Once, I saw a gorgeous picture of a Reptilian and I wanted to sculpture it badly. As I began, my Beings telepathically told me, "NO! Not that one." I told them that I really wanted to create one on my own, without their help, because I wanted to know that I had the artistic skills. They explained to me that the being I was making was a negative being and they would not allow it to be created. I sculpted it anyway and my Beings remained quiet. The sculpture turned out so perfect, I was now very confident in my abilities. I set the sculpture on the counter and turned to go get something. As I walked away, I heard the sculpture being moved. I turned around and watched as my Reptilian sculpture flew across the countertop into the air, and crash-land on the floor, completely smashing it. My Beings telepathically told me, "You agreed before you came here that you would help create these sculptures to help awaken people. These sculptures hold the frequencies of the ET created in order to help people see their truth and only those meant to have them will find you."

I have had many, many people contact me later on, telling me of their own personal encounters and experiences with these sculptures. They range from strange, vivid dreams to teachings, conscious contact and being awakened to their own true identities. The sculptures are alive and they carry their own consciousness. For example, in 2008, Mother Mary visited me to explain and verify that she puts her very own energy in the plaque I do known as the "Blue Lady." After this encounter, my psychic abilities increase significantly.

I was also taught by my Beings to look for characteristics of the ETs in the people that I meet. My Beings told me that there are certain traits that can be seen in people that signify their ET origins. I have learned about so many of these characteristics from all of the sculptures and ETs I have worked with. Then I began to receive invitations to do speaking engagements. People wanted to hear about my lifetime experiences of alien abductions, missing pregnancies, feelings of victimhood, followed by miraculous healings and incredible teachings that had forever changed my life. Yet the greatest lesson of all was the *truth* of who I was, why I am here on Earth, and about a mission I was to complete.

In early 2006, I woke up in the middle of the night to go to the bathroom. It was really dark in the bedroom, but there was a sliver of light coming in from the windows and the dim radio light. I saw a being standing right next to the bed. I saw another being looking at carvings on the fireplace ledge. Another being was standing in front of the radio, I could see his body was muscular. I walked around this being to go to the bathroom. I saw their heads were football-shaped, their eyes were large, they had a couple of antennas on top of their heads and thick "whiskers" on their chins. Once in the bathrom, I threw cold water on my face. When I walked back into the bedroom, the beings were still there. I knew they purposefully wanted me to see them. I jumped in the bed and covered my head with the covers. Usually when beings come to me and

communicate with me telepathically, I can feel their unconditional love. These beings were not communicating with me and I couldn't feel their love because of that. I telepathically told them if they wanted to communicate with me, go ahead. Next thing I knew, I was unconscious. One of my good friends has seen this same being face to face and confirmed this encounter for me. Later on, I found out that these beings are called the "Ant People." I later sculptured one of these beings and a known book author told me that he knew of these Ant People. The Hopi Nation know of them as well.

Telepathically, the Ant People told me that in the end of the old world and at the beginning of the new world, they will bring those that are meant to survive the catastrophic events to the inner-Earth. I asked my own Beings to show me what their inner-Earth city looked like, to get some validation on my encounter. That very night my Beings showed me the Ant People's home inside inner-Earth. They are incredibly clean and they dug the den and tunnels them-selves. They are more insectoid, but are very muscular. They have four serrated appendages, stronger than elephant tusks, on their hands that they use to dig with. I saw storage bins where they were storing food, water and other necessities. I asked my Beings how the Ant People would know which Humans to bring down for survival. They told me by using their antennas, they will pick up the frequency of the Human each one is meant to save, find him/her and bring them to inner-Earth. They further explained to me that this frequency is the person's soul frequency and does not change at the core, it is who you are.

I have been taken aboard medical motherships and saved from death many, many times. Mostly, I recall seeing Ashtar in these ships as I am being healed for one thing or another. Sometimes it is a completely different species that I see. My Beings will not intervene unless my life is threatened. When I was hit by that car while walking in the pedestrian zone, my Beings would not heal my body, they allowed my body to heal naturally.

They helped me heal after I received the lump on the back of my head that caused an aneurysm. I was told that it was an injection from the secret government and it was meant to cause an aneurysm. I experienced vomiting from the severe pain. At this time, I remembered that I was given implants from my Beings and they told me to call them if I ever needed them. So, while I was lying on my bed, I began yelling at them to come heal me if they wanted me to finish my mission here on Earth. Instantly, I was unconscious and woke up almost an hour later, completely healed from the aneurysm.

In 2006 I was in Oaxaca, Mexico. I get sick so easily and I am allergic to any type of bites. I had sciatic nerve damage before this trip and I could not sleep on a hard surface. I could not sleep in any one position for more that a couple of hours either. We were staying in a hotel that used to be an old Mexican jail. I told my Beings that I was done, I was ready to go, I have done what they wanted me to do and made all of their ET sculptures. I asked them, "Haven't I done all that I can and spoken my truth?" I was then met by the "Council of 5." I saw a male figure in the etheric realm, he looked very familiar. He had white hair in a crewcut hairstyle, a goatee and piercing blue eyes. Next to him was a female, obviously a Hybrid being. They were both wearing clothing made of hemp. They told me, "You cannot die. Why do you think we have healed you and why you have survived all of these times you should have been dead?" Then I remembered a car accident that I should have died in. My Beings made my car invisible or placed it in another dimension, so that I would pass through a semi truck. I don't know which guides or which ETs help me, I just know they are always there.

In the end of 2007, I had a virus attack my heart for the second time. Doctors say that people don't usually survive the first virus to the heart. I felt like I was on the edge of my life. I was in the tub full of cold water and I went into the etheric realm where I met a bunch of my guides and masters. We met inside a building similar to a South American Zigurat. When I came back from that meeting, I began to heal.

My Guides once showed me the New Earth. It was the most pristine planet, as if it was brand new. It showed no signs of destruction, or scarring by Humans. The air smelled so wonderful and the sky was just beautiful. Even the houses were very pleasant. They were made of the Earth, not like chucks of adobe, but they were domed-shaped and blended in with the Earth. My guides told me while watching this scene, "This is the new Earth, and this is where you will go." I told them that I wanted to go on my ship. They replied, "This is the place where those who have ascended will go. There will be no negative emotions such as anger, greed, fear and control. Everything will be made of natural, biodegradable materials."

My Galactic Family and Masters told me that I needed to teach others how to find their own truths. By sharing my story, I hope I am able to help *you* awaken to *your own* truth, not mine and not anyone else's, how to be in charge of your own life, realize how all beings throughout the Universe are connected to the same Source/Creator-God, and why our Galactic Family communicates with us as a collective. It's time you know why *you* are here and what *your* true purpose on planet Earth is. *You* matter so much!

Books that were significant to me:
The Only Planet of Choice by Phyllis Schlemmer
Voyagers and *Voyagers II* by Anna Hayes.

You may contact me at: *cynthiacrawford@msn.com*
My website: http://etsculptor.com

Laselena

I am an incarnate, not a Hybrid. I named myself Laselena, meaning "Leaf of the Stars," because I feel so close to the trees and I know that I am not from here. The name came from Tolkien Elvish, and is the name that I feel describes my soul the best. One can recognize us who incarnated not by how we look, but by the feeling around us. People feel relaxed, trusting and open to express themselves around us. Most of us here on Earth are born with almond-shaped eyes, of which the sides slant slightly upwards to the side of the head. There are about 50 of us on Earth, all over the planet. I can feel them mostly in California and the Far East, so I am trying to find them. We don't like to be recognized here on Earth because there are those who try to trace our energy and thought forms back to our home world, and we don't want them to have that information. Our original home world is now inhabited by someone else; we are renegades living among the Pleiadians.

We don't name ourselves or our planets, we simply are. We would be considered Pleiadian, but we are recognized by our energy patterns, which are unique to every being, as with any species. The stripes in our energy field is our name. Stripes are acquired from experiences each soul goes through. Trying to describe who we are is like trying to draw a third-dimensional object on a piece of paper. If I had an infinite number of drawings, it would still not be suitable to describe us. One's mindset, life perspectives, thoughts and emotions all show in their energy field, unless one is totally neutral. A being can only be neutral if they have complete knowledge of everything. You can see this energy in everything, conscious or not.

We have about 500,000 beings on our home world. We do have alliances with other species, mainly the Pleiadians, and we consider ourselves part of the Galactic Federation. Our race is a Hybrid one itself. We have some Andromedan DNA from a "Human" type race there and ones that look more like we do. Their eyes are blue and almost as big as the Grays', very pointy chin, hardly any nose and their skin is white. We are usually in a higher form and not visible on our physical home planet. However, some decide to incarnate into a physical form; and when we do, our form is similar to humans, but a flexible look. I think Tolkien knew my people because he describes us to a "T" and our planet looks

 almost exactly like Lothlorien. We are tall and thin, but we have more strength than we appear to have. We look like Elves in physical form. Our people's ears are somewhat pointed as it shows in those movies, but smaller. It is even a trait we have incarnated into a Human body. I have really small ears that go out at a unique

angle, and I have really good hearing. Our eyes are really big, similar to a human's shape, but smaller than the Grays'. Our heads are oval-shaped and larger than humans. When we are not incarnated on Earth, we are about 7 to 8 feet tall, have small noses, thin lips and a pointy jaw. We tend to be on the quiet side, but we are not afraid of partying. We don't sit in the corner at parties, we dance on the table, so everyone can be entertained as they laugh at us, we are jokesters. We speak telepathically and we travel by thought. We feel nothing except God, Love and Peace. Our food is the light. We have an amazing ability to understand anything we focus on. We absorb information fully and retain it. For example; whenever we need information about something, we just tap into that dimension and get it. The information is available to anyone at all times, you just need to know how to listen. It is a skill to relearn, you imagine what something could be and then you use your intuition for the rest. Whatever you see, ask if it is correct; sometimes the image will change in your mind, or you will get a "yes" in your gut feeling. You must relearn to feel and trust your intuition.

We use a planet that we're living on with the Pleiadians for contact experiences only. Some beings, when they visit us, feel more comfortable communicating with a physical form. Our diplomats usually go into physical form to communicate with other beings. Others chose to be guides and they travel to other places. For example, I have 10 guides with me here in ethereal form, to remain inconspicuous. On Earth, we only incarnate as Human. Our people will take a "vacation" and lower their vibration to the fourth or fifth dimension to experience things and get a different perspective. It is actually difficult for us to stay in one dimension. I am always shifting between the dimensions, even now. It is very difficult for me to be in physical form.

The only way we know to speak is through thought-form, telepathically. When we come in contact with another species, we will understand their thought forms as they speak, but then we have to learn how to use their language to speak back to them. Beings of all kinds have an instant trust in our people, even us incarnate on Earth. Because of this trust, we can place our finger on the being's forehead and send images through to them. We prefer this way of communication.

There is no such thing as ownership with our people. Humans have an instinct of ownership from birth, but even as an incarnate here, I don't feel ownership. So this creates problems for us in that we are not good about "respecting" other people's boundaries and items of ownership. It is just something that doesn't make sense to us. I am always wanting to meet more people who are like-minded in this way.

We cannot be isolated to the Pleiades, because there are over 400 stars in this system. We have two equal-sized stars that are just far enough from each other that they don't sap off of each other. We have a larger planet that circles around both of these stars. This is a planet in another system, very close to only one star. This planet comes so close to one of the stars while orbiting that they pull on each other's gravity and the orbit is erratic. It is just close enough that we are comfortable and it does not cause us damage. We do have gravity, but it is not as strong as Earth's. Our home planet is slowly dying, but it is still warm. Our water is still very much alive in our rivers and streams. Since the core of our planet is cooling, there hasn't been any new formations on the planet for a while. We have hills, but it is not rocky and mountainous.

We are peace loving and we don't get involved in wars. If someone attacks us, we do not run or fight back, we just protect ourselves by using a type of shielding. We live among nature. The places we move to have mostly vegetation and we like it that way. We find that vegetation is always very harmonious. It is hard to fight with a plant. The plants on our world actually cradle us like we are their children and it was not uncommon to fall in love with a tree or plant, similar to how Humans fall in love with a place or an idea. The plant life are probably the wisest beings on our planet. They all have their own energy and personalities, but they are all similar. They have a consciousness and are very much alive. They are huge in size and more observant than anything else.

When a traveler comes to our planet, they will not see much besides the plants and trees. Our trees look similar to the California Redwood, except a little grayer in color and 100 times bigger. A lot of our plants came from other planets and only grow in certain areas. The ground color in the forest is almost black, but everywhere else, it is a brownish, yellow, red all mixed together. That is where our shrubs are located. A being of a higher vibration would see us, but we would look something like heat and very bright light. If someone were sensitive to energy, they could feel us, since our energy is strong. Someone in the third dimension that was not sensitive would not see anything. There is no need for religion or currency. We have no need for technology, nor do we have buildings. We live basically the way the Hippie movement wanted to. We are free and loving. We actually appreciate the practicality of the Human mind. We tried to copy one of the sea ships during the time of Atlantis. We did well with the design, but we couldn't stand having to hurt a tree in order to make it, so we never made another one.

As I recall these memories, I realized an event that left me disgusted by the Insectoid species. What happened is that some Insectoid species found our planet and saw all the food there, which was our plants. They started to eat away at our forests and we were very upset. They couldn't see us and didn't know that we were there. I do not feel this way about all Insectoids, it is just a personal "grudge" I have about that one particular event. It was a very traumatic event for us. Imagine having your mother eaten from the inside out.

I was born from my mother by C-section because my brother was going to be born breached, so I was, too. My mother is ET as well, she just doesn't know it. We are both super sensitive to anesthetic. My mom isn't meant to know her identity this lifetime, but she came here as a general helper, that is why she is a nurse. So I am a Starseed, an ET soul in a Human body. The term Starseed has another important meaning for me because our people birth stars. I remember taking astronomy and I would always skip over the Earth bit and go right to the "Star Classification" information. I wanted to be an astrophysicist when I was in college. However, I am over-aware of the ethereal world and this led to medical problems in college because I would often go out-of-body. You are wherever your mind is. Very few people are in their bodies and, if they are, I feel bad for them.

*   *   *

Since I was the age of 2, I have had ethereal communication with my people in one form or another. I would randomly cry or laugh when I was a baby, and now I know it was during my communication with my people. When I was a little older, I didn't have any friends that were human. I would just sit and talk to my people, even play games with them. Our communication was out loud as well as telepathic. They could read my thoughts and always knew what I was doing or thinking. I always have communication with my people even now. It is similar to asking a question and having an image just pop into your mind. I focus in on their dimension and I can see them—my guides that came with me.

One experience I had was when my fiancé and I were together and we could feel each other's wings, then suddenly we were back in the past. He is an incarnate Reptilian Hybrid and has scaly, ethereal wings. Although he is from my home galaxy/"quadrant"/school. School means that we were in the same lesson at the same time. We have been together for a very long time and through many lifetimes. We originally met while we were both working in a similar star system. His race of Reptilians are mediators and consider themselves "knights in shining armor," but are always helping other races. In his race's organization, he is of a high ranking. I believe his incarnation on Earth was a result of rape between his "mother" and the negative race of Reptilians who are on Earth now. He volunteered to incarnate into that baby's body because he is gifted at controlling urges and he knew urges would result from the negative Reptilian DNA. He lived through a devastating childhood, but is today the most loving man I have ever met.

I recalled a life during the times of Lemuria, where I mated with a Reptilian being. It was during the bombing of Lemuria and mud huts were flying everywhere. We were together during the bombing and he was very loving towards me. He took me up on a ship and took care of me for the 10 and a half months I was pregnant. We had a Hybrid son together and when I died about five years later, my son lived on.

My dad just got out of the Army and was an engineer in the 1970s. He was invited to a special event and accidentally walked into the wrong room. He walked into a meeting where they were discussing how to create a black hole outside of a spacecraft, so it would pull it faster. The guards realized he was not supposed to be there and eventually escorted him out. If we incorporate spirituality into science, we wouldn't even need a spacecraft. Ships are for the physical plane.

I have my own stories and I never really decided whether they were true or not. My father had his own stories as well. Then, Doreen Virtue did her own study on what she calls "Star People." Virtue, herself, is an incarnated Angel from the 11th dimension. I read her book called *Earth Angels*, and it talks about the kinds of souls that are incarnated on Earth right now. Someone told me I was a "Rainbow Child" and I didn't know what that meant until I read her book. In *Earth Angels,* it says the auras of Star People are rainbow rays emanating from their skin. I instantly recognized that and I knew what it meant. I looked at my aura and it was not like that, so I said, "Okay, I am not one of those then." I later came to understand that Doreen Virtue is still doing her research and that she doesn't know everything that is out there. She hasn't found all of the resources yet, so there is good reason to use discernment when researching the information in any book.

I watched the movie *What the Bleep Do We Know?* and they stated that the Human mind perceives only what it wants to see. I knew this was true when I heard it. So I decided to go outside, look at the sky and see what was really there. I started to feel all of these energies and started to feel overwhelmed. Then I asked my MUFON friend about this experience and started to research things, such as the man who fought the Gray ETs in Mexico, and Valiant Thor, an ET from Venus. These stories struck me as true. Then, suddenly one night, it just came to me "The Elves = The Pleiadians." That was just two weeks ago, but I have always had these memories of my home world and of my past lives. I followed the *Lord of the Rings* movies and it made me sad, I just wanted to go home.

My mission is to help heal people and to help those who ask for help. I can't actually heal people, they have to heal themselves. People not only have to be accepting of the healing, but also they have to continue what I have done for them. It is not until the unconscious, subconscious and conscious mind agree that we can feel complete union and do whatever we want. At that point, the law of attraction is instantaneous.

I am a musician. I have been one ever since I can remember and I have always been attracted to instruments. Music comes naturally to me, it is like a gift or from an implant that was given to me as a tool to use. When I play my music, colors surround me and heal me. It also affects those that are nearby. I also have a strong affinity for colors, like color therapy. I do energy therapy for chakras, and I help people visualize. I practice my color music for personal groups, it is much stronger that way and those who need it come to me.

I have been on Earth ever since Humans have been here. The reason was to see how much we could learn on this plane of existence. Earth is of a low vibration, and we know that the lower the vibration, the more we learn. I remember how difficult is was in the beginning, trying to get an entirely new genetically engineered species off the ground and have successful incarnations. We had to work on this and I was one of the volunteers. We were a big group of beings that volunteered for this project, not just our species, but many. There is an influence on Earth of basically every race that is out there (in the Universe). I was in Atlantis and Lemuria before Sanskrit was invented. I was in Egypt as a high priestess for several lives. I was actually a double spy during the "Cold War" in my last life before now. I am here on Earth not only as a teacher, but also a connector, someone who brings people together. I feel this is why I have such good memories. I am gathering the 50-plus people that are from my home world. They are located around Earth, except China, eastern Russia and Singapore. A lot of us are located in Switzerland (the neutral country, of course), and also the USA, since it is a strong, powerful country. We want to go to China, but it will be rough because of the situation there. Our people have no tolerance of not being able to know what we want to learn. For example, in China they have restrictions on the Internet, allowing only limited research and knowledge. The Internet is an integral part of life for us and that would cause us great hardship.

Spiritually, I believe in the unity of all living things. Together we make up Unity or God. And love is the ultimate power. In order to reach any kind of harmony, one first has to love thyself. We are all reaching toward personal goals whose levels are infinite, and therefore irrelevant. What people call God is Love. Love is the type of power that makes you feel stronger, it is also electricity, it is also matter. It is energy and power within itself. Notice that when you feel hatred, or the absence of love, that lights flicker. If my people had a name they call God, it would be "Universe." It is too beautiful to put into words.

Books that are significant to me:
The Kryon series of books by Lee Carol.
Earth Angels by Doreen Virtue
Chinese Astrology and Palmistry books

Websites that are great to research:
Google Images and YouTube (use much discretion)—just type your research topic in the search line.

You may contact me at: *laselena@gmail.com*, or my cell phone (520)979-2531

Shenai

My people are called the Annunaki. We are very slender and we range in height anywhere from 13 feet to 30 feet. Our eyes are dark brown to black and we have no hair. Our skin is off-white in color and our heads are round, but elongated in the back (represented by the Egyptian Goddess Nefertiti). Our enlarged brains support the brain power we require to fire up the 24 strands of our DNA, and also opens many abilities to us, similar to those Christ has. Some of us have two fingers while others have three. We have ears, a nose and a mouth, all similar to a human, but very small compared to our heads.

Our people, the Annunaki, are a genetic mix of Human and the Dog, Lion and/or Cat Beings. For example; the Egyptian God Thoth is a Dog-Human Hybrid and the Egyptian Goddess Sekhmet is a Lion-Human Hybrid. There are other species that are considered Annunaki as well. My Star mother looks more like the original Annunaki species, similar to Nefertiti. Although I do not fully recall my mother, I know she is of royal blood.

My people have yet to reveal to me my Annunaki name. I am aware that there were safe-guards put into place while I am here on Earth. Not revealing certain information to me is one way my people keep me safe and "under wraps." I know I will receive the information when it becomes appropriate. At this time, they are allowing me to have more understanding of my mission, and I am focusing on that. I lead spiritual groups and UFO groups as a part of this mission.

When I started awakening to this information about who I am and all of these memories I was recalling, I actually questioned myself, wondering if somehow I was making it all up. I have assured myself over the years that all of this knowledge is true and very real, for it comes from the super-consciousness.

*   *   *

I incarnated by way of birth canal and had an Earth mother and father. They are no longer on the planet, so I have my ET mother that communicates with me often. I am not a Hybrid, but I am from an ET species and I remember coming to Earth on my own free will.

I am part of the royal family from the Sirius star system and also from the planet-ship called Nibiru. Each exists in the sixth-dimensional reality; however, they are multi-dimensional up to 10-D.

Sirius A is where the Dog Beings live and Sirius B is where the Lion and Cat Beings live. Each species has males and females of its own kind. The old saying, "Fight like cats and dogs" originated from the Sirius star system. My father, Anu, is half Lion and half Human. Anu has the ability to shape-shift his form and this is why he looks and appears differently to many people. For me, Anu is approximately 22 feet tall, has a huge golden mane, lion paws, a tail and walks bipedal. He is always loving, always helpful, always comforting and never negative. Both species of Dog and Lion beings eventually migrated onto Sirius C, which is a very small planet.

I was brought to Nibiru with my entire family after only a couple of incarnations on Sirius. Nibiru is a planetary ship created and controlled by my people, the Annunaki. There are 200 to 300 different intelligent species that live inside Nibiru along with us. When we travel to Nibiru, we enter through a portal that exists on the inside of the planet where we live. Within Nibiru is a binary sun system, so it is never dark. Nibiru is still in orbit around Earth's sun and is coming around again, and it is getting close.

When I first landed on Nibiru, I landed in the desert area. It is three times the size of Earth and has every type of climate and tundra you can imagine. I saw three types of animals that look similar to a camel. I began to shave his "muzzle" and I asked the three Ambassadors who were standing there why I was doing this. They told me because I took care of all of the animals on the planet, I also genetically engineered animals on Nibiru. (In my current life, I had been a dog groomer for 34 years. I have an infinity for dogs and cats.) My job was genetic engineering and my father taught me this science. My other job was taking care of the animals on Nibiru, so I understand the animals here on Earth as well. These Ambassadors and I got on the camels and walked to the city. Our cities are all crystal cities, that is the architecture of the entire planet.

There are thousands upon thousands of see-through crystals. There is also much marble. I have been to the Crystal cities under the ocean as well as inside Mother Earth.

We have a language that is called the Annunaki language. I sometimes wake up speaking my language, although I do not know what I am saying. I speak this language with a friend of mine who understands what we are saying. It is a universal language and, at a future time, we will all begin to speak this language.

We travel by way of portals, which are also referred to as Stargates. We know how to create these portals and they can even be created in your home.

Clothing and uniforms vary greatly with our people. My mother wears a tight-fitting uniform and my father is just a big Cat and prefers not to wear any clothing.

Love is our religion, unconditional love towards all races is what we live by. We have alliances with the Pleiades, Orion, Arcturus, Andromedans, and many others. On Nibiru alone, we have made alliances with the hundreds of different species living there. There are as many names for each alliance as there are alliances themselves, to include The Nibiruan Council, The Council of Nine, and many, many others.

The weather on Nibiru is controlled by the Annunaki. Although it varies, Nibiru does not have the extreme cold nor hot temperatures. Our skies are usually blue and purple hues, and one cannot see the stars from living inside Nibiru.

Our technology amongst the species varies as well. We are very technologically advanced; however, when we need something, we simply visualize it and it materializes. Anything from housing, food and clothing, we have mastered physical manifestation.

My brothers Enki and Enlil are the sons of God Anu. Anu sent both his sons to Earth to inhabit and take control over the Milky Way Galaxy. This was Anu's gift to his two sons. We came to Earth by using a portal on Lemuria and Sumer, at the time. Both Enki and Enlil began genetically creating a worker race of beings on Earth. This is the reason Humans were created. Anu sent me to Earth with my two brothers and it was my job to mix the blood and DNA to create a working-class Humanoid. I brought what people call the "Bengal" and

"Siberian" tigers with me from Nibiru. We used to ride on the backs of the Bengal tigers. I have a Bengal tiger spirit animal, who is always beside me, her name is Sheena. Sheena is my close friend and she exists on the etheric level. Sometimes when I am sleeping, I can hear her purring. My father Anu and my mother stayed behind on Nibiru; however, they visit back and forth as they please.

In the late '80s, I was having communication with the Ascended Masters, such as Melchizedek, Yogananda, Sananda, Maitreya, Maka, St. Germain and others. The being known as Christ is from the Pleiades, and while on Earth, he was under the Order of Melchizedek. Many Ascended Masters incarnated on Earth, but many did not. Maka is actually an ET.

After reading the book *We Are the Nibiruans* in 1996, it really "struck a note" with me, and I began to experience ET contact. The first contact I had was with the Zeta Reticuli beings and I welcomed their contact. These Zeta beings came to take and use my DNA. I gave them two Hybrid children for their "cause." I had given permission for them to do this from the beginning. The Hybrid babies were incubated in my body for three months, then the Zeta beings took them out of me. After those two, I told the Zetas, "No more DNA from me," and they complied. I have not seen my Hybrid children nor the Zeta beings since then. I didn't ask to see my children because I knew they did this just to have my DNA. I also don't feel a need to see them, since I am being visited by so many types of ET beings.

These Zeta beings were kinder with more feeling than the other, similar ones. The Zeta were small, with big "buggy" eyes, and they were even playful with me. I would catch them peeking around the corner at me, and I would tell them to come on out, I was not afraid of them. They seemed to have more emotion than the other, colder ones. Sometimes as I would wake up, I could see the Zeta beings leaving. This happened during my sleep-time and I don't remember a lot of it. Sometimes I would wake up and notice two or three needle marks on my stomach, near my belly button. I knew then that I had been visited by the Zeta beings. I had a friend take a "black light" to my hands and could tell that my hands had been worked on. Using this black light, we found "spots" on my neck and arms that are more of a blue color than the rest of my body.

*   *   *

My mission when I first arrived on Earth was to monitor the two boys, Enki and Enlil, from fighting. However, that was something I never accomplished. They both have an aspect of their souls on Earth today, and I am still trying to get them together. My mission now is to gather and bring together Starseeds. I wasn't aware that I was doing this before, but now I am fully aware of this gift of mine. This ability and my mission are paramount right now. I organize a big group that meets in the major city I live in, and it is a lot of responsibility. I seem to call Starseeds right to me and I seem to bump into them. I do recognize my Star family immediately and I bring them "into the fold." Beyond my ability to unite our Star family, I also lead them, I have been a leader for a very long time. I call them up and say we have to meet at a certain place and time, and they all come. I give many workshops, including multi-dimensional travel. Manifestation is another ability that I plan to teach people.

There are other Annunaki here on Earth, and we have already united, although there are some still coming. The family itself is not huge, but the children of the Annunaki are very many. Our family has not united like this for 15,000 years. There is something coming up, and soon. We will be called into action to serve. We have the Annunaki family, the Arcturian family, the Pleiadian family, the Andromedan family, and the Orion family. They are all coming back together again, in a big group. These families have not been together for 15,000 years. Once we unite, nothing will stop us; together we are stronger and more able.

Earth has everything. She is a paradise and not many planets like Earth exist in our universe. Once we get her cleaned up, she will be a paradise again. That is also why I am here, uniting us Starseeds, so we can do this altogether. I have to remind myself often that it is not just me. I have my part to do, and all I need to do is my part, I don't need to take on the entire world.

Regarding 2012, I see that our abilities will have returned to us and we will be getting things turned around here on Earth. It may not happen exactly in 2012, it may happen after or before (Now would be a good time). I don't think that I will be going home during or after the "Shift." I believe I will be going on board the ship for maybe a week or two. Then I will be put back down on Earth to finish what we started here a long time ago. We have to clean up this planet. I would love to run away and be off this planet, but I have taken on the responsibility of our mission and to finish what we started.

Spiritually, I believe in loving everything, the good and the "bad." To be unconditionally loving is the concept I am promoting in all parts of my life. I very much believe in reincarnation because I have all of my memories of who I am. This helps me learn and to teach others not to make judgments about "good or bad" people, because we have all played the perpetrator and the victim. We are not perfect yet, but we are working on perfection. And soon, in the fifth world, we will have what we want (*our freedom*).

Books that are significant to me:

Jelaila Starr's *We are the Nibiruans*, and her website: www.nibiruancouncil.com

You may contact me at: *Shenai44@yahoo.com*

Niara Terela

I have a lot of memories of my home planet in the Lyran system. This system is also called Lyra or Lyran. It is still very emotional for me to talk about some of these memories. I do not personally know anyone else that is here on Earth that is also from Lyra... perhaps my Earth Dad was. I am sure that there are some of us here, I just haven't met them that I know of.

Our people looked very human, just more like an ethereal human. We had a translucence to our bodies, like a light or a glow about us, but not transparent. We were in the fifth dimension, living in fourth-dimensional bodies. We were very slender and most were fair-skinned, with fair-colored hair, large blue and green eyes (larger than humans). Some were more slender than others, but we were not obese people. I feel that on Earth people put weight on as a source of energetic protection.

There were lots of different life forms on Lyra because Spirit/Source Creator wanted to experience these forms. We had whales and we brought the whale DNA to Earth, we brought many animals to Earth. Lyra was green, really lush and alive. I remember the rainforests, but I don't remember any deserts, which I dearly love on this planet! We had beautiful mountains and it was rich with every type of life you can imagine.

We were aware of other beings in the universe, but they seemed like newer races and we are a very old race, as sequential, linear time is measured. We had a tangible, conscious connection with our planet. I was young, before the equivalent age of 10, when I learned how to consciously contact the planet. When I made this connection with her, we co-created a craft for me. It was grown for me out of the consciousness of myself and the planet. It materialized from the planet's elements, although it was a co-creation by the two of us. It was created for my frequency specifically. I could get in this craft and it was as natural to fly it as it was to use my arms or legs. It was really special. The craft had its own consciousness and even looked out for me, especially when I was younger.

I remember how I was conceived. My parents spent a day in a creative meditation to create me, their daughter. They were sitting across from each other with their hands out towards each other. They were holding an energetic space between the two of them. They playfully began to create my form between them in this space, laughing and having fun saying, "She needs this quality from you, and this from me." They were deliberately manifesting certain qualities between them and into my form. Then I was 'born' or fully formed by the end of that day. I was created as a baby. I believe I grew up faster than a normal human child would. We enjoyed living in bodies because of the things we could do and enjoy, but lots of times we would go into meditation and exit our bodies. We would travel this way, in the higher dimensions. We lived in our bodies very lightly and were not anchored to our bodies like humans of Earth are now.

We didn't have written language and we didn't really have names. Everybody had their own unique vibrational signature. When I would walk into the room where my parents were with eyes closed in meditation, they knew it was me because of my vibration. So it did not seem necessary to have names. We feel that naming someone limits their being. My star name now, Niara Terela, is the closest sound to my true vibrational frequency.

I worked a lot with energy and how to use our hands to move energy through the chakras, including healing as well, though it was rarely needed back then. When all of your faculties are open and alive in you, you can see energies in everything. We could see and feel when energies were unbalanced and we knew how to correct them quickly, before they became problematic.

The best example to show people the vibrational difference between resonance and dissonance in a vibrational way is with music. I play various multiple tones for people to listen to and ask them how it feels inside to hear these tones. I play tones that do not harmonize, that clash with each other, and everyone can feel the dissonance of that. Then I play tones that are in harmony and that vibrate well together, and people can feel the resonance of this. It does not mean that you will hear the "sound" of every vibrational input you have, but you will feel it because your body is mostly water and water is sensitive to vibration. When you are aware of these feelings and sensations, you can pick up for yourself whether something is dissonant or resonant for you. This helps your decisions in life greatly.

Science was linked to spirituality, they were the same on my home planet, both a discipline and a philosophy. We had an understanding of things at the core of their energetics and their vibrational nature, we could do things far, far beyond what scientists here on Earth do. Science here on Earth is really crude, it only deals with the physical, though that is just beginning to change. Earth scientists are starting to realize that the physical is an illusion, that between the atoms that make things solid is mostly space, that our observation of atoms and subatomic particles affects them. That area of science, called quantum mechanics, is in its infancy, but it is really reaching those scientists who have a personal spiritual foundation. Eventually science and spirituality will be a single discipline and philosophy here on Earth as well. But today, there are a lot of people that want to deny quantum realities.

Our ships look similar to our mothership, a cross between a sphere and a disk. They are like two different size bubbles put together, but not perfectly round, with no sharp edges. There are docking ports and bays near the center of the ship. Our architecture was similar to our ships, they were all grown in cooperation with our planet and had organic components. The craft, motherships and scout craft alike, served a common purpose—they would allow our minds free for other pursuits while keeping us safe, enclosed and traveling where we wanted to go. As spiritually aware beings, we could travel without craft if necessary. But there is a lot of joy in taking a journey by a vehicle carrying your form to its destination.

We didn't have any roads. We flew everywhere in our crafts which had a field around them so insects or birds could avoid collision and were not injured or killed by our crafts. Our homes were like bubbles of quartz glass that were formed out of the natural elements of the planet, She would form them for us. We had windows in our homes where other life forms could come inside too. We had natural lights that we would use in the dark hours so you could see the homes at night, but in the daylight our homes blended almost seamlessly in with the environment.

We had three moons that were whitish in color, similar to Earth's moon and I think other beings would visit them. One had an atmosphere where the other two did not. They had different topography. One was completely smooth. We had a binary sun system. Our planet was light most all the time. At "night" it would get just a bit darker but no extra light was needed to see. Besides, "seeing" was as much a faculty of sensing vibrationally as it was with eyesight. Every seasonal cycle we would have a few "complete nights" where both suns were on the other side of the planet. Our atmosphere protected us and shielded us from the two suns' harmful rays. Our air had a quality of shimmery light in and of itself.

We had no use for currency on our planet, nor religion, we had 'living spirituality.' Our needs translated to intent and were co-created with our Lyran planet. Like the replicators of *Star Trek*, only without any replicator devices.

We lived on Lyra eons and eons ago as sequential, linear time is observed on Earth. (These memories are emotionally charged and are equal to any memories of this lifetime).

What happened on our planet that forced the outward expansion and colonization of other worlds was that an opportunistic and aggressive Reptilian race came to Lyra. The Reptilians met with our elders and asked if they could mine some of the elements from our planet. Mining was such an alien concept to us, it was something we never needed to do because we knew our planet was formed the way She chose to be. However, we did want to help them. What concerned us was the fact that they had some kind of block on their consciousness or thoughts and we could not 'read' them, nor their intentions. We had not experienced vibrational dissonance like this before. This made us nervous, so we gave them a very small and specific area to mine. We told them they could mine in this area of the planet and only take a limited supply. This went on for a while with no problems until some of our people found that the Reptilians were mining in other areas, outside the specified area. A few of our elders went to confront the Reptilians about this violation, and several of them were killed.

The Reptilians suddenly unrestrained themselves and began mining wherever they wanted to and took what they wanted from the planet. This action really changed our people's consciousness. Before that, we had not encountered death or violence. It was very frightening to us and the vibration of fear locked our consciousness into our bodies more like here on Earth. We could not come and go into the higher realms like we did before. (This is so real to me that I relive this event when I talk about it). So, when we became frightened, it lowered our frequencies to a lesser fourth-dimensional vibration and we couldn't leave our bodies with such ease anymore.

Some of us wanted to learn to fight back on the Reptilan terms, others disagreed and reminded the others that we couldn't do that, it wasn't who we were or what we were about. We weren't warriors, we never had to be. Regardless, some tried to fight back and stand against the Reptilians, but they were all killed. The Reptilians just became more violent and began killing more of our people. My parents and my uncle wanted me safe from these Reptilians and decided to put me on a ship that was leaving for Earth. The mission of this ship was to seed life on Earth. My Uncle was the one that was teaching me advanced sciences and I was really enjoying the teachings; however, I was not done. They were rushing to get me to this ship before it left. I was in shock from leaving my parents, my uncle and my home planet. I also knew that they did this at the cost of their own lives.

The ship was full of young people and we were still on the mission to seed life on Earth, but we were all in shock. Everything we knew was being left behind and possibly destroyed. I think that my home world was completely devastated. I hope that someday I can go home to a fully restored Lyra. Someday, when my mission is over, I will be able to go back to Lyra. I imagine I'll fall down weeping and hugging the ground. I really want to go home, a vibrational home, to resonate with the people there who really accept and love who I am, as I am. An end to the isolation I've felt on Earth.

I remember landing on Earth in the land called Lemuria. I threw myself at the ground and grabbed onto her. I really needed to be close to a planet again. I eventually formed a deep bond with the Earth and it helped in my healing process. I was working with the scientific teams in creating intelligent life on Earth. We were working on creating a human-like species similar to our own. It was on-the-job training for me, but we were considered geneticists involved with creating single-celled life in the beginning. We were living in our ships, which eventually became our domed city while we watched life evolve. This original work we did gave rise to some of the body types and characteristics on Earth today, although now characteristics from different ET origins have all pretty much merged. Where we landed, there were no other beings nearby. We knew of other groups out there, but we did not contact them. My impression was that we were not the first group of beings on the planet, but we were among the first groups that appeared around the same time. We may be considered in Earth's prehistory as the Annunaki, but I am not certain. We are not Reptilian.

So I lived on Earth for a very long time. We didn't even have to give up our bodies, except that I wanted to. I wanted to experience life in some of the bodies that we were creating. I chose to incarnate into the Human Lemurian civilization, where they also lived a very long life. My next few lives were incarnations in Atlantis. I can vividly remember my last life there. I was a temple worker where this huge crystal was standing in the center of the temple. It would probably take 20 people holding hands to encircle the diameter of this crystal. There were 12 pillars in a circle around the crystal and a hole in the roof, to not interfere with the energy emitted from the crystal. I was a really young initiate in this temple and our Order was telepathic. Our elders were the priesthood and were working with the government, or political people.

The government was getting destructive and out of control. They approached our elders in the temple and said we must use the crystal chamber to keep the energy balanced and stable while they continued their experiments. I had a lot of clairvoyant gifts at the time and I knew that what the government was doing was going to end in disaster. I had a 'vision' that a huge tidal wave was going to come in and take out the entire sea coast where we lived. Because our Order was telepathic, the elders knew I had this vision and forbade me to exit the temple grounds. They were concerned that I would tell people what was going to happen.

There was a young male priest that I was in love with and he was in love with me. It was forbidden for us to be together because they were afraid that it would lessen our psychic abilities. When chaos hit the city of Atlantis, I knew I could not get away from the destruction. I telepathically connected to the male priest I was in love with and we met at the beach, where the huge tidal wave was going to sweep over Atlantis. I remember it so clearly. It was wind-swept beach on a misty morning, not a lot of sunshine. There was a high cliff behind us with a row of really tall, thin cyprus trees growing on it. I was the first to arrive, standing there alone, taking in the whole scene, sharp and clear. We took each other's hands and looked out to sea, where we could just see the wave coming. We stood there watching it approach. It was scary to watch it coming and when it hit us, at first there was an immense crushing sensation, but only for an instant. Next thing we knew, we were both out of our bodies and in a place of pure light. After this life, I have not come back to Earth for a long while. I actually remember having some lives in the Pleiadian system, which is an offshoot colony of the early Lyrans. This was another place besides Earth that our people settled after escaping the Reptilians on Lyra. It was more natural for me to be in the Pleiades than on Earth.

In this lifetime Native American spirituality really resonates with me and from my father's side of the family I am part Cherokee. I went on a trip to Arizona in 1990 and it turned out to be a very special trip, where I began to truly discover "my medicine." Many special things happened for me on this pilgrimage. I drove down to Tucson, then ended up in Sedona. I did my first sweat lodge. The people putting on the sweat lodge experience were a part of Solara's "11:11: Opening the Gateway" project of the early '90s. After the sweat lodge, a Native American woman gave each of us a reading, and when it was my turn, she told me I had once lived in the Boynton Canyon vortex area as a Native American in a past life. So that was my next stop. Out there, I took a walk, putting up my hands to try to sense or feel where the vortex area was, and by following the direction where I felt a tingle in the palms of my hands the most, I ended up climbing a small hill and discovering a medicine wheel up there, next to a small cedar tree. This was my first time in this life of tuning into "energies" and to find a medicine wheel on the vortex area I was feeling my way to was profound. I stayed sitting quietly there until sunset.

Later on, back home I connected with more of the 11:11 community in Las Vegas, Nevada. I was born in the 11th month, on the 11th day, at 11AM, so I decided it was a sign for me to be involved with this 11:11 event. We were to do a meditation for our 'Star names' and I received mine very clearly. It sounded like little bells or chimes, then the sounds shifted into my name, Niara Terela. So, I have been going by my star name since 1991, and legally since 1993. I went on a date years later with a guy who had looked up my name on the Internet. He told me that "Niara" was West African and meant "Woman of high purpose."

I discovered the 11 AM birth time on my physical birth certificate at age 17, when I was ordered to get a passport. Being born in an 11th month, 11th day and at 11 AM has always had me wondering what that might mean for me in my life. Eleven is a "Master number," as are 22, 33, and other twin digit numbers. When later on I did the numerology on my star name, all the vowels in Niara and Terela respectively also each added up to 11, and the consonants in each name both added up to 5, respectively. Elevens have followed me around my entire life, especially since my move to Colorado, like some master time keeper arranged my birth to some cosmic clock where 11 or some other twin digit would crop up in my life at significant times.

     I have genetics from my Earth mother and my Earth father, but I know that I have something else in me as well. Something that was added, so I have a little more ET DNA than a normal human. I had a psychic tell me also that my father was an 'abductee' when he was a kid, almost weekly, by the Zetas. He had an interest in the ET phenomenon too, and gave me Erich Von Daniken's *Chariots of the Gods* books to read when I was a teenager. If there was another Lyran on this planet, I feel my Earth father may have been one of them. He and I were kindred spirits.

     My awakening began in my early teens with that first vision of standing on the beach, watching the huge wave come in and destroy Atlantis. From there, I began to gradually receive more and more memories of who I was. I look around at other people now and I just feel so different from them.

     From earliest childhood I remember an intense drive to understand what life was about, what my relationship might be to the universe, to the world around me. As soon as I could read, I started reading about the sciences, especially all the geological sciences, paleontology of all kinds and archaeology and anthropology. Science class in school was almost an effortless subject to move through.

     I was also experiencing a "larger reality" when out in nature, a non-physical, energetic connection to all life around me. I tried to find the answers about that at first in the Lutheran church and Sunday school, though even before I was out of childhood I knew that it was far too restricted a venue for learning to give me the answers to my questions in this area. Late in my teens I discovered astrology and more esoteric branches of metaphysics that showed much more promise of real discovery.

     But my passion and drive to learn, and to know, set me apart from everyone else, both family (except possibly my father) and my peers at school. I always felt different. In fourth grade, my teacher came up to me and said, "I notice you don't play with the other kids and you don't seem to get along with them and I was concerned." I just looked at my teacher and said, "I have birds, animals, insects and the plants in my backyard. They are my friends. I don't need other kids" He looked at me strangely. He never brought up the subject again after that.

Kids at school were not very tolerant of my difference from them. I was teased and made fun of a great deal. I didn't like it at all. It hurt, but instead of compelling me to conform, I pulled away from them even more, not wanting to be like them in any way. I felt that they were cruel and mean. It was horrible for me to see people hurt each other, from my dad's alcoholic violence towards my mother to seeing other, less popular kids getting picked on in similar ways to me at school. I knew how much that hurt and learned to be a warrior-defender. I would step in to help people that were being pushed around, verbally or physically, by bullies and I would physically fight them if necessary, even though I was always small for my age.

I have always felt like a stranger here, like an outcast on this world. I had to learn to toughen up, to become a warrior here. It was an important survival skill to acquire. I have an astrological chart that helps support that side of me, with Mars in Aquarius in the first house. An altruistic warrior, one who wants to right the wrongs of this world.

Learning to be a warrior at such an early age naturally had me gravitate to serving in the military later on. The other primary consideration was learning a trade. In my mid-20s I joined the Air Force. My excellent science background matched me up with being an auto-track radar technician. I was stationed at Nellis AFB, Nevada, on a unit that worked out on the Air Force Bombing and Gunnery range. This range was adjacent to the Nevada Test Site, where Area 51 is located.

It was more than 10 years later, after being out of the military for quite some time, that I discovered I had three months of missing time, where I couldn't remember any details of my life at all. I had hypnosis to recover some of my memories of that time.

While stationed at Nellis and assigned to the auto-track radar unit, I was taken out in the desert in the middle of the night—not my usual duty time. I was on a crew of people who were not allowed to speak to each other. They told us that we could not speak to each other beyond what was necessary to run the tests. We were given fatigues to wear with no rank insignia, name tags or any identifying marks of any kind. We were testing the auto-track, surface-to-air missile radar that I was working on, to see if it would track ET craft that were flying in the sky that night. They couldn't be tracked, not with that radar. They moved so fast and they seemed to be able change places in space and time instantly. The radar could not lock onto them.

When I looked up, I saw several 'saucers.' One was quite close, 100 to 150 feet away, hovering low overhead. It was glowing orange on the bottom. It looked like it had a translucent metal skin on the bottom with an orange glow from inside. It had a smaller circular section in the center of the underside. There were lights under the metal skin that was lighting up in sequence in a circular pattern. This made it appear that the bottom of the craft was spinning. There was a specific sound coming from the craft, it sounded like rock concert speakers when they are on, but no sound is being played through them, like a deep hum with soft, intermittent static crackling here and there. While they could have been back-engineered ET craft, I felt at the time that they were actual ET craft, being piloted by ETs. As I was looking up at these craft I was terribly scared... not of the craft, but of the circumstances under which I was seeing them. What was frightening was the way we were being treated by the superior officers. They wouldn't make eye contact with us, they would order us here and there, being very curt with us, even threatening. I only had a secret security clearance and I knew what we were looking at must be classified way above top secret. I was afraid for my life.

Next, we were put on a bus and taken to what I believe was Area 51. When we arrived at Area 51, they took us to a medical facility. We were directed to sit in a waiting room where the lights were turned off. One by one they would call us into a room off to the side. When it was my turn, I walked into the room and was told to lay on the stainless steel examining table, fully clothed. I noticed an armed security guard in the room with me. I laid there feeling really scared, almost terrified. Next, I saw this guy walk in wearing a white lab coat, he passed the security guard, walked around up by the right side of my head. He said, "Stay calm" about three times in an expressionless voice. He raised his hand up to the side of my head and, using a syringe, injected something into the side of my neck. I felt a rush of something go straight up to my brain.

Later on I had more hypnosis about what happened after the injection. My body immediately went into shock. A couple of security guards came in and took me out of a different door than the one I came in from. They took me down a very long staircase, it had to be somewhere underground. I was dumped into a small room with the door shut and locked behind me. The room was completely empty except for a one-way mirror on my side, and I'm sure an observation window on their side. I knew they were watching on the other side of this glass. I went through the effects of that injection in that small room. Strangely, I don't remember feeling pain, but I did feel like I was going to come apart at the molecular level and I was shaking violently. I laid down on the floor, my arms wrapped around my knees, trying to hold myself together in a little ball. I screamed. Finally, the injection started wearing off.

I also had a soul-level regression to get other details with a shaman friend of mine. My inner-dimensional teachers, which are my Lyran family; my father, my mother and my uncle, are with me all the time. They were there with me during this time as well as a Native American spirit guide. Looking at this experience from the soul regression level, they were holding hands, forming a circle of light around me when I was going through that experience. I feel their energy may have saved my life.

Once the injection's effects subsided, security guards came in and dragged me out of the room and placed me on a black vinyl couch, where I was raped by both of them. There were eight people sitting in the room watching all of this, including a Gray ET. He was pale gray in color, had big black slanted eyes and was wearing a pale color human shirt with buttons, which didn't look right on him. I remember when all of that was going on, I could hear this Gray's thoughts in my mind, he was wondering, "Why would these people do something like this to one of their own?" I don't think he was necessarily communicating with me, I just think I was able to pick up his thoughts. (There is another Area 51 witness who speaks of a Gray ET being out at the Area 51 complex and that he may serve as a technology consultant.)

I could sense that some of the people there did not want to be watching, but maybe they were made to for some reason. One of the guards, the one with blond wavy hair that sexually assaulted me, was a like a sociopath—he enjoyed inflicting suffering. By contrast, the other dark-haired one simply did what he did and backed off, done and finished.

This seemed part of a series of things done to shock and traumatize, to get me to splinter away and bury the memories of what happened. There were other flashbacks of things they did to me, like using electric shock cattle prod types of sticks in the neck and shoulder areas. There was also interrogation, where I was threatened with more sexual assault and death. They even threatened my then-preschool age daughter with such treatment. All this to traumatize me into burying the memories.

During these three months of missing time, I believe these episodes happened multiple times. The blond security guard seemed like my 'handler.' He was present for almost everything that happened to me and often involved in the various types of abuse that were inflicted. I had this very strong feeling that the people who had picked me to be part of these 'tests' knew I was an ET abductee, maybe they even knew that I was a hybrid. While this was not covered during hypnosis sessions, I feel strongly that I was told this at some time during these episodes over the three-month period in which these events occurred.

I feel that other crew members on the radar or other enlisted personnel unfortunate enough to be dragged into this area were probably put through the same procedures I was afterwards. I think I may have been the only woman or one of a very, very few.

I had a psychic tell me that the things I have endured as a child, being taken by the Grays, was like torture. It was really uncomfortable and scary at the time, but I don't see it as torture. It was never done in a violent way. It was cold and clinical, but there was never any gloating of me being in their power or anything like that, such as there was with the blond security guard. It was strictly being a study subject in a variety of ways. So I don't place that judgment on it of being tortured. I know I am still having contact with ETs, likely still the Grays, or Zetas as I've come to call them, and what I call 'my own people,' more human-looking ETs that feel more like my own Star family.

I have awakened different times in my life with strange marks, including a scoop mark which later filled in on its own. I woke up with some pretty severe nosebleeds as a child and still wake up with minor ones from time to time.

Recently, I woke up with three finger-like bruises on my upper right inner arm. Also just recently, I woke up with a half-inch long red scrape underneath my nose, just above my lips. This mark comes and goes. I knew this was an acupuncture point, so I looked it up in a book to see what the point corresponded to. It turned out to be a point for relieving foot and leg cramps and—interestingly—it's also a point for 'opening up consciousness.'

I believe this may have been done by the Zetas. I have been a part of their culture beginning with early childhood, and I think I am still picked up from time to time. According to hypnosis sessions, I have had hybrid fetuses harvested from me over my adult, fertile childbearing years, as many as 17. I think very few of them lived to become adults. At first I was disturbed by this and resisted it, but now I have come to accept that I am a part of a very different, extraterrestrial culture as well as my Earth-human culture.

The Zeta beings are different sizes, some small and some much taller. They would stand around me when I was having examinations. There was a hybrid Gray who is the father of all my hybrid children. He has very thin, white, wisps of hair on top of his otherwise bald head. He has very large, blue eyes that looked similar to the large black Zeta eyes, but vivid blue. And he was not circumcised. I would have sex within a very clinical way. I would be laying on one of their tables and he would be standing at the end of the table between my legs. He definitely had emotions, but not like or anywhere near as strong as human emotions. I knew he would try to make me more comfortable by sometimes placing his hand on my stomach or hip area during sex. It was pretty uncomfortable for me sometimes. The sex felt good, but I was with somebody who didn't look human, so it didn't feel right. The only way I can describe what I was feeling is that it was like having one foot on the accelerator (good feelings) and the other foot on the brake (disturbingly strange emotionally to have such intimate contact with an obvious non-human), pressing them both to the floor at the same time. I still feel a bond with him somehow, though. There is a connection there for me and always will be. When I think about him, it seems like a type of long-term relationship. He was always there on my encounters. He was the only one that I was with sexually.

Some of the ways in which they were collecting human sexuality study data was really difficult for me. There were times when It seemed like they were stimulating me sexually for specific—though to me unknown—reasons. It was really uncomfortable because, again, I was with beings that did not look human. This has caused me difficulty with my own sex life. It was very disconcerting to experience the powerful feelings of sexuality under such circumstances. I remember waking up from an intensely erotic 'dream' having an orgasm, which I never had from only a dream any other time. When I looked at that under hypnosis, I was with my hybrid Zeta lover. Hovering over me in a weightless state was another classic Gray with the big black eyes. He was watching me and studying me as I was having these sexual feelings. Again, it was uncomfortable and unusual.

The sexual experiences are not easy for me to talk about, but I feel that it is necessary to help others. I think there are a lot of people who could be trying to cope with such memories, silently and secretly, and there are sexual issues that arise for human beings from close encounters of the "intimate kind" with ETs that range all the way from frigidity to sexual addiction. This must be opened up for people to talk about, so they can create understanding and healing for themselves around these parts of their encounters.

Lots of times the Zetas would project screen images to me. These screen images would not work for me in many cases. I think this happened because of my own ET background of being Lyran, incarnating as human. I could see right through their screen images while they were projecting them to me on the ships at the time they were happening. However, once back in normal daytime waking consciousness, the screen image would be what I remembered. I would tell them I knew that wasn't my sister when I would start to see the Zeta form that was trying to project her image to me. There were times when they didn't want me to pay attention to something going on, so they would try to distract me with sexual stimulation when projecting images failed to work on me.

I have learned to live with all of this at this point. It is just a part of my life and if it helps their species to survive and grow in a new direction, then it's worth it. I feel that life should be preserved and if a species has a way of preserving themselves, why shouldn't they take the opportunity? If they asked us openly for our permission, humans would most likely say no. One of the things I have learned in my healing journey is that we have given them permission, from a soul-level agreement we made with ourselves and them before we incarnated. This is done on a level that most humans don't remember consciously.

                                    *   *   *

My feeling about implants is that I have perhaps three or more. I have an implant behind my right ear, like a little bump. Sometimes it seems to move outwards more than it normally is most of the time. Once in a while it feels sore. I think one of them collects physiological data for hybridization research; glandular functions, hormone functions, neuropeptide levels, etc., for the Zetas. This is so that when they combine my human genetics with their own, they can check for consistency and proper functioning; so the glandular and neural peptides activity works properly in the hybrid. One implant I feel may be for tracking where I am at any given time. The one that collects the physiological data likely also supplies tracking information.

Another implant, put there by my own people—the Lyran-Pleiadian group—may be a two-way device that could be responsible for downloads of information into my subconscious where it 'bubbles up' when needed. This happens when I'm writing or communicating (like right now is a great example), and it also sends them information from me, about my experiences as a human being on this planet. They need this kind of information from me and many others to understand what it's like for all of us living here, to keep their collective fingers on the pulses of us down on the planet. They know all the things that have happened to me, what I've experienced in my lifetime here and how it's affected me and my life and helped facilitate my own spiritual evolution, all from that implant. I also think it interacts in some way with my pineal gland—*how* I'm not yet sure.

Possibly connected to implants is a sense of having on-going contact now and a constant ringing in my inner ears. I feel it's a communication download, possibly coming in on a super-conscious level. It's getting a little frustrating not knowing what is going on, on the conscious level. I trust it, however, because it feels good. These encounters, largely in the astral, I feel are on-going because I have stepped into an ambassador and educator role about ET contact. I feel they are really happy about that. I astral travel to the ships at night to learn specifically more about how I can best be of service. I learn things with them that I later will use in my articles. Sometimes I really don't know where the information is coming from in these articles I put out. I truly feel it is them helping me and the multidimensional learning I experience with them on the ships at night. At the edge of my consciousness, I believe I also have Pleiadian contacts. I feel they are closer to being my real family, since these Pleiadians are an offshoot from the Lyran civilization.

I am trying to help the people of this planet, trying to smooth the way to contact with my articles and other writing. Sometimes I have to be careful when writing these articles because I have the temptation to differentiate myself from humans. I'm not sure how people I'm trying to educate would respond to that! In this life, even though I daily remember more of where I came from, I am still a human being of Earth also.

I feel that some of my lives on Earth are simply because I got caught up in a Karmic cycle. There are some things I experienced in this life that I know are to balance something I have done earlier.

I know I wanted to come here at this particular time to try to help educate people that life is life everywhere. It is about love; integrative, cooperative and sustainable. While these are concepts and ways of living people are beginning to understand on this planet, these are well-established ways of being and living with most life out in the galaxy and universe. There is a Galactic Federation and all the cooperative races understand that love is the primary principle that the universe is founded on. So I do my best to educate about ET contact, about what I feel is the meaning of life in a body: to learn to give and receive unconditional love. Having had to deal with moving beyond fear in this lifetime, I now teach others how they can face and move beyond fear and allow their awareness to open up and evolve, and their consciousness to expand.

It feels like someone flipped a switch in me about three years ago. Suddenly I lifted up my head, looked around and said, "Oh! This is why I'm here." That is when I started publicly speaking out about my military experiences. I felt like I had to do something to turn things on this planet back in a positive direction. I can't be silent. To be silent is to give personal power away to fear. I am passionate about educating people on ET contact, so they don't fear it. I really dislike the Hollywood movies that portray violence and fear regarding human contact with ETs. I tell people that the ones we have to worry about have already been here and have created a great deal of the trouble we see in our world today. The ones we will be meeting soon are the ones we *want* to meet... our expanded Star family. Contact will be about discovering who we really are.

I did Buddhist vipassana meditation for eight years. Also called "insight meditation," much of my spirituality was greatly enhanced by this practice during those years, and since. If we can come to the conclusion that love is the most powerful energy in the universe through our various spiritual practices and paths on Earth, about how where and what we put our attention and intention on increases, then wouldn't ETs—that don't have to deal with the heavy Earth veil of illusion on their conscious awareness—understand this even more completely? Of course they would.

On Earth we have the strong preying on the weak. More primitive civilizations become the prey of stronger and more technologically advanced ones. And that has been the way of it on this planet. A lot of Earth people are conditioned to think it is all about conquest. The government plays on that fear and the movies play on that fear as well. People are conditioned into fear about ET contact, thinking they are going to be conquered, enslaved or even eaten. This just is not the case with what is coming. What I am trying to do is to help people understand that nature is not something that just applies to nature here on Earth. Nature extends out across the galaxy and beyond. Nature understands cooperation, synchronicity, synergy and that these things work together as a whole. Extraterrestrials that have evolved to the point where they have space flight and conscious organic technology understand those principles of integration and cohesiveness, of *unity*—of *everything* Which means they are not coming here as conquerors, they are coming here as our extended family to invite those of us who are evolved enough to join them in community. They are willing to help us to solve our problems here, once we have learned the lessons about what a mess we have created on our planet out of our unconscious and fear-based behaviors.

I had a soul contract to come into this life as an Earth human. I am an ET Wanderer soul that decided to incarnate as a human at this time, to really help humanity learn, grow and evolve into their full potential. Part of my soul contract was to experience the 'abductee' experience with the Zetas, because they had a key role in activating my consciousness. The other part of my soul contract was going through the difficult experiences with the military. That was something that, by going through it and processing it, helped me to awaken. At a higher level I feel that I am in contact with my own people, the Lyrans and Pleiadians.

I look back on my life and I see that all of it was leading to where I am today, to this place, to do this work at this particular time. I am content with that. I think ET contact is coming soon and that people need to be prepared as much as possible so that when open contact does happen they will have a foundation of understanding. I hope to step into a fuller role for this as time goes by. My life experiences helped me awaken to who I am and to step into my place as an ambassador for contact.

Souls volunteer to come to Earth to experience disconnection from Source. They do it so that they can find their way back to Source and experience it as more profound, more real. We are always connected to Source, but we want to understand what it is to feel disconnected. On Earth we experience this disconnection and learning Love creates our journey home to Source. That is why coming here is so difficult. We are all one, with All That Is. Even the parts of the universe that show up as negative are really here to teach us more about ourselves and provide the evolutionary pressure that we need to evolve to the full potential that we have. Maybe we, as Lyrans, manifested the negative Reptilians that frightened us so badly so long ago. Maybe we needed that experience to grow into a fuller expression of who we could really be and those beings were just playing a role. Maybe it was even a difficult role for them to play. I want to look at the highest level possible, not the lowest. I was born with an intense desire to know the universe and my place in it. This desire has guided my whole life, giving me my passion for learning and discovery and preparing me for my work in this world today.

There is a beautiful unity and cohesiveness to the universe at the most fundamental levels that we are discovering through quantum mechanics. Beings that have a mastery of such knowledge, while I don't guarantee all are good or positive, I would say that the majority of them are. Any organism, on up to civilizations that are so opportunistic that they become a threat to the very life of their ecosystem, are not sustainable, they would kill themselves off over time. Going against nature is ultimately destructive. For all to live and thrive in nature, symbiotic or mutually beneficial relationships are developed. Love is built into the operating principles of nature and the universe. The ETs that are our extended family understand this well. I welcome them!

You can read a more indepth version of my story in my upcoming book,

Facing the Shadow, Embracing the Light, due out in 2010.

Books that were significant to me:

Lyssa Royal— *Prism of Lyra, Visitors Within* and *Preparing for Contact*

Michael Talbot—*The Holographic Universe*

DVD that was significant to me: "What the Bleep Do We Know?"

You may contact me at: *gaiatribe.niara@gmail.com*

Niara Terela

P.O. Box 4448

Durango, CO 81302

My blogs:

http://durangoexopolitics.blogspot.com

http://encounterswithhealing.wordpress.com

DISCLAIMER:

The views expressed in this essay are solely those of the author and do not reflect the views of any organization with which the author may be affiliated.

Peanut

My story is short, but then so am I! At only 4 years old I don't have a long story to tell, but it is still an impressive one. I have had many experiences that my family has witnessed and documented for me. My hopes in sharing my story are to inspire other parents out there to listen to their children, ask questions, and be open to all the truths of the universe.

My experiences at first seem insignificant, but as I aged, my ability to verbalize my thoughts expanded and therefore so did my stories. What I once called "bad people in the dark" became "Aliens" and eventually "ETs." If nothing else, it allowed my parents to ask the right questions and finally understand what I was experiencing. I will start by mentioning that my verbal skills have always been advanced for my age and that these stories are very accurate. I mention this because you may wonder at some point if it is more my parents talking in these recollections than I. It is true that they have recorded, compiled and written them for the sake of this book, but it is truly I that is in the details. My gift of speech early in life has enabled me to give very detailed accounts of my experiences. So please sit back and enjoy.

The first of my experiences occurred late one night while living in Colorado. My mother and I were in the kitchen, cleaning up after dinner, and I started by asking her a simple question: "Mommy, who are the bad people who hide in the dark?" You can imagine her response—that is, after I peeled her up off the floor. She immediately asked me who I saw in the dark. I was about 2 at the time and just repeated to her, "The people who come in the dark, Mommy, and just look at me." My mommy then inquired more about them and I told her that "they are nice people, they just are in the dark, they are my friends … they have dark eyes." (Remember that at this time I didn't understand the true meaning of "bad". I labeled them "bad people" only because this is what people in the dark usually were, not because of their actions towards me.) At this point, my mother concluded the conversation by saying that she was glad they were nice and friendly.

A few nights later, I spoke about the bad people again. This occurrence happened one evening just after my mother had read me my bedtime story. I once again asked her who the bad people where in the dark in my room. She asked me if they were there then, and I replied "no." I told her that they came in the night, when I was sleeping, and just watched me with their dark eyes. She once again asked me if they were nice, and I reassured her that they were. She kissed me good night and that was the last I spoke of the "bad people."

By the time I spoke of ETs again, I was approaching my third birthday. At this time my mother was pregnant with my brother. She had taken me to McDonalds' for a fulfilled afternoon when, in line, I surprised her yet again. I patted her on her eight-month belly and told her that "Chip was in a spaceship with the aliens." She quickly responded with, "Excuse me?" I clarified by telling her that "Baby Chip was in a spaceship with the aliens," but that it was okay "because he would be back." She never asked who Baby Chip was, but I think she understood.

About three months later, my mother came into my room one morning to say "good morning" and see how my night was. I told her that I had a great night and then proceeded to tell her about my event with Ceto. A little background information on this story is that I had in the mean time received a book about an ET named Ceto, who was a Gray that came to Earth to play with a little girl and boy. I tell you this now so that you know that Ceto was a familiar name to me, and the name I perceived for what many call a Gray ET. Now back to the story. I told my mother that the night before Ceto had come and taken me up in his ship. We flew around in space and Ceto even let me drive, but I crashed the spaceship down to Earth and hit a "twig" on a tree.

My mother quickly asked if I was okay, and I told her I was, because Ceto fixed the spaceship and brought me back home. My mother also asked me to describe what Ceto looked like, and I told her that he "had big brown eyes." Since my mother was used to seeing ETs with black eyes, she pointed to the picture of Ceto in the book and asked if I meant black eyes like his in the book. I said, "No, they were like his, but brown," and that Ceto was like the one in the book, but not the same one and that he was my friend.

This event took place at the mere age of three years and three months. My mother quickly called her ET expert, to tell her of the incident. The expert asked my mother if I had any physical changes. My mother told her no at first, and then remembered that I had awakened that morning with a little dried blood in my nostril. She thought this point insignificant, even though it was my first and only nosebleed to date. However, the expert asked if it happened to be my right nostril, and wouldn't you know, it was!

My mother found out then that this is quite common with "contactees" that have been implanted. Although I think this scared my mother a bit, she just gave me a hug and we moved on. Following this incident, I would often point to the sky during the day and say, "Look, Mommy, a spaceship." She was never able to see what I was seeing, but knew there wasn't a plane in sight.

One of my favorite new things that I had received was a book all about ETs. I would often show people my new book and tell them what the pictures were. All of my friends and relatives were shown the book upon visiting my house. Shortly after receiving the book, I ran in one day and said, "Mommy, Mommy, I have something to show you." I quickly ran and got the book. I turned to a page with a Reptilian being drawn on it, and told my mom, "Look, Mommy, it's my friend!" She instantly smiled, knowing herself that the person who sent me the book is a Reptilian being themself.

The last story I am telling you happened recently, after going to see the movie *Monsters vs. Aliens* with my Daddy. One day, Daddy said to me, "Hey, let's play monsters vs. aliens. I'll be the alien and you can be the monster." To this, I instantly replied, "Silly Daddy, you have to be the monster because *I'm* an alien!" It seems my Daddy still needs to learn!

These are all the stories I have to share at this time in my life. My parents are pretty certain they are not the last. Why, just the other day, I was telling my mommy how much I missed Ceto. She asked me if I meant my Ceto doll that I have. I told her, "No, I miss when Ceto came to visit me in the night. He would pat my cheek, but be gone when I awoke. So I would run to my window and say, 'Ceto where you are?' " My drawing (above) depicts this for you. You can see me with my curly hair, looking out my window into the night, looking for Ceto while he is in his space ship in the stars.

My favorite books are *Ceto's New Friends* by Leah A. Haley and *The ABC's of E.B.E.s* made for me specially by my favorite Reptilian

You may contact my Mommy through the Compiler, Jujuolui, at:
faquian@gawab.com

Norji

I am Sirian, but I do not know if I am from Sirius A or B. I was also told I am Sirian by an ET Hybrid friend of mine. I am not sure if I am 100 percent Sirian, I am still awakening to who I am. It feels like a rebirth, an awakening or a higher spiritual connection. I know what my people look like, but I am not certain what I would look like in my pure Sirian form.

I feel like a genetic Hybrid, both ET and Human, as well as a Starseed. I don't look anything like my family. For one, I am so much taller. I have always felt like I didn't belong here on Earth, that I belonged somewhere else. I know I have another family "out there" and I am still looking for specific answers. I also believe, from my ET experiences, that I am a sperm donor for Hybrid children.

The beings I see on a regularly basis are dark brown in color with bald heads, and large, round, black eyes. They stand about 4 and a half feet tall. They have three protrusions on top of their heads; one in the center and one on each side of the center one. Their mouths are small, their chin more like a human's and their body is thin and bony. I remember noticing how bony their rib cages were, they looked anorexic. Their fingers are long and look like sausages. There is some type of appendage that bulges on the end of their fingers. They have three fingers and a thumb.

In one encounter, I remember seeing them wearing a type of gray-colored headdress. The material was very thin and looked like canvas or thick paper. There was a long slit in the cloth over each eye. This hood covered their entire head down to their chest area. They also wore this same material over their torso, but their arms were totally exposed. I could tell this being was the same one I would always see in my encounters. He has the same energy and this is how I recognize him. Later on in my experiences, he told me his name is "Elbi." That is the closest I can pronounce it. I am assuming that these are my people.

These beings took me on two ships and I was allowed to fly one of them. I was told by Elbi that I was programmed from birth to fly the ships, me and thousands of others on Earth. We will be taking people off Earth to another dimensional "Earth." He did not say when this was going to happen. That is a question I plan to ask him the next time I see him.

Elbi only lets me ask just a few questions each time I see him. Then he cuts me off, "That's all for now, I will contact you at a later date. We will reveal so much to you, but just a little bit at a time." I feel that he doesn't want to overwhelm me. I have seen him so many times, I don't like calling them "aliens," I really feel that he is my brother or even a father figure. That is the feeling that I sense from him, he is definitely family. He has never told me where they are from. That is another question I plan on asking him next.

When I was 3 years old, I disappeared out of the house. My whole family was around and they said one moment I was there and the next I was gone. The doors were locked and there was no way I could get out of the house. I was gone for about two hours. The neighbor found me nearly two blocks away, just standing in the road.

Before I went missing, I was playing a game with my siblings. Recently I asked them if they remembered the event. Both of them did and told me the same thing, we were all playing a game together, they turned their head and turned back at the game, and I was gone. That quick, I just disappeared.

I received more information about this event during a hypnotherapy session. I always had a fascination with our front door. When I was a kid, I would often put my face against it, wrap my hands around my eyes and look outside. During my regression I realized that what I was looking at was a "man" beckoning me to come through the door. I don't remember how I did it, but I found myself on the other side of the door with the man I called "my friend." He was small like I was, and we would walk around the corner together. As we turned the corner, I would start lifting into the air. I would look back at my friend, who stayed on the ground, and I waved good-bye to him. I kept going higher and higher. From what I can remember, he looked like a little Gray ET. That is all the information I recalled from hypnosis, I couldn't get past that.

When I was 13 years old, I had a being come to me while I was at my uncle's house. At about midnight, I woke up and saw this being staring down at me. He stood about 6 to 7 feet tall, bald head, pointed chin, the eyes were large, round and black, and his skin was a pale white. I don't remember him wearing any clothing at all. The being reminded me of the ET face on the front cover of Whitley Strieber's book *Communion*. However, I have seen another picture that is more exact to the being that was in my room. The picture is listed as a "Sirian A" in Stewart Swerdlow's book *Blue Blood, True Blood*. This being did not do anything nor say anything to me, telepathically or otherwise. I was just lying there in my bed, shaking. A few mintues later, I closed my eyes and wished him to go away. After a few more minutes, I had the nerve to open my eyes and he was gone. That event was very traumatic for me at that age. I still remember to this day what his face looked like. I do not know if these are my people or not.

Right after this encounter, I started having "dreams," which I know weren't actual dreams. All of a sudden. I would see a male alien and he told me, "Get up on the table, it is time." On the table lay a scrawny-looking, near-anorexic mannequin doll, and I was to have sex with it. The male alien never said anything else to me, he just stood over in the corner, watching the whole time. This event continued happening to me until I was at the age of 35, when it ceased. The event happened probably 25 to 30 times total. The doll was pale white, inky looking, with scraggly, sparsely long blond hair and big, round, black eyes. This doll did not move the entire time. It was like a machine, possibly just taking samples of me. It just laid there and didn't seem to have any life to it. The male alien just had me have sex with it each time—that was it. What always made me remember this encounter was that I would always jump out of bed afterwards and have to use the restroom. I also felt the need to change and clean up. I would always notice a clear, lime-green substance in my groin area. I do not know if this event happened on a ship or not. All I remember was a white room and this table in the room where the doll was lying. I really believe I have Hybrid children out there; I feel like I am a genetic experiment. Someday I hope to see my children.

After I graduated high school, I moved to a different state. Every two weeks I would make the drive back to visit my parents. On one trip in August, I was driving to visit them. At about midnight I saw this massive white flash of light. It lit up the entire inside of my truck. When the light was gone, I was sitting in my truck in a ditch. Later, under hypnosis, I could see myself standing next to my truck that was in the ditch. There was a house and a barn nearby off of this dirt road. I was watching this big white glow and I could make out the shape of a craft sticking out of this glowing light. That was all I could get out of that hypnosis.

After that encounter, I would have recurring "nightmares" that lasted for years and years. It always started out that I was walking up these stairs into this round "building" that was floating in the air. The building was doughnut-shaped on the inside and there were windows on the inside wall about every 10 feet. I could see "ribs" of the building going from the center area, in between these windows and down into the floor. I was walking around and I could see people just lying unconscious on the floor, along the inside and the outside walls. They were a variety of people: kids, adults, male, female, white, black, etc. Some were dressed and some were naked. I walked about halfway around and saw a doorway that led to the center portion of this doughnut-shaped building. There was a very narrow stairway that went downward. I walked down and it led to a hallway. As I walked down this hallway I became very anxious. Near the end of the hallway was a door that was slightly ajar. I stopped and looked at this door and I felt very scared. All of a sudden, I ran past the door to the end of the hallway and I could see it turned and continued on. I could see there was someone inside the room when I passed that open door, but I don't know who it was or what they were doing. I continued down the hallway to the end, where it turned again. I ran down that hallway and it dead-ended. There was a door at the end of the hallway, so I opened it and stepped inside. It was a room about 20 feet by 20 feet. In the center of the room there was an armless chair sitting on a pedestal. Directly in front of this chair was what looked like a chalk board attached to the wall. I looked at this scene and became frightened again. I ran out of the room and back up the hallways. I was so scared, I thought I was going to explode. I reached the door that was slightly ajar and I stopped. I wanted to get out of there, ASAP. I took off running again, looking into the room of the open door as I ran past it. I could see someone still in there, but I didn't know who. I ran to the stairs and back up to the top. I felt a lot better, but people were still lying on the floor. I then walked back to the door where I came in at. I walked down the stairs to the ground and I woke up. I had this dream so much, it feels like a nightmare. I would usually wake up sweating and scared.

The very last time I had this "dream," everything was the same, up to the point where I came back to the door that was slightly ajar. This time, I pushed the door open. It was a white room with nothing in it but what looked like a gurney. There was a male being lying on this gurney, it looked very similar to the doll or mannequin I was made to have sex with, but this being was real— alive. It was definitely a male and was only about 3 and a half feet tall. My fear and anxieties left and I calmed down. This doll started speaking telepathically to me, even called me by name. He said to me, "Don't worry, everything is going to be okay, I just wanted to talk to you." Then we just stared at each other in the eyes. I felt like he was downloading information into me, like a computer download. I don't know what he was putting into my brain, but it felt like he was pumping me full of information. I felt like I was in a trance, my entire body was buzzing. When he was finished, he told me, "We'll meet again. I don't want you worrying about this, everything is going to be okay. We'll see each other again in the future." Then I said goodbye to him. I was sad that our time together was over, but I walked out the door and back up the stairs. I was totally calm, it felt great. All of the people were still on the floor, I never recognized any of them. When I woke from this "dream," I never had it again.

One night we were having a barbecue at my boss's house. It became late and I decided to drive home. While on the freeway, I noticed a huge, almond-shaped craft hovering in the sky. I used one of the pullouts off the side of the road to stop my car and take a better look at this craft. Suddenly, this craft started zipping and zooming around. Instantaneously, it would be in the valley and then suddenly above a mountain. Next, it approached me, almost right up to me. It scared the heck out of me. Then it zipped back out on top of the mountain again. I had enough and decided to drive home. When I got home, I tried to find it again from the back yard, but I couldn't see it, so I went to bed.

As soon as I fell asleep I had this "dream." The covers seemed to move on their own and moved down towards the foot of the bed. Then I started to levitate off the bed and towards the door. At that point, I noticed there were six Grays in my room, three on each side of me. They were about 3 and a half feet tall, bald heads, almond-shaped black eyes, tiny mouth, tiny nostrils, spindly fingers, and were light blue in color. I don't think they were wearing any uniforms, but if they were, it was skin tight. I don't remember any details on their bodies; however, their bodies were a yellowish-white color compared to their light blue heads. I could see my dresser and my TV, too. I levitated out to

the living room and the Grays followed. I could see the dining room table and
the TV in the living room. Then I drifted out the front door and towards my car
that was parked in the driveway. I could see the trash can by the road. I looked
up and I could see this almond-shaped craft above my house. This looked like
the same one I had just seen on the freeway. I tried to scream and to wake up,
but I couldn't, I was totally paralyzed. I told them to leave me alone. I then
started to float up towards the craft. I had been floating on my back until then,
but now I was standing upright and floating up in this light. As I started to enter
into the ship, I heard *Wham!* I hit the floor next to my bed as if I had been
dropped. I hit the floor pretty hard. I was totally naked and wringing wet with
sweat. I was so anxious, I thought I was going to blow up.

I got up, turned on the lights, the TV, and took a shower. After a while,
about 2 AM, I went back to bed and fell asleep. Immediately, I found myself in
this round room, lying on this couch upon a pedestal. Everything was a misty
white light inside. All of a sudden, *Wham!* again. I found myself having been
dropped on my bedroom floor again, naked. I was in a cold sweat again and
took another shower. It was now 6 AM and I decided to stay up for the rest of
the day. I don't remember what happened for those four hours of time on the
ship. There was no telepathic communication between me and these Grays.
Every encounter I had with these beings has been "rough and tough," like they
had a mission to do and I just had to put up with it.

I had a Gray pop into my living room one night, when I was sleeping on
the couch, because I quit sleeping in the bedroom. I sat straight up and looked
over at the door to see this little Gray, the same exact type I saw on the ship. All
of a sudden, the door slammed open against the wall and the little Gray was
gone. He was lightning fast. I couldn't believe how fast that guy moved. I ran
over by the door and grabbed the baseball bat that I kept there. I ran outside and
looked all around me, but nothing was there. There was nobody running away. I
realized later that I should have looked up, not around.

A lot of weird things were happening to me that I felt were done by the
Grays. One night I woke up, hanging halfway out of my window. Another night
I woke up on the clothes washer. Sometimes I would wake up, totally paralyzed
with a bright light behind my head. I would try to scream, wake up and move,
but all I could move were my eyes. That happened so often and it still happens

to me today.

My whole life has changed in the last three years. I feel like I am going through a metamorphosis. I used to be real blunt and kind of snotty. Now I am mellowed out and I don't do any hunting, I refuse to kill anything any more. I will go to step on an insect and I catch myself. I have no reason to kill it and my thoughts say, "Let it live, they have a purpose." One day I saw this pale white praying mantis on a window. It was very long, about 6 inches. These couple of kids were going to kill it and I stopped them. I said, "No, don't kill it. He is your friend, these are good to have." I stuck my hand out and the praying mantis walked right up onto my hand. I took him to a flower garden nearby and let him climb off my hand onto a bush. I was trying to convey love to these kids, instead of just killing something for fun. I like this change in me, I feel better about myself. I am more in tune to my surroundings after my ET contacts. I am becoming more aware of everything around me and I like it.

At one of the recent UFO conferences I met a woman called Umma, who had art work of the very ET that visits me on a regular basis. It was a dark brown being, with big black eyes and looked almost exactly like Elbi. Umma called this art work a "Sirian." As I was standing there, looking at this art work, Umma interrupted her conversation with two other people and came directly over to me, saying, "Oh my gosh, you're Sirian." She grabbed me and was checking out my ears and nose and said, "You are 100 percent Sirian." Umma recommended that I start meditating to get more information from my encounters.

That very night at about 1 AM, I fell asleep on my couch. Immediately, I was paralyzed, only this time I could not even open my eyes. I was scared and tried to force myself to move. Then I felt a warm sensation and a feeling of calm come over me. My whole body was vibrating at a high frequency. I could hear three or four separate beings just walking around touching things, like kids. I then felt these long fingers on my head, moving all over my head and face. I was totally calm and at peace. Next, I felt these fingers touching my feet and felt something bumping the couch. Then I heard the sound of clicking behind my head, "Click, click." It sounded just like the Mexican castenets. I didn't receive any telepathic communication or anything. I don't know who they were or what they were doing, but I felt like they were doing something to my head. I heard what sounded like my dinette chairs moving across the floor. This event lasted for about 12 minutes and then everything was quiet. The paralyzation started to wear off. I opened my eyes and no one was there, but the one dinette chair was on the other side of the living room. I would have loved to have seen those beings.

In June 2008, I was lying on the couch in the dark. Suddenly, this bright beam of light came through the ceiling and down through the floor. It was a beam of about 4 or 5 inches in diameter. It was only there for a few seconds, but I noticed dark things inside of the light, like shadows from another dimension. This light plays an important part of my on-going encounters. The next month, I saw this beam of light come through the living room again, only it was not as bright as the first time. It moved across the living room and I could see a being following it. I was watching this from my couch.

On another night, this same beam of light appeared and a being was manifesting itself in the living room. I could almost make out what it was, then it was gone.

Then, on September 11, 2008, I went to bed and started to "dream." I was standing face to face with this ET being that was always following the beam of light in my living room. I was only about an inch away from him. I couldn't move and I was receiving a telepathic message from him that everything is okay. My whole body was vibrating strongly again and I could feel that I was being downloaded with information again. I have no idea what he was putting in my head, but we were just standing there for a long time. His eyes were solid black, maybe there was a lens over his eyes, but he was using his eyes to download me. He then called me by my name, told me not to panic, that he would show me more later on, and it was time that I find out what is happening to me.

The very next night, September 12, this ET came back to me again and the same thing happened. I was buzzing again and he was downloading more information into me, which lasted about 10 minutes. Then everything turned into a fuzzy white. Next thing I knew, I was sitting in the same chair that was facing the blackboard on the doughnut-shaped ship in my recurring "night-mare." I was there in that same room. The ET was standing in the corner of the room, in my peripheral vision. I couldn't move anything but my eyes, and I was trying to look around the room. The ET telepathically told me to look straight ahead at the "screen." A row of six symbols appeared in front of me on this screen. Every now and again, a symbol would change to a different symbol. I would just keep watching as these symbols would change. I had no idea what these meant, but there were all types of geometric shapes and squiggly lines and more. This continued on for a while, then everything turned fuzzy white and I was back on my couch again. Whenever I would have these encounters, everything seemed to be a hazy white, like an opaque light. It is a strange feeling, like I am in a different world. All of my recent encounters are all like this.

On the third night, September 13, I was face to face with the same ET again, and I was feeling that whole-body buzzing sensation. He was downloading more information into me. After 10 minutes or so, he told me telepathically that that was all for tonight, it was time for me to find out who I was and what was happening to me. Everything turned fuzzy white again and I was back on the couch.

These encounters are a little bit frightening, but I really wasn't that scared. I found out later that this ET being was Elbi.

On September 28, I had a UFO sighting. I was talking religion with a friend outside when I noticed an object coming from the east and heading west. It was moving real slowly and it was a large, bullet-shaped object. When it was right overhead, I could see three bumps on the back of it. There was a band that went around the back end and I saw a rosebud-shaped, orange flame coming out the back of it. There was a big, long contrail that went as far as my eyes could see. The ship was right above my yard tree, about 50 feet above us. and I could see a round porthole window in the ship. Inside was lit up and I could see a dark brown being staring at me, the same being that I was having contact with. Then the entire ship just blipped out. I will never remember seeing him as clear as I did that day.

In November 2008, I was driving near a dam and I saw a huge, round object. It was like a translucent ball, and it must have been the size of a football field. It went behind the mountain top and I could see the glow of light from the ship through the trees. I raced to see if I could see it again, but I never did.

In December 2008, the dull white beam showed up again after I laid down on the couch. I could see a being was following the beam. I had realized by now that this beam of light meant I was soon to be on the ship and I would automatically go unconscious. This was like their "calling card," saying, "We're here!" I was standing in a void, where everything was a fuzzy gray color. I noticed a machine nearby and a pedestal about 3 feet high. I saw this disk sitting on top of the pedestal and a beam of light coming out of the top of the disk. The beam was about 2 feet in diameter and it seemed to go forever. On the other side of the machine, I now noticed about 13 aliens standing around, looking in different directions. The one that I know from my contacts walked over to me and said, "Hi" and began to tell me that I was in their dimension now. He further explained that they don't travel in Earth's dimension, the machine nearby permits them to "dimension hop." They took me to the machine and instructed me how to operate it. I was to move my right foot forward in the spot on the ground and, when I was ready to return, I had to pull my right foot back. So I tried; all of a sudden, I was in the mountains somewhere. I saw Army personnel nearby and one guy about 100 feet away saw me and pointed at me, saying, "There he is, grab him." I moved my foot back and immediately found myself standing next to the aliens at the machine. I thought that was really neat. The being told me to try it again. I moved my right foot forward again and instantly I was back in the mountains. The same Army guy was a lot closer this time, about 30 feet away. He saw me and yelled out, "There he is again, grab him quick!" I hurried my foot backwards again and I was back with the aliens in their dimension. I was thinking to myself that I wanted to try this again and see if I could land on top of one of the Army guys. Then I got the telepathic message, "No, you are not doing that any more."

I asked him where they were on Earth. He showed me symbols in my mind and I could actually read them. The symbols said "Siskiu." I said, "You are in the Siskiu Mountains, aren't you?" He told me, "Yes, we are there all the time, your government is always trying to find us. We are always there, just in a different dimension, our ships are also there." I was surprised that I knew exactly what those symbols meant. This must have been a result of prior training with their language.

Then he started explaining to me that this is how they travel great distances. They don't travel from Earth to another planet, they can't do it that way, they have to do it by dimensional hopping. When people see a UFO in the sky and in the blink of an eye it is gone, it is because they slipped into a different dimension. This is what he explained to me. He continued to tell me that they will show me much more, this was the very beginning and that there is much more to come. Then, like usual, everything turned fuzzy white and I woke up on the couch again.

In February 2009 I saw the light appear again. This time I had a sensation of moving, I could feel G-forces and it became worse. Then I found myself sitting in that same chair again, facing the chalk board. I was watching symbols as the aliens were standing over in the corner, not saying anything. I could only move my eyes. When I was done, I woke up on the couch again.

In March 2009 I saw the light again and I went unconscious. When I come to, I was on the inside of a ship, looking at one of the aliens sitting at the-console. I assumed he was piloting the ship. I was standing next to my ET being, Elbi. I could look right out of the ship and I could see all of the stars. Then we began moving and I could feel the heaviness of the forces again, almost to where I couldn't stand it. The stars were moving so quickly and then turned into white streaks of light. I passed out because of the g-forces. Then everything turned fuzzy white and I was back sitting in the chair, looking at the blackboard. This time I was seeing six rows of six symbols. The symbols changed regularly, but I didn't know if this was a story they were telling me or their alphabet. That went on for some time before I woke up on the couch.

In April 2009, the dull light appeared in the living room and I found myself inside a laboratory. I saw these same dark brown beings wearing the hooded gray clothing and torso clothing that left their arms exposed. I could see that there were more of them than usual here, about eight or nine. I knew these beings just by their energy, and I felt that I am very much related to them. There were also Humans in this lab, wearing white lab coats and inter-mixing with the aliens. I could see computer equipment monitors all over the walls, tubes hanging from the ceilings and all types of apparatuses around the room. In the middle of the room was a table and above the table was a clamp that looked as though it fit around a person's waist. This clamp had rods coming off of it. This ET came up to me and told me he wanted to look at my back. He told me to get up on the table and lie on my belly. I wasn't afraid because I was getting used to these beings. One of the Humans came over and put the clamps around my waist and I remember how very tight they were. He then tied straps to my arms and legs, and attached them to the rods on the clamp. When he was done, the clamp started moving me around in different directions. The ET told me not to panic, all they wanted to do was look at my back. He reassured me that everything would be okay. This clamp moved me around more and then stopped, leaving me in a hunched position. The ET got up on my back and positioned himself where his face was behind the back of my head. I could really smell him and it was such a different smell, like a dirty, burnt formaldehyde smell. Next thing I saw was his three bony fingers going over my face and into my mouth, up against the roof of my mouth. His fingers tasted like mud. He ran his fingers up and out of my mouth, over my face and to the top of my head. He continued to telepathically tell me not to panic, that he had to do this for my benefit. He did this motion three times and then got off of me. Next, he went over to my ear, where my implant was. I remembered at that point wanting to have Roger Leir take the implant out of me and I had scheduled this to be done soon. This ET (who was Elbi the whole time), took my ear into his fingers and pulled on it. He told me again not to worry or panic. He took a ball about 4 inches in diameter, shoved it in my ear and started twisting it around. He then rubbed the implant with his finger, saying very sternly, "This is your implant, *do not* have it removed." He didn't tell me what it does or why it is there. I decided at the time just to leave it in.

Then the Human came over and unhooked me from the clamps. I jumped off the table and everything looked real fuzzy white. It was as if I was half conscious and all I could think about was wanting to sleep.

Elbi came up to me and handed me a device that looked like a ping-pong paddle. It had three bumps on the end of the paddle part, they almost looked like lights of some kind. He told me to hang onto that and *do not* let it go. I could tell he was very serious, like when he told me not to take my implant out. Next, we went into this room, where there were about 15 Humans sitting in chairs that were lined against the walls. The very end chair was empty and Elbi sat me down in that chair, telling me to wait there and *do not* let go of that device. I had a death grip on the thing. The guy sitting next to me turned his face towards me and said, "Man, you have no idea how lucky you are, no idea!" I wondered what he meant by that, then the aliens walked into the room with my sister. She didn't look conscious and was holding a board that was about 2 feet long and 6 inches wide. This board had three things coming off of it that I did not know what they were. It sort of looked like three puzzle pieces hooked together. I called out her name, but she couldn't hear me. Then the aliens left and three others came in. One was holding a box with some type of cable coming off of it and what looked like a microphone at the end of the cable. The three aliens stood in front of me with this box and other equipment I didn't recognize, I was still only half conscious. Then the three aliens left. Elbi came into the room and picked me up from the chair. He reminded me not to let go of the device and hang onto it tight. We left the room together and went back into the lab. I saw all of the Humans and aliens talking and doing all of these activities together. Elbi told me not to panic, they wanted to take me on a trip somewhere, they wanted to show me something. At this time, Elbi told me his name. He let out this awful, high-pitched, screeching sound (felt like nails on a chalk board). After that screeching noise, he told me, "My name is Elbi. It is time that you know what is happening to you. In time we will reveal things to you, but now we have something to show you and we need to go."

I followed him down a dark hallway and I saw two droids hovering in the air. They had lights, tubes and other gadgets on them and were bullet-shaped. They hovered beside me now as Elbi and I were walking. Elbi told me he was going to take me to this place and "they" would be there shortly to pick me up. Suddenly, I blacked out after things turned fuzzy white. When I came to, I was standing on what looked like a tarmac or runway. I could see big buildings and hangars way off in the distance. It was really dark and I could see the stars shining. Then I received a mental message, "Don't panic, don't move, we will be there shortly to get you. Do not let go of the device I gave you." I still had a death grip on it. My sister was lying on the ground next to me, still holding onto that board, but she was totally unconscious. Another voice spoke to me, "We are almost there." Then I passed out as everything turned white and I woke up on the couch. My sister didn't remember anything about those experiences. I believe that my sister is also a Hybrid like me, and I think she and I are from the same family, the same as what I am a part of.

In August 2009, I fell asleep on the couch after seeing the light beam. I was with Elbi and we were both standing, looking out at the stars on this huge ship. Elbi told me it was time for me to know what I am to do. He told me, "You have been programmed at birth to fly a ship to take Humans off Earth to another dimensional Earth." He did not say when, but I can't wait for my next experience. He had me sit in this black chair that was molded from the floor, it was one piece with the ship. I placed my arms on the armrests and *Boom!* Elbi told me we were going to go on a little trip and dimension hop. He said I would feel g-forces at first, but once we dimension hop we would not feel it. I was sitting in the chair and Elbi was sitting beside me. We started accelerating and hopped into one dimension after another. We did this eight or nine times. Each time we hopped into a dimension, I could see the scenery for a couple of seconds. In one dimension I saw a city, another one was in the country some-where, another one was on a completely different planet, and so on. At the last hop, we were sitting in the middle of the universe and I could see a galaxy with its awesome spiral arms. It was breathtaking. Elbi said, "Okay, now we are going back." When we arrived back, he told me that this is what I will be doing in the future, me and thousands of others on the planet. Elbi told me that all the information is now in my brain and I had completed the programming. He finally said to me before leaving that he would be back to reveal more to me.

I did manage to ask a question at our last encounter. I asked Elbi to tell me about "Bigfoot." Elbi said, "I won't tell you now, but I will tell you all about Bigfoot in a later meeting." I feel Bigfoot has a part in all of this UFO/ET phenomena.

I keep pretty quiet about my ET identity and encounters. I just don't talk to anybody about these events because they will think I am a nut or on drugs. Once I joined MUFON, I was able to speak out more about my experiences. Since then, I have really connected with some awesome people. I have met a lot of other Sirians as well. They have an implant in their ear, just like I do. One guy even told me that his job is to pilot a ship and take people off this Earth to a dimensional Earth, the very same things my people have told me. I just wish my people would give me more information.

Everything started to subside for a few years. Then recently, my encounters have come back with a vengence. It seems for other people that once you get to a certain age, the contact stops. Not me, it seems to really be just starting with me.

I had a few government experiences. I had a brand new, white, Chevy Suburban parked right outside my house for about three days. I don't know why he was there, unless he was reading my emails, hacking into my computer and listening on my phone. I was emptying my trash one day and saw him parked there. I did a doubletake on him and he quickly drove off. I noticed he had government plates and every single window was blacked out, even the front windshield. I was told by people that the CIA use the white cars, while the NSA and FBI use the black cars. The following day, I saw him parked a block down the street from my house. He would sit there for three or four hours at a time. The good thing is, I have become really aware of my environment and people around me.

Another time, I drove up to the entrance gate of Area 51. I was parked at the famous sign that is posted there. A Dodge Caliber pulled up and two guys got out. The driver was an Asian male and they weren't friendly. They walked around us, seeing what we were doing. I said "hi" to them, but they didn't say anything. They soon left after checking us all out. Later on, I was at the Luxor in Las Vegas. I turned the corner of some slot machines and ran right into this same Asian guy. We actually bumped into each other. He didn't say anything, which was very strange. Even during these two events, I felt safe, like I have a bodyguard with me all the time. I know my people and especially Elbi are always near me and I feel very protected.

There is something happening. I can feel something is going to be revealed to me real soon, I actually have an anxiety towards it. Something is going to happen. I think this is connected to 2012, but it could happen before that time. I don't think it will be anything catastrophic, I feel it will be a very spiritual thing. It is like the doors are going to be opened all of a sudden. There are chosen people on Earth, maybe the Starseeds, maybe the spiritual people, I wish I had more answers. Some people know the Earth will be splitting and the chosen will go to this higher dimensional Earth. I know whoever these chosen ones are, I will be the one to fly them to the New World.

Books that were significant to me:
Bud Hopkins' *Missing Time* and *Witnessed*
Ed Walters' *Gulf Breeze Sightings*
Travis Walton's *Fire in the Sky*

You may contact me at: *Realworld112353@yahoo.com*

Jaeya

I am a Starseed. I came to Earth by way of the soul. I am also aware that my genetics are not the same as my family's. I sort of remember having some type of DNA strands attached to me at one point. It could have been while I was in the womb, I'm not sure. This DNA was of my future Bluestar self, and maybe Sirian DNA as well.

I have a Sirian connection. I graduated from Sirius before I came to Earth, so one could say I am of Sirian origin. I may also have a Reptilian connection going back a long, long time. Although the being who I was back in Sirius wasn't Reptile, I was more of a Humanoid Dolphin.

I was born to a mother who is a Starbeing herself. Even though she is not aware of who she really is, she still remained "open" to all things. Her psychic abilities also pretty much remained with her, so she unknowingly helped me keep in touch with everything paranormal and so forth. One of my grandparents and great-grandparents were also Starbeings, so it runs in the family. I only found this out recently, so it could be that Star-children are allocated to certain lineages. Growing up, I always knew that I was different from all of the other kids and I kept to myself. I also grew up in an abusive family. I was an outcast in my own family and school.

Around 4 years of age, I was always with my ET guides in South America, in the fourth/fifth dimension. I was also working with a Reptile at this time, sending light energy to different places. I was able to emit a form of electricity from my hands and I was just learning to fly or levitate (not very high, maybe a meter off the ground). I had various other psychic abilities as well, inherited from the genes I have.

Unfortunately for me, the men who wore black clothes knew about me and my capabilities in the other dimension. I am always stopping the "MIBs" in their negative creations, as well as dismantling the inter-dimensional machines they put in the skies which help cause humanity to be rather comatose. So the MIBs went to great lengths to take me out. One night a man in a black suit took me from my bedroom. When I got into the car, I remember thinking how odd it was that the driver's side was on the left, because it is on the right side where I am from. It was dark and we drove and stopped at the front of a white building where many other black-suited men were walking around.

Not too far in front of me, there was a Blue Starbeing staring at me. Then the black-suited man leaned over to me and said something that made me retaliate at this Blue being. I became extremely angry and I launched at the Blue being with huge bolts of electricity, hurting it very badly. While I was basically killing this being, I remember beginning to feel ashamed. I didn't feel like me any more and I knew something was different inside of me.

The MIB began laughing loudly at me. Hurting this Blue being really meant hurting myself, as it turned out to be my future self. Our bodies are immediately connected, so whatever happens to this entity happens to me. When I finally realized what I'd done, I began walking away in shame and sadness. The MIB looked at me and said, "You're normal now," in a very "Ha, I've got you back" sort of tone.

After that event, I,could no longer emit electricity from my hands and I could no longer levitate, I could no longer do nearly everything I'd inherited from my Star-genes, and that upset me. This was the MIBs' master plan, and they succeeded. By doing this to myself or "selves," I tore one of my inner-dimensional bodies. Ever since then I have had parasites attach to me and take control of my torn-body in the other dimension. To some degree it affects me here, both emotionally and physically. I've realized now that there was a good reason why it needed to happen. I am broken, but not incapable.

Around age 6, I cut myself off from the other worlds and the other dimensions, because I had given into the amnesia veil to which many children succumb. Before then, I was working with a Reptile each night, sending light-energy to different places. I was friends with him until I cut myself off. After that, I guess I ignored him. I am supposed to be working with him even now, but I've basically only just got myself back together, so maybe I will eventually. The Reptile is from the fourth dimensional Earth; he and his race are native "Terrans" (from Earth), even more so than Humans.

*   *   *

When I was 14, I began questioning reality, myself and the world. I began searching for information anywhere I possibly could. I began working on myself psychologically, polarizing negative elements of my subconscious and eventually regaining the memories of who I really am. I have been on the "awakening journey" these last three years, and the memories have nearly all come back. I'm returning to my state of "Is and Knowing." I almost can't believe I forgot about it all. I remember a lot of it like it was yesterday. Earlier this year, I contacted Jessica Schab, who helped me be as I am, and be more comfortable talking about these things with others. I am still working on myself and regaining my memories, even more as I go. My guides and other inter-dimensional beings are now helping me heal the old internal wounds all the way back from the time of my MIB incident.

I am still pretty young, so I don't really do much when it comes to a career or anything like that. I sketch, I love art, I also like composing music. I recently left school, as it was a waste of my healing time, and I feel it is not necessary in my path. Another reason why I left is because I need to begin gathering as much money as possible so I can leave for South America by myself. I have a connection with some natives there, who are intermingled with an ET group. They sort of let me know it was time to get there. From a soul perspective, I am returning home, since my soul lives there in South America, in the other dimension.

The natives I know in South America have an ancestral lineage going back to a star constellation near Andromeda. Although I don't entirely remember yet, their planet may be called "Apu." The "Apunians" live among some of the tribes in South America. They are actually inter-mixed and living with one another. They look identical to the natives; you can't tell the difference between them. I think a lot of the natives around the world are having ET contact, and others actually have ETs living among them.

The Reptilians are not so different from the Human shape. However, Reptilians are a lot more muscular and taller, about 6 to 7 feet. They usually wear robe-type clothing. Their scales are rough and can be brown, or a very dark green in color, almost black. Their eyes are large with a cat-like pupil.

Their irises vary from yellow to green, to maybe a reddish color. Reptilians are extremely sensitive, like those people who you have to be careful about saying certain things to them because of their reactions.

The Reptilians are extremely intelligent, however, and some of them you wouldn't want to approach in a single chance. Many Reptilians are lightworkers, but others work for the dark polarity—about 30 percent of their race is negative. There is a lot of racism going on aimed at them, by other beings, because of what the negative ones do. Their whole race is being blamed (sound familiar?). Some of the positive Reptilians are being manipulated by the "bulls," and, unfortunately, being forced into doing the things they do. Even the one I used to work with is being manipulated to some degree. Hopefully, I can help him as soon I begin working in the other dimension again.

The Reptilians live underground, in the fourth dimension. They are capable of coming here to the surface if they ever wanted to. Many of them do not think very highly of the Human race. They were here before Humans and Earth is actually theirs. Humans invaded their territory long ago and they are still quite frustrated by this. I don't quite understand why, since they have had billions of years to come up and tell us to leave.

It is my understanding that, in the future, there will come a great Blue Star. Miriam Delicado has also mentioned this star. It will change the color of our skin to a very deep blue and our forms will become very different; we will

 begin producing children that are unlike us physically. I do not know when this will occur, it may be our great-great-grand-children that experience this.

Imagine a more human face on the Nefilim Child statue. Our eyes aren't that large, and we don't have ears per se, we have slits on each side. My Blue Star self did not have hair and had some interesting star symbols written around his shoulders and arms. That comes pretty close to what we will look like, when the Blue Star comes.

I recommend reading and watching Jessica Schab's material,
as she holds an important base that is valuable on all levels:
http://www.jessicamystic.com/
http://www.youtube.com/user/jessicamystic1
http://www.facebook.com/jessicamystic

I like connecting with other Star-people. You may contact me at:
Jaeya.Blue@live.com

Last Thoughts

If you would like more information about our book,
we have created a website for you to explore:
http://weareamongyou.tripod.com

Please keep in mind that you may relate to one or a few of these stories within, but you have your own special story. We do not wish for anyone to feel threatened by this information by comparing it to your own life experiences (as so many of us do). We only wish to encourage feelings of love, unity, positivity and self-empowerment by sharing our stories with you. If it helps you to expand your perceptions on life and about yourself, perfect.

It is Time — Starbeings are uniting all over the world, in preparation for things to come. Contact any Starbeing you wish within our book, we welcome all sincere correspondence. We hope to connect with others like ourselves and with those who are ready to receive this information. Knowledge can be "poison" to those who are not yet ready to digest it.

Below is the "New ET Quiz" in its entirety. This is a guideline, a tool. It is created by a Starbeing who is also a well-known researcher and has many books available on the subject of Starseeds. Have fun with it! Our ET guides are usually telling us that we of Planet Earth all take life too seriously. Remember who you are.

The New ET Quiz
Created by researcher Scott Mandelker

New and revised, this questionnaire gives those of you who prefer the scientific method (*just kidding!*) a more quantitative way to decide if you are a Wanderer or ET soul. Simply answer "yes" or "no" to the following 20 questions. In my own personal experience, as well as my teaching and counseling, I've found that most Wanderers and ET Walk-ins fit the following profile:

Your Childhood

		Yes	No
1	Did you often think about, daydream, or fantasize about ETs, UFOs, and other worlds?		
2	Did you feel like ordinary things around you were somehow strange, like the human body, the color of the sky, trees and nature, human architecture, and adults?		
3	Did you ever feel as if your parents were not your real parents, that you had a missing brother or sister, or a home some place far away?		
4	Did you have magical dreams of flying, invisible spirit friends, or receiving special guidance and protection?		
5	Did you look up at the night sky with longing, and sometimes say: *"Take me home... Why am I here?"* or ask *"Why am I so alone?"*		

Your Personality

		Yes	No
1	Are you kind, gentle, peaceful, and non-aggressive — not just sometimes, but almost always?		
2	Are you hurt, saddened, and confused by all the human evil and cruelty in the world?		
3	Do you feel that money, possessions, and a successful career are not really that important?		
4	Do you sometimes feel more comfortable with plants and animals than with people?		
5	Are you generally sensitive, considerate, generous, and concerned about others around you?		

Your Experiences

		Yes	No
1	Have you felt different, out of place, or somewhat alienated from human society all your life?		
2	Have you had dreams, visions, or sightings of UFOs that inspired real spiritual growth?		
3	Have you had dramatic dreams of Earth changes, geological and social upheaval, the end of the world, or future civilization?		
4	Are you logical, scientific, non-emotional, and somewhat confused by hot passion and desire?		
5	Have you had a clear and uplifting contact with benevolent, kind, and highly evolved ETs?		

Your Interests

		Yes	No
1	Are you interested in science fiction, epic fantasy, angels, high technology, and world prophecy?		
2	Are you interested in Atlantis, Lemuria, channeling, pyramids, New Age ideas and UFOs?		
3	Are you interested in meditation, alternative healing, or bringing love and light to the world?		
4	Do you believe human society is ignorant or the spiritual truths that you know to be true?		
5	Do you have a strong sense of purpose and feel that your mission is to help Earth and humanity?		

Scoring Your ET Identity

For each YES answer, give yourself 5 points. For every "somewhat" answers, give yourself 3 points. Then total your points:

100-75 points — In my view, you definitely are an ET soul, but perhaps you are not surprised!

75-25 points — You may or may not be a Star Person, and you need more reflection to know for sure.

25-00 points — You probably are not an ET soul, but why are you interested in these matters?

Remember, *only you can know for sure* if you are from elsewhere, and knowing your cosmic roots is only the first step. After that, it's essential to consider *why you're here* and *what is your purpose*. Being on Earth gives all Wanderers a perfect opportunity to develop ourselves, to refine our understanding and expression of love and wisdom, and to help the world in our own special way.

Jujuolui Kuita

I have been into Ufology since I was young, but I began actively investigating in 1995. My thirst for knowledge and truth started out on a self-health and spiritual path that quickly led to my Starseed awakening. ETs are my life because I, myself, am an ET/Human Hybrid.

Since 1995, I have passionately investigated the subject of UFOs and ETs through reading books, attending conferences, counseling experiencers, doing on-line research and having many personal experiences. In 2003, I became a Field Investigator for MUFON because I wanted even more hands-on learning. I used my report writing and investigation skills from my prior law-enforcement job and applied them towards investigating UFOs. A few years later, I became the organizer for our bi-monthly MUFON meetings. I have since left MUFON to focus on my new path of sharing knowledge with others. I am more metaphysically focused in life and I prefer to research sightings and encounters with that perspective.

Jujuolui Kuita

I have had some media exposure that includes a few articles printed about me, being interviewed on radio shows and filmed for a Starseed DVD. Starseeds are a section of Ufology not widely understood nor accepted, and I believe we need to open the minds of Humanity to that reality.

During the major UFO conferences, I participate as a "vendor," lending my ear and offering my knowledge to those who seek some clarity and information regarding their experiences. My knowledge is offered in a humble manner, for learning is a never-ending journey. My new path has led me to teach Basic UFO Filed Investigations at the International Metaphysical University. We are teachers mostly because we wish to learn ourselves.

Made in the USA
Charleston, SC
30 March 2010